Anti-Aircraft Artillery in Combat, 1950–1972

To

Harpreet, Prabhleen and Gurleen

Anti-Aircraft Artillery in Combat, 1950–1972

Air Defence in the Jet Age

Colonel Mandeep Singh

First published in Great Britain in 2020 by
Pen & Sword Military
An imprint of
Pen & Sword Books Ltd
Yorkshire – Philadelphia

Copyright © Colonel Mandeep Singh 2020

ISBN 978 1 52676 208 5

The right of Colonel Mandeep Singh to be identified as Author of this work has been asserted by him in accordance with the Copyright, Designs and Patents Act 1988.

A CIP catalogue record for this book is
available from the British Library.

All rights reserved. No part of this book may be reproduced or transmitted in any form or by any means, electronic or mechanical including photocopying, recording or by any information storage and retrieval system, without permission from the Publisher in writing.

Typeset by Mac Style
Printed and bound by CPI Group (UK) Ltd, Croydon, CR0 4YY

Pen & Sword Books Limited incorporates the imprints of Atlas, Archaeology, Aviation, Discovery, Family History, Fiction, History, Maritime, Military, Military Classics, Politics, Select, Transport, True Crime, Air World, Frontline Publishing, Leo Cooper, Remember When, Seaforth Publishing, The Praetorian Press, Wharncliffe Local History, Wharncliffe Transport, Wharncliffe True Crime and White Owl.

For a complete list of Pen & Sword titles please contact

PEN & SWORD BOOKS LIMITED
47 Church Street, Barnsley, South Yorkshire, S70 2AS, England
E-mail: enquiries@pen-and-sword.co.uk
Website: www.pen-and-sword.co.uk

Or

PEN AND SWORD BOOKS
1950 Lawrence Rd, Havertown, PA 19083, USA
E-mail: Uspen-and-sword@casematepublishers.com
Website: www.penandswordbooks.com

Contents

Abbreviations vi
Preface viii
Introduction ix

Chapter 1 Korea 1950–53   1

Chapter 2 Vietnam   27

Chapter 3 India Pakistan War 1965   68

Chapter 4 The Six Day War   88

Chapter 5 The War of Attrition   105

Chapter 6 The Bangladesh War 1971   124

Chapter 7 Conclusion   152

Appendix I: The Soviet View of the North Vietnamese Ground Air Defense 169
Appendix II: Vietnam War   178
Appendix III: The Bangladesh War 1971   182
Bibliography   184
Notes   191
Index   211

Abbreviations

Above Ground Level	AGL
Airborne Early Warning	AEW
Air Defence	AD
Air Defence Artillery	ADA
Air Defence Direction Centre	ADDC
Air Force	AF
Anti-Aircraft	AA
Anti-Aircraft Artillery	AAA
Armour	Armr
Armoured	Armd
Brigade	Bde
Commander	Cdr
Control & Reporting	C&R
Division	Div
Egyptian Air Force	EAF
Electronic Counter Measures	ECM
Electronic Intelligence	ELINT
Electronic Warfare	EW
Electronic Warfare Officers	EWO
Far Eastern Air Force	FEAF
Indian Air Force	IAF
Infantry	Inf
Israeli Air Force	IAF
Mobile Observation Unit	MOU
North Vietnamese Air Force	NVAF
Pakistan Air Force	PAF
People's Army of Vietnam	PAVN
People's Liberation Army	PLA
Royal Air Force	RAF

Standard Operating Procedure	SOP
Surface to Air Missile	SAM
Suppression of Enemy Air Defences	SEAD
Squadron	Sqn
Territorial Army	TA
Vietnam People's Air Force	VPAF
United States Air Force	USAF
United States of America	USA

Preface

Nobody writes about Air Defence as it is not sexy enough, thus lamented Dr Kenneth P. Werrell when he wrote *Archie, Flak, AAA, and SAM*, the operational history of ground-based air defence in 1988. Not much has changed since then. There are not many books available on Air Defence Artillery which cover its combat employment though air power and its application are the subject of many a book. Even while discussing the employment of air forces it is generally the offensive operations that are the favourites rather than the less sexy defensive operations, although what can be discerned from even a cursory reading of the history of air power is that the defence has had an upper hand rather than the offence. As will be discussed in greater detail in the book, it is quite clear that the ground-based air defence weapons have held their own against the attacking air forces though the balance seems to tilt in favour of the attacker in recent times. However, in the period covered in the book, that is from 1950 to 1970, air defence was quite dominant.

The year 1950 was an obvious choice to be selected as the beginning of the narrative as the Korean War started that year, the first war involving the jet aircraft in combat, although the AA was primarily the vintage Second World War era guns. Covering the Vietnam War and the conflicts in South Asia – the Kashmir War of 1965 and the Bangladesh War – it was but obvious to include the Six Day War of 1967 and the War of Attrition which ended in 1970.

The Yom Kippur War of 1973 is not included in the book as it is, in my opinion, the first war in which the air defence missile played a pivotal role and it heralds the beginning of the Missile Age. That is left out, to be included in the next book of the trilogy.

Before the book, just one more thing. Why the name *Ack Ack in the Jet Age*?

Well, it is just an attempt to sex it up and make the name a bit more appealing.

Happy reading!
Mandeep Singh

Introduction

The jet age made its appearance just before the start of the Second World War when the Heinkel He.178 became the world's first aircraft to fly under turbojet power on 27 August 1939, although this was not the first time a jet aircraft had taken to the skies as the *Ente* (duck) designed by Alexander Lippisch had made its first flight using rocket power as early as 1928. It was, however, not a jet aircraft per se – as the Ente was originally a glider which had been re-designed as a rocket-powered seaplane. Even though the Ente was not developed further, other rocket-powered aircraft were developed in the intervening period of which the Opel RAK.1 is notable as being the first aircraft to have been designed and developed ab initio as a *rocket* aircraft. It made its first flight on 30 September 1929. The rocket-assisted aircraft did not find much success, however, and it was the turbojet that was used to power the new generation of aircraft and which would find wider acceptance leading to the development of true jet aircraft.

The first patent for using a gas turbine engine in an aircraft was given in 1921 to Maxime Guillaume, a French innovator, but the complexities involved in his design made it a rather impracticable idea and it was never adopted for any practical use in aircraft. The credit for developing the first practical turbojet goes to Frank Whittle and Hans von Ohain whose efforts led to the design and development of the Gloster E.28/39 and the Heinkel He.178 aircraft respectively. Experience gained while developing and testing the Gloster E.28/39 paved the way for the first true British jet to become operational – the Gloster Meteor which entered operational service on 27 July 1944. Unfortunately, Heinkel's design was not patronized by the German establishment and it was the Messerschmitt Me.262 which would go on to be the first jet aircraft to become operational, entering service on 19 April 1944. Of these two, the Me.262 saw more extensive service during the war and was regularly used against Allied bomber streams, and also against ground targets. The Gloster Meteors, which served with No. 616 Squadron Royal Air Force, were initially used for the air defence of the homeland and moved to continental Europe only in January 1945. Even then, they were forbidden to fly over German-occupied territory, or to go east of Eindhoven, to prevent a downed aircraft being captured by the Germans or the Soviets. Not surprisingly, the Me.262 became the first jet aircraft to be shot down by anti-aircraft artillery in October 1944 when being used for attacking Allied airfields in continental Europe.

After the invasion of Normandy, as the Allied troops moved towards the hinterland, the need for close air support operations necessitated advanced landing grounds being constructed as far ahead as possible. The Airfield Construction Service made well over seventy-five advanced landing grounds (ALGs). These were used by the Allied air forces in conjunction with liberated airfields. The British advanced landing grounds (prefixed by the letter B and given numerical identity) were defended by light anti-aircraft squadrons of the Royal Air Force Regiment equipped with Bofors 40mm L/60 LAA guns. One such ALG was at Helmond, near Eindhoven in The Netherlands, and was defended by 2873 and 2875 Light Anti-Aircraft Squadrons, RAF Regiment.

As with other advanced landing grounds and airfields, Helmond was attacked regularly by the Luftwaffe. On 26 November 1944 four Me.262s of III*Gruppe*/KG 51 *Edelweiss* attacked the airfield in the morning at about 10:00am. It was cloudy and overcast with visibility severely restricted. As the Me.262s strove to attack the landing ground, the guns of 2873 and 2875 LAA Squadrons opened up, hitting one of the aircraft. The badly damaged jet, piloted by *Unteroffizier* Horst Sanio, crashed near the airfield, making it the first jet to be downed by anti-aircraft artillery.

The war diary of 2875 Light Anti-Aircraft Squadron records the incident as:

Weather very cold indeed and rather overcast. Another Me 262 very unwisely visited the airfield – with fatal results. Squadron guns opened up and the crew of B11 gun was successful in shooting it down. During the evening a personal message of congratulations was received by the squadron commander from the Air Office Commanding 83 Group.

The Royal Air Force Regiment went on to claim five more Me. 262 aircraft before the war was over, three over Helmond and two at Volkel. Considering that the Me.262 had a speed of over 900 kilometres per hour, it is creditable that an anti-aircraft gun was able to shoot down these jet aircraft, although these were not the only instances of the jet aircraft being shot down by guns. An Me.262 was shot down on 2 February 1945 by gunners of the 441st Anti-Aircraft Battalion of the US Army with their 0.50 quad M-16 anti-aircraft guns and, in another instance, Pfc Ralph Caputo of 559th Anti-Aircraft Battalion shot down an Me.262 using an MG-51 machine gun on 21 April 1945 near Klotze, Germany.

Though the anti-aircraft guns shot down fewer *jet* aircraft compared to the number shot down by fighter aircraft, the guns were more effective when the *total number of enemy aircraft* shot down is considered. During the Second World War, more aircraft were shot down by anti-aircraft guns than by any other weapon system but it was not always so and the capabilities of anti-aircraft guns were rather limited in early years.

Ground-based air defence systems precede aircraft and had already made their debut before the first aircraft took to the air. The first ground-based air defence systems were in the form of anti-balloon guns used during the American Civil War and the Franco-Prussian War although they made hardly any impact and had limited deterrent value. The Prussian anti-balloon guns were able to shoot down only one of the sixty-six balloons launched by the French during the siege of Paris. The performance in other conflicts before the Great War was equally unimpressive with the first aircraft falling to anti-aircraft gun fire only during the Italo-Turkish War of 1912. With the aircraft yet to mature as an offensive weapons system, it is hardly surprising that anti-aircraft systems were not high in the priorities of most nations. During the period leading to the Great War of 1914–18, it was Germany alone which paid some attention to the development of anti-aircraft guns and even then, had only eighteen of these when the war started. The other countries fared worse. As the war progressed and the air threat manifested itself with increasing efficiency, almost all countries devoted efforts to develop not only the guns but the associated technologies which included mechanical fuzes, sound ranging and searchlights in order to come up with more effective anti-aircraft defences. The number of guns employed for anti-aircraft defence against the German Gotha bombers and airships also increased with the United Kingdom alone deploying 480 guns for the homeland defence – more than the number of aircraft deployed for the same purpose.

The German bombing campaign against the United Kingdom notwithstanding, the air threat was more tactical than strategic during the Great War and it was continental Europe that saw more employment of anti-aircraft guns. During the war, over 2,600 aircraft were shot down by anti-aircraft guns with German gunners alone shooting down 1,588 Allied aircraft. Amongst the Allies, the French army shot down the greatest number of enemy aircraft (500) while the US gunners were most economical – using just over 600 rounds to down one aircraft, although the total number of aircraft shot down by US Army was only fifty-eight.

The years following the Great War saw rapid advancements in aviation technology while the progress in anti-aircraft artillery lagged behind. The gun technologies developed during the Great War were not able to keep pace with advances in aviation and, in the years preceding Second World War, it was the aircraft that dominated the guns. It was not that efforts were not made to develop better guns. One such attempt was to upgrade the calibre of guns to enable them to take on faster and higher aircraft. From the existing 3-inch calibre, almost all countries changed over to 90mm calibre with Germany adopting the 88mm gun and Britain adopting 3.7in (94mm).

A major factor that had a bearing on development of anti-aircraft artillery was the theory of air power as propounded by Douhet, Trenchard and Billy Mitchell which envisaged the use of strategic air power to crush the will of the people by destroying the enemy's vital centres. As these theorists believed that there was no defence against the bomber, the belief that 'the bomber will always get through', as the British Prime Minister Stanley Baldwin put it in a speech to the house of Commons on 10 November 1932, made the air defence seem redundant with only offensive air power seen as the panacea against enemy air power. It was thus not surprising that anti-aircraft artillery was relegated to secondary importance during the 1930s. With severe restrictions imposed on them that barred them from developing or retaining any air force by the Treaty of Versailles, only the Germans paid greater attention to the development of anti-aircraft guns. The real development could only take place after the ascent of Hitler in 1933 as even the development of anti-aircraft weapons was inhibited under the terms of the treaty. The initial focus may have been on developing the air defence guns for protection of the fatherland but the experience gained in the Spanish Civil War made Germans realize the importance of light flak and its use in the ground role. By September 1939 Germany had the largest air defence system in the world with over 6,700 light and 2,600 heavy flak guns. Compared to this, the U.K. had only 540 heavy anti-aircraft guns at this stage.

After a relative low-key performance during the period of the Phoney War, British anti-aircraft artillery first came into its own during the Battle of Britain when it claimed to have downed 357 of the total of 1,733 German aircraft shot down. Though anti-aircraft guns shot down fewer aircraft than the Royal Air Force, its real impact was psychological as the ack-ack fire unnerved the German fliers, forcing them to fly higher and reduced their bombing accuracy. Moreover, ack-ack was the main defence against the night bombers, destroying 85 per cent of the German aircraft shot down at night.

An interesting concept tried out during the war was the all-gun belt from which all aircraft were excluded. This was developed to counter the growing V-1 threat, and to engage the flying bombs away from the urban areas. The British deployed almost 600 heavy AA guns along the coast, between Dover and Beachy Head, augmented by American 90mm guns and SCR-584 gun laying (GL) radars. This concept worked well with the guns shooting down over 80 per cent of the observed missiles. Britain also tried out unguided multi-barrel rocket launchers as air defence weapons but they were not too successful.

German anti-aircraft artillery was not only the largest air defence system but it was an equally potent one. From the 9,300 guns it had in September 1939, German *flakartillerie* grew fast during the war and, by June 1944, the Luftwaffe had 10,900 heavy and 22,200 light guns deployed in the west alone. One advantage the German flak personnel had was the experience gained during the Spanish Civil War, making them the most potent of all air defence gunners. Even during the Western European campaign of 1940, German flak had claimed 854 aircraft, a number which went up to 5,381 aircraft by October 1941.

The best known flak gun was the 88mm Flak 18/36/37 AA gun, which was equally effective against tanks and as a standard artillery gun and formed almost 60 per cent of the total heavy flak guns held by Germany. Though the flak made use of the technological advances like the radar, sound detectors, grooved projectiles, double fuzes and sabot projectiles, it faced problems also in terms of scarce resources. Poor personnel quality forced it to use even civilians and auxiliaries, who formed almost 44 per cent of its ranks in August 1944. Shortage of ammunition was another problem area, severity of which can be gauged by the fact that, by 1944, German flak was resorting to restrictions on firing and was using inert material in shells. In spite of these shortcomings and problems, German flak was one of the most effective anti-aircraft artilleries and downed almost two-thirds of all the Allied aircraft losses by 1944–45. The US Army Air Forces alone lost 7,821 aircraft to flak during the war, as against 6,800 to aircraft.

The measures adopted by German flak, like the use of civilians and auxiliaries for air defence duties and controlled firing of guns due to shortage of ammunition, would be resorted to by North Korea and Vietnam in the 1950s and 1960s.

American anti-aircraft artillery, even though a late entrant, performed well during all the campaigns. From shooting down ninety-six aircraft of 682 sorties during the Normandy campaign to 366 German aircraft downed in the Battle of the Bulge, American gunners were effective during the war and were credited with an impressive number of German aircraft shot down.

The Soviet Air Defence Forces (*Voyska Protivovozdushnoy Oborony, Voyska PVO*, formerly *Protivovozdushnaya Oborona Strany, PVO Strany*) was the air defence branch of the Soviet Armed Forces. Formed in 1941, it was one of the largest air defence forces in the world and played an important role in defeating the Luftwaffe on the Eastern Front during the Second World War. While confirmed figures of its performance and number of kills are not available, studies of individual battles indicate that it had achieved mixed results. During the Battle of Stalingrad, anti-aircraft guns shot down 273 German aircraft, i.e. 37 per cent from 10,000 sorties. While this number may not be as impressive as the performance of Western countries, it needs to be remembered that, technologically, the Soviet Union was at a disadvantage. This can also be seen from the number of rounds used to shoot down German aircraft, especially at night when the German aircraft would simply fly above the reach of searchlights and guns. In 1941 Soviet guns fired 715,000 rounds of medium calibre ammunition, downing only eleven aircraft and making for a poor performance – 65,000 rounds per kill. The performance of the guns with PUAZO fire-direction equipment was far better when it was claimed to have used just 313 rounds per kill.

Soviet AA guns were used in anti-tank role also, as was the German flak, and did equally well in this role. Again, similar to flak, the Soviets employed rail-mounted AA guns. One tactical concept tried out by the Soviet was the 'Hunter Batteries' or 'roving' guns. These tactics were later used by the North Koreans when faced with a technologically superior adversary in the Korean War.

The experiences and lessons learnt during the Second World War regarding employment of air defences were used during the later conflicts, primarily by the Communists.

Following the Second World War the United States accelerated the development of long-range jet bombers capable of carrying nuclear weapons. The B-47 Stratojet, supported by aerial refuelling aircraft, with its extended range could strike deep into the Soviet Union and became the mainstay of US strategic forces. By the mid-1950s the USA was capable of targeting the Soviet Union with over 2,000 nuclear bombs using 1,200 bombers. The B-47 was followed by the B-52 Stratofortress which posed a more significant threat to the Soviet Union with its greater range and payload. The Soviet Union was forced to develop intercontinental platforms as it could not station its bombers closer to the United States. The first long-range bomber was the Tu-4 Bull bomber which was given an aerial-refuelling capability to extend its range but, as these piston-driven bombers were vulnerable to air defence systems and jet interceptors, the Soviet Union began development of the 3M Bison and Tu-95 Bear which were its first true intercontinental delivery systems. These developments affected the development of anti-aircraft systems leading on to introduction of the first surface-to-air missile system as the existing air defence systems, with its aircraft and anti-aircraft artillery, were not capable of taking on the new threat.

The USA had started working on Project Nike in February 1945, well before the end of the Second World War, and it led to the development of Nike Ajax which entered service in 1954, becoming the first operational surface-to-air missile system. It was followed by the Soviet S-25 Berkut surface-to-air missile which first entered service in 1955. In the following years the real strides in surface-to-air missiles were taken by the USSR, which faced a far more serious bomber and reconnaissance aircraft threat than the United States.

It was not that surface-to-air missiles were a new concept. Nazi Germany had worked on both guided and unguided flak rockets during the Second World War. Four guided flak rockets, viz. *Enzian*, *Rheintochter*, *Schmetterling* and *Wasserfall*, were developed, of which *Wasserfall* was the most promising project. Designed to have an operational range of twenty-five kilometres, *Wasserfall* could not be fielded during the war due to technical problems faced in refining the guidance system. It was to have a simple radio-control manual-command-to-line-of-sight (MCLOS) system, but problems in telemetry and disappointing test results forced cancellation of the project. Moreover, the missile did not have a proximity fuze. That in itself was a big drawback and it is doubtful if *Wasserfall* would have succeeded even had it been fielded. Not only *Wasserfall*; by early 1945 all four guided rocket systems had been cancelled.

The unguided flak rockets fared better with both the *Foehn* and *Taifun* seeing operational service. Foehn was designed to engage low-flying aircraft and was fired from a 35-barrel launcher while Taifun was launched form a 30-barrel launcher mounted on an 88mm gun carriage. Three batteries of Foehn were commissioned and are credited with at least three confirmed kills. After the Second World War, the German flak rocket technology, as with the V-1 and V-2 rockets, and captured German engineers and technicians were used by both the USA and the Soviet Union to develop their own missile systems.

While the two superpowers were developing their respective missile programmes, a new factor that posed an additional threat to USSR and had to be factored in by the Soviet Union, was the high-flying spy plane, like the U-2 used by the USA to keep an eye on the Soviet Union. As they flew way beyond the reach of anti-aircraft guns, missiles were the only counter to these aircraft. For long, the US believed that the Soviet

Union did not have the capability to shoot down its spy planes but it was rudely shaken out of its belief as the Soviet Union developed the SA-2 Dvina missile system that was capable of shooting down an aircraft flying at altitudes of more than 20,000 metres. The SA-2 entered service in 1957 and achieved its first kill on 7 October 1959 when a Taiwanese Martin RB-57D Canberra was shot down over China by a salvo of three V-750 (1D) missiles at an altitude of 20,000 metres. The SA-2 went on to become one of the most widely deployed and used surface-to-air missiles in history and played a prominent role in South East Asian and Middle Eastern conflicts.

With the surface-to-air missiles becoming operational, the anti-aircraft guns seemed to be pushed back, destined to play a secondary, inconsequential role in all future wars. It was not that new guns were not developed. Based on experiences gained during the war, the major powers took their own routes to develop new weapons. The USA started work on a number of programmes like the quad .60-calibre Stinger gun system, 37mm Vigilante Gatling gun system and the 40mm M41-mounted Duster but it was only the 75mm Skysweeper and 20mm Gatling gun that became operational. Of these, Skysweeper was used for a relatively short period as Army studies in the mid-1950s indicated that guns could not provide adequate protection against the expected threat and that guided missiles would be more effective for the role of air defence in forward areas. The Army phased out its last anti-aircraft guns used in continental defence in mid-1960. Later efforts, like the Division Air Defence (DIVAD), to develop a self-propelled anti-aircraft gun system ended in failure and the US ultimately gave up on anti-aircraft guns as a weapon of choice.

The Soviet Union, on the other hand, with its tradition of reliance on artillery, developed a number of anti-aircraft guns in the years following the Second World War. One reason was also the fact that the surface-to-air missiles did not enter service until the mid-1950s and the Soviet Union had to rely on its anti-aircraft artillery as the ground air defence means, not only into that period but beyond into the period of deployment and expansion of SAM sites. It developed and fielded the 57mm and 100mm AA guns to fill the technological gap created by new Western weapons. Plus, it adopted the eight-gun battery concept from the earlier four-gun concept to provide greater density and effectiveness. Other measures were the gradual replacement of the 37mm AA and 12.7mm DShK M1938 AAMG by the 57mm AA gun and 14.5mm AAMG. All these weapons systems would play an important role in the wars to come, the first of which was the war in Korea.

The other two developments that took place during the Second World War, and which would influence air warfare and anti-aircraft artillery in the jet age, were radar and electronic warfare.

When the war started, the UK had developed and networked the radar into a nationwide command and control system and it had played a decisive role in the Battle of Britain. Chain Home, the early warning system, was used effectively not only by the Royal Air Force to take on the Luftwaffe but it proved to be invaluable for the guns in neutralizing German aircraft and the V-1 flying bombs. With the use of gun-laying radar introduced in 1939, British anti-aircraft artillery was able to improve its performance in downing the Luftwaffe night bombers and was using only 4,000 rounds to achieve a kill as against 30,000 rounds earlier. The guns had not been effective against the V-1 initially but as the defences were developed along the coast, the guns coupled with improved radars and use of proximity fuze were able to down almost 84 per cent of the V-1s observed, up from the 48 per cent earlier.

Germany used a two-tier radar network that warned fighter-interceptor squadrons of the impending arrival of enemy bombers. The first tier was the network of Freya early-warning radars which first picked up the Allied bombers, followed by the second network made up of Würzburg. In addition, a third network was used by ground controllers to guide the *Nachtjagdgeschwader* (night-fighter squadrons) pilots – usually flying twin-engine Messerschmitt Bf.110s, Junkers Ju.88Gs or Heinkel He.219s – towards Allied bombers until they picked them up on their airborne radar screens (*Lichtenstein*) or actually saw them. Integrated with this network was the Flak (*Fliegerabwehrkanone*, i.e., anti-aircraft artillery) with the 20, 37 and 88mm anti-aircraft guns aided by radar-controlled searchlights.

Radar was to go on to become the backbone of a modern air defence network although it needs to remembered that, in the first couple of decades following the Second World War, countries with a rudimentary radar network were able to take on a technologically much superior adversary.

The early wars, in Korea and Vietnam, were between unequal adversaries. The United States and the states supported and armed by it were confronted by technologically inferior adversaries during these two wars, more so in the air. In such asymmetrical conflicts, it was the anti-aircraft artillery that proved to be the nemesis of the airmen, causing more casualties than anything else. Adapting simple and yet effective measures like anti-aircraft ambushes and traps, anti-aircraft gunners rose to the occasion as they challenged and denied a free run to the air forces. There were times that, in face of anti-aircraft artillery, air operations failed to achieve their objectives. The strategic bombing campaigns simply did not work in South East Asia and proved to be of little use to break the will of the people and end the war. In fact, the resolve of the people rose as the campaign gained momentum. The AA gunners were the symbol of opposition and national resolve in this struggle.

In 1950, when North Korea crossed the 38th parallel at dawn on Sunday, 25 June, it was the beginning of the first war in the jet age. Both opposing sides used jets extensively. Although many older aircraft did take part in the conflict, it was jets all the way. North Korea did not have any credible air force to take on the United Nations' forces in the air until it got the support of People's Republic of China and the Soviet Union. Initially, the MiGs dominated the skies over Korea but were found to be wanting once the North American F-86 Sabre came on the scene. The onus of defending, and taking on the challenge of UN air forces, fell on the North Korean air defences armed with Second World War AA guns, and they performed admirably, given the limitations they had. Of the 1,041 combat-related losses of UN forces' aircraft, 816 were shot down by AA guns and small arms while 147 were shot down in air combat, i.e. almost 80 per cent of combat losses were due to AAA and only 14 per cent were lost in air combat. The threat from AA guns, especially at low level, where all tactical aircraft would have to fly, was still very real and potent. What was of import was that the maximum attrition was caused by light AA weapons – 79 per cent of aircraft destroyed by ground fire were by light flak and only 7 per cent by small arms and 14 per cent by heavy flak.

In the first jet age war, the AA guns had proved their mettle.

It may be argued that as the surface-to-air missiles had not been used in the Korean War, it was but natural that the losses would be accrued because of AAA. While it can be accepted that, in the absence of missiles, only guns would be the threat to the aircraft but what needs to be understood is that the AA guns, and not aircraft, were the *main* threat. Even in a scenario where both sides used jet aircraft, the main threat in the air was ground-based anti-aircraft weapons.

While the AAA did claim the maximum kills over adversary aircraft, the technologically advanced air forces (primarily the US Air Force in this case) at times gave them more credit than they deserved. All this was to deny the rightful credit to the Red Air Forces, manned and operated by the Soviet Union and the People's Republic of China. This was to project the Red Air Forces as inferior, and technically and tactically no match for the US Air Force. While it was true to some extent, the Communist forces were not as inferior as portrayed. In any case, the air defences that defeated the US Air Force were all red-blooded communist trained and equipped forces. Years later, during the War of Attrition, also, it was the Soviet air defences that denied the victory to Israel and made it accept the ceasefire agreement.

The air defence weapons developed and perfected by the Soviet Union, especially the missile systems, proved themselves time and again during this period. The failures, as they happened, were more because of tactical reasons and employing the wrong weapon system – as happened with the SA- 2 missile system when it failed against low-flying fighter aircraft, something it was never meant to counter.

The argument about whether guns or missiles were a more serious threat was partly answered in the Vietnam War. Of all the 2,255 aircraft combat losses, as per the USAF Operational Summary of November 1973, a total of 1,433 aircraft were lost to AAA while 110 were shot down by SAMs. Though the losses to SAMs are at times given as 205, the fact remains that almost 89 per cent of all losses in Vietnam were to AAA and less than 8 per cent to SAMs. In the case of rotary wings, all but nine of approximately 2,400 helicopters were lost to AAA. Only seven helicopters were shot down by SAMs, and two by MiGs. Over North Vietnam alone, 72 per cent of the 1,100 aircraft lost were to AA guns, while 19 per cent were to SAMs and only 8 per cent to MiGs.

Only during the LINEBACKER campaign did the AA guns not get more kills than the SAMs but then it was the B-52s which were the main workhorse of the campaign and they flew way above the effective ceiling of the guns. During LINEBACKER II, overall US Air Force losses included fifteen B-52s, two F-4s, two F-111s and one HH-53 search and rescue helicopter. Navy losses included two A-7s, two A-6s, one RA-5 and one F-4. Seventeen of these losses were attributed to SA-2 missiles, three to daytime MiG attacks, three to anti-aircraft artillery and three to unknown causes.

The use of precision-guided munitions should also have similarly reduced the attrition due to AA guns but a 1968 study indicated aircraft dropping PGMs took two to three times the number of flak hits as those dropping dumb bombs.[1]

All throughout, the AA guns proved themselves to be the most reliable air defence weapon, immune to jamming and other counter-measures but they lacked the range and accuracy so very vital to make a real impact. Still, it was the guns that scored almost all the hits during the wars in South Asia. The rare use of SA-2 missiles by India – Pakistan did not have any surface to air missile during the two wars – made no impact, the dozen or so launched during the Bangladesh War achieving just one probable kill to their credit. Again, it was the AAA that was responsible for almost half of the Indian Air Force's (IAF) losses during the Bangladesh War, during which the IAF so dominated the skies.

It was a similar narrative during the conflicts in the Middle East. The Six Day War of 1967 saw the SAMs deployed in large numbers by the Arab countries, especially Egypt. However, they were one element of the air defences that fell short. Thirty-eight of the total of forty-eight Israeli Air Force aircraft lost in the war were to AA guns with only one to a SAM – and that to a HAWK missile of the Israeli Air Defence when it shot down a F-4 near Dimona nuclear reactor in a case of friendly fire. On day one of the war, i.e. 5 June, when the IAF suffered maximum losses, thirteen of its aircraft fell to AA guns and none to SAMs.

It was during the War of Attrition that the SAMs were more successful, but still the AA guns outperformed them. As per US sources, Egyptian Air Defences shot down fifteen Israeli aircraft during the war – seven by SAMs and eight by AA guns.

Whatever be the number, and percentage, of kills achieved by the AAA, the real impact of the AAA lay in forcing the opposing air force, just by its potential to inflict losses, to use tactics and types of ordnance that were less than optimal, degrading the capabilities of the air force and denying it the freedom of operations the air forces so desperately sought.

While the SAMs may have made an impact, they were yet to arrive in a big way on the centre stage and the importance and relevance of AA guns could not be understated as yet. In the first three decades of the jet age, more aircraft were lost to AA guns than to any other cause and it was primarily the AA guns that called the shots.

Chapter 1

Korea 1950–53

On 25 June 1950, 507 Anti-Aircraft Artillery (Automatic Weapon) Battalion at Camp McGill, Japan, was ordered to organize a detachment for an 'air transport mission'. Three officers and thirty-two men were air-lifted with four M-55 quadruple-mounted 0.50 calibre AA machine guns by C-54 transport aircraft with the stated mission 'to establish air defence of an airfield in Korea'. Detachment X, as this unit was called, reached Suwon airfield, twenty kilometres north of Seoul at about 9.00am on 29 June and immediately got down to organizing the air defence at their new base. No sooner had the Detachment finished with their immediate deployment actions than the North Korean Air Force attacked the base. Four Yak-9s, 'looking like P-51s', came in from the north-east, attacking the airfield from about 1,400 feet. A pair of Yak-9s was in front, followed by two in single file. They made three passes and strafed the airfield, also dropping three medium bombs. The Detachment X gunners got into action, shooting down two Yak-9s. These were the first shots fired by US troops in the Korean War.

One of the pilots of the aircraft destroyed, a major in the North Korean Air Force, managed to bale out but was captured. At 8.00pm the airfield was again attacked, this time by two Yak-9s. The AAA engaged them but could not hit either of them. However, both North Korean Yaks were shot down by USAF F-80s.

Detachment X was evacuated from Suwon in face of the advancing North Korean Army and was moved to Taejon on 30 June and, later, to Japan for re-equipment.[1]

Just five years after the Second World War, war returned to Far East Asia as the North Korean Army crossed the 38th Parallel, pushing back the South Korean Army to the Pusan Peninsula, threatening the very existence of the Republic of Korea. The US troops hurriedly sent from Japan tried to stem the rout even as the Eighth US Army in Korea (EUSAK) held on to the Pusan bridgehead. Detachment X, mentioned above, was part of the force moved in from Japan.

This was the first war between the two major blocs and the first test of their resolve to defend and propagate their ideologies. Although the 'Iron Curtain' had descended in the West, dividing Europe into two camps, it was Korea that was to be the first battleground as the US-led coalition was to try and stem the spread of communism. Korea had been occupied by Japan in 1910 and, following the defeat of the Axis powers, was divided into two along the 38th Parallel, which was the de-facto border. North Korea was ruled by the Communist regime of Kim Il-sung, backed by the Soviet Union. Its People's Army was equipped largely with Russian tanks and artillery. The presidency of Syngman Rhee in the South was a 'democratic' state, although it believed in 'unity through force'. It had a poorly equipped army with no tanks or combat aircraft and was more of a glorified gendarmerie. The 38th Parallel had seen a series of violent and bloody clashes ever since the division of Korea and matters came to a head in June 1950 as North Korea launched a full-fledged attack on the Republic of Korea. By the end of August, South Korea was on the verge of collapse. The US troops sent from Japan were not of much help as the Eighth United States Army in Korea tried to hold on to the Pusan bridgehead.

Meanwhile, the United Nations Security Council decided to send a coalition force, with personnel from twenty-one countries, to Korea while declaring the North Korean act as an 'act of invasion'.

The UN counter-offensive was launched in September 1950 at Inchon, cutting off the North Korean communication lines and forcing them to withdraw back North. The hot pursuit by UN forces rattled the Chinese, making them cross the Yalu in October 1950 and enter the war directly. This in turn forced the UN forces to retreat and it was only in spring 1951 that UN forces could make any headway and advance northwards. The war was now more a stalemate and a war of attrition.

The war in the air was, however, a different ballgame. The superior US Air Force and UN forces simply drove away the North Korean Air Force from the skies. The bombing campaign destroyed much of North Korean industry, razed its cities and crippled its transport system. Even Russian-built MiG-15 fighters flown by Chinese airmen could not sustain the initial successes and the US Air Force restored its supremacy over the skies, challenged only by the ground-based air defences.

After three years of a bloody war, an armistice was signed on 27 July 1953, creating the Korean Demilitarized Zone to separate North and South Korea and allowing the return of prisoners. In the absence of a peace treaty, the two Koreas are technically still at war.

The Air War

The jet aircraft was central to the air combat in Korea for the first time and this made it different from all previous air wars. When North Korea invaded the Republic of Korea, it was supported by a vintage air force flying prop-driven Soviet Yakovlev Yak-9s and Lavochkin La-9s. The UN forces, on the other hand, had jets like the P-80 Shooting Star, F9F Panther and Gloster Meteor, making it an uneven fight. The balance was restored to some extent when the Chinese intervened directly in October 1950 and MiG-15s joined the fray. The presence of MiGs forced the UN forces to switch to safer, but less accurate, night bombing of targets as the USAF B-29 Superfortress bombers suffered heavy losses to the MiGs. It was only with the arrival of F-86 Sabres that the USAF had the capability of taking on the MiGs. Even though outnumbered, the F-86s took on the Chinese and North Korean air forces, coming out on top.

The Korean War also saw participation by the Chinese PLA Air Force and the Soviets in support of the Korean Air Force. During the war Soviet pilots claimed to have downed 1,106 enemy aircraft, including 650 F-86s, as against 335 MiG combat losses. China's People's Liberation Army Air Force (PLAAF) claimed 211 F-86s shot down and reported its own losses as 231 combat aircraft, mostly MiG-15s, and 168 other aircraft. The KPAF reported no data, but the UN Command estimated KPAF aircraft losses at 200 in the initial stage, with seventy after the Chinese intervention.

The USAF on the other hand claimed, and continues to claim, an F-86 Sabre kill ratio in excess of 10:1, with 792 MiG-15s and 108 other aircraft shot down by Sabres, and seventy-eight Sabres lost to enemy fire. The USAF disputed Soviet and Chinese claims of 650 and 211 downed

F-86s respectively. However, one unconfirmed source claims that the US Air Force later cited 230 losses out of 674 F-86s deployed to Korea. The total of aircraft actually shot down was, however, never confirmed.

While the jet aircraft being central to air combat was a marked departure from the Second World War, the reliance on strategic bombing as a means to an end was a continuation of air doctrine of yore. During the strategic bombing campaign, starting in June 1950, US forces dropped more bombs than it dropped during the entire Pacific campaign of the Second World War and destroyed almost every substantial building in North Korea, reducing the entire country to heaps of rubble, and forced most of the factories, schools, hospitals and government offices to move underground. US Air Force General Curtis LeMay even went on to comment: 'we went over there and fought the war and eventually burned down every town in North Korea anyway, some way or another, and some in South Korea, too.'

The severity of the bomber offensive can be gauged by the fact that US forces stopped the bombing of Pyongyang as there were no worthwhile targets left to bomb. According to one assessment, 'eighteen of twenty-two major cities in North Korea had been at least half obliterated.' Towards the end of the campaign, US bombers simply jettisoned their bombs into the sea or took on innocuous targets like footbridges. Another first of the Korean War was the large-scale use of helicopters like the Sikorsky H-19 for medical evacuation.

The overall impact of the air operations on the conduct and outcome of the war in Korea, however, is subject to divergent views. While the earlier view was that 'without question, the decisive force in the Korean War was air-power,'[2] a number of later analysts are of view that the air war never played a decisive role. As Robert Jackson asserts 'Allied air power, apart from blunting the communist offensives, never played a decisive part at any time of the conflict ...'.[3]

While the role played by the air has been debated, the contribution of anti-aircraft artillery in the air war is but a forgotten chapter, even though anti-aircraft artillery played a vital part at every stage of the air war – in the success and failure of air operations.

The air war in Korea was the first major post-Second World War conflict which saw extensive air operations, that too by the new rivals, the

USA and the Soviet Union. Within two days of the North Korean act of aggression, the air war started with nine North Korean aircraft attacking Kimpo and Suwon airfields. The strike was engaged by seven USAF aircraft making it the first aerial engagement of the Korean War. The first anti-aircraft engagement had to wait for a couple of days more as the US anti-aircraft detachments were yet to arrive from Japan. On 29 June a strike by four North Korean Yak-9s on Suwon airfield was engaged by Detachment X of 507 Anti-Aircraft Artillery (Automatic Weapon) Battalion, making it the first US Army unit to fire in anger during the war. One Yak-9 was shot down by the US Anti-Aircraft Artillery although the subsequent months hardly saw action involving the US ack-ack as the North Korean Air Force operations petered off.[4]

On the other hand, North Korean (and later the Chinese and the Soviet) anti-aircraft artillery was in the thick of battle throughout. North Korea had only twenty 76mm AA guns in June 1950 which were used for air defence of the rear areas while the field formations depended on the 12.7mm heavy machine guns to take on the enemy air. It is a different matter that the North Korean troops had no doctrine or training for countering a hostile air act. The US Air Force pilots were surprised to see North Korean soldiers stand up on being strafed and fire back with their rifles. For the American pilots, it was a 'foolhardy thing to do' but the North Korean soldiers caused enough damage to the attacking US aircraft to be taken seriously. Although the North Korean Army had infantry weapons only for air defence they proved lethal enough. More aircraft were lost by the USAF during the war to ground fire, especially small arms, than any other cause.

In the early months of the war with the initial push by North Korea driving back the South Korean Army, it was the US Air Force that stood between the North Korean Army and an outright victory. As the US Air Force took on the Reds, it faced stiff resistance from the Communist anti-aircraft artillery. The ack-ack was particularly effective at low level which made it difficult for the US Air Force to take on ground targets and reduced bombing accuracy. The B-26 light bombers not only found it difficult to manoeuvre in the small valleys of Korea but the hostile ground fire was causing substantial losses and damage.[5] The ground fire was the cause of some serious attrition. During a raid by twelve B-26s of 3rd Bombardment Group on a railway yard at Munsan airfield near the 38th Parallel on 28 June, the strike element suffered a loss of three B-26s – an attrition rate of 25 per cent.[6] It was not an isolated incident. During a low-level attack on Communist concentration near Pyongtaek on 7 July, three B-26s managed to destroy a number of trucks and left six to ten tanks burning but they also lost one of the three B-26s.[7] It was increasingly becoming evident that the light bombers could not afford low-level bombing raids and had to operate at medium altitude if they were to have any chance of survival.[8] The war was not yet one month old and already the primitive ack-ack had started taking a heavy toll.

In spite of hostile ground fire and heavy losses, the USAF did continue its operations, both close support and interdiction, and the ferocity of continued daytime attacks compelled North Korean units to resort to attack under cover of darkness.[9] The tide seemed to be turning in favour of the US Air Force and the absence of effective AAA was taking a heavy toll on the communist ground troops. The adverse effect on morale and disruption of supply system were serious enough for the North Korean Army to start taking air defence in right earnest. The field orders now instructed troops to take necessary precautions against hostile air – by way of camouflage and cover and, more importantly, on greater emphasis on using all available ground weapons in anti-aircraft role. The orders issued by the 25th Rifle Regiment for the crossing of the Naktong river are illustrative. The Field Commander's orders directed that

> The Anti-aircraft defence will be provided by the Regimental anti-aircraft unit supplemented by one heavy machine-gun section from each battalion. When enemy aircraft appear, 50 per cent of the infantry weapons will be diverted for anti-aircraft defence.[10]

Dependent on hand-held infantry weapons and, at best, the tripod-mounted heavy machine guns, this was the best North Korea could do as regards anti-aircraft measures. Things changed only after the Chinese People's Liberation Army (PLA) intervened directly.

China, in 1950, was economically in dire straits and its military was not prepared for a war, least of all with the USA. One thing in its favour, however, was the readiness of the Soviet Union to support the cause of war in Korea. The intervention by China in the Korean War was made only after an assurance by the Soviet Union of military and economic aid. The first intervention by China was on 14 October 1950 when two People's Liberation Army (PLA) aircraft carried out a raid at Kimpo airfield at 4.00am and again at 9.10pm. No damage was caused but China had made its intentions clear.[11]

Soon enough the PLA anti-aircraft artillery was to join the battle. On 15 October four US Mustang aircraft that were sent to search for the origin of this raid were shot at by flak from across the Yalu river, shooting down one Mustang. This was the first US Air Force aircraft shot down by Chinese anti-aircraft fire.[12]

The Chinese ack-ack would shoot at all aircraft that appeared along the Yalu river. This became a routine feature during any and all raids by the US near the Yalu and proved to be a hazard for the US Air Force aircraft. Restricted by orders not to cross the Yalu, the flak proved detrimental to the US air effort and soon it was obvious that the results of the US interdiction strikes were not commensurate with the effort applied.[13] The ack-ack was sporadic but effective enough to keep the bombers above 18,000 feet and damage the occasional bomber.

It was not only the flak that was changing. UN air forces had a more capable adversary in the air also. Although 1 November was just another day of US air raids over Korean targets when F-80s attacked Sinuiju airfield, destroying several Yak fighters on the ground for one F-80 shot down by anti-aircraft artillery located across the Yalu, things changed when, later in the day, six MiG-15 jets appeared for the first time in the war and fired on a T-6 and a flight of F-51 Mustangs in the Yalu area.[14]

With the arrival of the Chinese PLA, the flak with the field forces was more effective. Kim Il-Sung, the Supreme Leader of North Korea, ordered the raising of 'Hunter Groups' using volunteers. These groups were armed with infantry heavy machine guns and were accorded special privileges, including the decoration of 'Hero' and grant of furlough if they shot down three US aircraft over a ninety-day period. North Korea also used an elaborate system of 'flak traps' as they made dummies using parachutes, straw figures and strips of lights to lure US aircraft to take on 'convoys of trucks'. In addition, they had aircraft warning sentries at an interval of 300 to 400 metres to warn of raiding aircraft. These measures may seem pedantic but they did cause serious damage to US aircraft.[15] As the Reds used Hunter Groups, the US Air Force F-80s operated in pairs as 'Truck Hunters'. In the standard flight, the two F-80s were armed with rockets and .50-calibre machine guns. The leader flew 100 to 300 feet above ground level while the wingman flew at 1,000 feet. The Shooting Stars used rockets for flak suppression and the machine guns against the trucks and vehicles. Even so, the new flak measure had started taking a toll of US aircraft, forcing the US Air Force to initiate serious anti-flak measures. Flak suppression measures were soon to become the norm and it was routine to use a massive 'pre-bomber' strike to suppress flak at the target before sending in the bombers. The strike on Pyongyang airfield on 23 January 1951 was one such occasion. The 49th Fighter Bomber Wing of the US Air Force sent forty-six F-80s to suppress the flak deployed at the airfield wherein the F-80s used a combination of guns, bombs and rockets and, once they had finished, twelve B-29s were sent in to bomb the airfield.[16]

In the field the Communists were using new measures against the US Air Force. There was a marked increase in the number of flak guns. The armed reconnaissance missions started noticing an increasing ground fire, which was particularly lethal at low level. The increase in ground fire can be attributed to the anti-aircraft guns provided by China, and the Soviet Union to North Korea. The Koreans had asked for ten anti-aircraft regiments but were given only five.[17] Even so, it was again making its mark in the battlefield and in the air. This forced the US Air Force to change its tactics. The Truck Hunters were one such example. The RF-51s were now being sent in pairs on all missions for one to fly higher looking out for ground fire as one carried out survey and reconnaissance.[18]

The long-range interdiction missions were flown by four-ship formations with one element acting as lookouts. Thunderjets varied their attack patterns, all this to minimize loss to ground fire. It was not that the Communists were not adopting new methods of protecting their assets.

They started to hide their vehicles in tunnels. In case no tunnels were available, they built log reinforced bunkers in inaccessible ravines to hide the convoys. The movement of the vehicles was so planned that they moved from flak protected areas to bunker zone in one night, from the bunker zone to front lines on the second night and back to flak protected areas on the third night. The state was such that 'no truck was found in the open or protected only by camouflage'.[19]

There was a marked increase in the anti-aircraft weapon with the forward areas and along the supply routes. Earlier the forward troops had been armed only with 12.7mm machine guns but, with newly arrived Chinese and Soviet weapons, the truck-towed Soviet 37mm M-1939 anti-aircraft guns were used by the Communists along the supply routes. While the 12.7mm machine guns were effective at low altitudes only, the 37mm anti-aircraft guns could effectively engage aircraft up to a ceiling of 4,500 feet, firing a 1.6lb projectile at a rate of 160 rounds per minute against the aerial targets. This light flak gun was to become the mainstay of the North Korean air defences in the field. The change was not only in employment of better weapons but the density of flak was also increasing. From the early days when North Korea had only about twenty anti-aircraft guns, the US Air Force Intelligence could plot 252 flak guns and 673 automatic weapons in May 1951.

The other anti-aircraft guns added to the inventory were the Soviet 85mm Model 1939 gun, later supplemented by the 85mm Model 1944. The 85mm Model 1939 was capable of firing fifteen to twenty 20lb shells per minute at a muzzle velocity of 2,625 fps to an effective ceiling of 25,000 feet, while the 85mm Model 1944 had an additional muzzle velocity of 325 fps and an increased altitude capability of 4,000 feet. These were used in the rear areas including airfields. Although there was a remarkable jump in numbers, only a few of these guns were radar controlled.[20]

The increase in flak density was due to the preparations made by North Korea during the preparations for the 'fifth Phase' offensive. North Korea inducted new Soviet 37mm anti-aircraft guns and also auto-weapon anti-aircraft companies armed with Soviet 12.7mm heavy machine guns and, by May 1951, had built up its AA inventory to 252 heavy anti-aircraft guns and 673 automatic anti-aircraft weapons. The new flak positions picked up by US Air Force Intelligence were these weapons. The heavy anti-aircraft guns were mostly deployed at fixed sites while the 37mm anti-aircraft guns were used along the main supply routes. In April-May 1951, the North Korean anti-aircraft defences shot down fifty-nine US aircraft.[20] The better performance of Communist flak was due to better and more weapons, but equally important was the rapid augmentation of its flak defences by inducting regularly organized anti-aircraft regiments.[21]

In his book *Archie to SAM* Werrel mentions that some allied airmen reported the use of unguided flak which could reportedly reach an altitude of 10,560 feet but there were no indications of any successes. The reports of these flak rockets fizzled out by December 1952.[22]

The numbers may have increased many fold but anti-aircraft guns were grossly inadequate, not only because of their vintage but even their increased numbers were inadequate for the task at hand. The inadequacy of North Korean anti-aircraft resources to take on a modern air force like the US Far Eastern Air Force (FEAF) equipped with jet aircraft can be well appreciated by comparing the North Korean defences with what the Allied air forces had to face in Europe during the Second World War. Nazi Germany deployed one of the most dense air defence systems ever seen and it was routine to see more anti-aircraft guns deployed at one select target than in the entire North Korean inventory.[23] It was, therefore, no surprise to see the Far Eastern Air Force not taking the North Korean air defences seriously. It is a different matter that the Far Eastern Air Force paid a heavy price for disregarding the hostile air defences in the initial stages of the war. As the air war progressed, UN forces took to counter-measures to control their losses to hostile air defences – with good results. Even so, they lost a large number of aircraft to anti-aircraft fire which was by far a bigger threat than the North Korean Air Force. One reason for the continuing losses was the fact that North Korea kept improving their air defences, adapting new measures and making them more sophisticated. To discourage night attacks, the Communist forces strung lights on cliff faces to trick pilots into thinking they were attacking a truck convoy. Cables suspended over ravines could chop the wing from an aircraft. Anti-aircraft fire, even from small arms, constituted an ever-present threat.[24]

The battle between the US Air Force and the Communist anti-aircraft artillery was turning out to be a battle of wits with both sides using new tactics and methods to out-guess the other.

While this game of one-upmanship was going on, the Communist AAA had a new responsibility. China was building four new airfields ostensibly for use by the Soviet Air Force. The newly arrived AAA regiments of the PLA were given the responsibility of protecting these airfields. China employed most of the Communist Party Volunteer (CPV) anti-aircraft artillery units (a total of eleven regiments), along with the Soviet troops (eight regiments) to protect these airfields. This did not leave very many AA regiments for protection of the supply routes but then the priority of the defending the airfields was considered to be higher as compared to the supply routes.[25]

The air war was undergoing changes, subtle though they may have been. The Communists were building up their AAA and the Chinese, and now Soviet, air forces with their MiGs had started taking on the USAF, no longer shying away from a good fight. The MiGs were integrated with radar-controlled searchlight batteries, AAA and an early-warning radar network making it a formidable air defence system by mid-1951. The efficacy of this system was tested on 10 June 1951 when four B-29s on a SHORAN-guided bombing mission against a railway bridge at Kwaksan were illuminated by twenty-four radar-controlled searchlights, assisting twelve MiG-15s to engage the B-29 bombers and, into the bargain, shooting down two of them. A third, badly damaged, barely managed to get back to its base at Kimpo. The fourth B-29 managed to get away as it used electronic counter-measures to break the searchlight lock.[26] This was not the only raid which faced the now formidable communist air defences. Perhaps the most devastating raid occurred on 23 October 1951, when a swarm of over fifty MiGs mauled a force of nine B-29s. The unescorted formation lost three B-29s shot down and five heavily damaged. This attack resulted in the end of daylight missions for FEAF Bomber Command as the luxury of carrying out raids in the daytime, unchallenged, was no longer available to the USAF.

The USAF interdiction campaign was faring no better. No matter the effort, the communist supply route remained operative and the bridges and railways were soon enough repaired by the Reds, frustrating the USAF planners. The accuracy of fighter-bombers was severely affected, lowered to an abysmal level of only 7 per cent of the bombs dropped by the Thunderjets cutting the railway tracks.[27] The losses were mounting. According to one report, the Fifth Air Force of the USAF alone lost 115 aircraft during a four-month period (August–November 1951) to ground fire while 750 aircraft were damaged. (The losses were twenty-six fighters lost and twenty-four damaged in August, thirty-two lost and 233 damaged in September, thirty-three lost and 238 damaged in October and twenty-four lost and 255 damaged in November.[28] The high attrition, including a large number of aircraft damaged, appreciably lowered the aircraft serviceability and availability rates. If this was not frustrating enough, the flak suppression was proving to be not very effective. Though each fighter-bomber mission used a part of its ordnance for flak suppression, it only drove the flak gunners under cover for some time but rarely, if ever, destroyed or damaged the AA weapons.

A new phase of the air war started in November 1950 when about 100 Soviet MiGs joined their communist comrades. The balance of power in the air was shifting. The USAF losses also mounted as the new Soviet aircraft, the MiG-15s, took on US aircraft. The Soviet Union had about three fighter divisions by April 1951, operating from airfields just across the Korean border.[29] The Soviet 5th Guards Independent Air Division (GIAD) of Moscow *Protivo Vozdushnaya Oborona* (PVO) Division was the first Soviet air formation to be moved to China and was redesignated as the 151st IAD. The Soviet presence slowly built up and, by April 1951, there were two air divisions supporting the war in Korea. The aggressiveness of the Soviet pilots forced UN Bomber Command to curtail B-29 raids in North Korea unless they were accompanied by fighter escorts, and eventually only at night. The Soviet MiGs also began systematic attacks against UN fighter-bombers, thereby impeding the UN rail interdiction campaign then under way. At the same time, Chinese pilots also joined their Russian comrades in air operations, and so did North Koreans. At any time, from November 1951 onwards, the Communist air forces maintained three to four Chinese air divisions, along with two Soviet air divisions and one North Korean air division, totaling 350 to 400 MiG-15s, at the airfields on China's side of the Yalu. This preponderant force frequently launched as many as 100 MiGs at a time, flying them over the skies of North Korea to provide protection for the supply lines and bridges. Although there was a need to form a joint command from the military point of view, the Soviets refused, continuing to operate independently throughout the war. The lack of a single command system and co-ordination between Soviet air units and

Sino-Korean forces caused confusion. On occasion, Chinese or North Korean anti-aircraft artillery units blasted away at Soviet MiGs, while Russian pilots mistakenly shot down Chinese MiGs falsely identified as enemy Sabres.[30]

In addition to the air divisions, 64th PVO (Air Defence Forces) Corps included two Soviet AAA divisions (87th and 28th) along with 10th Searchlight Regiment. Each AAA division consisted of five AAA regiments with four batteries of six 37mm AA guns and four batteries of eight 85mm AA guns. They were assisted by target acquisition and director radars. The primary responsibility of Soviet AAA was to provide air defence to the four airfields used by 64 PVO and the airfield and bridges at Andung.[31]

The strength of Soviet AAA divisions, according to other sources, varied between one AAA division (67th AAA Division comprising of four AAA regiments, viz. 1982nd, 1986th, 1990th, and the 1994th Anti-Aircraft Artillery Regiments) to six AAA divisions as an Intelligence report claimed that

> Anti-aircraft strength, estimated to exceed six Soviet-style anti-aircraft divisions, is disposed at strategic points throughout Communist held territory.[32]

Wary of a direct war with the US, the Soviet Union insisted that its troops would not be used in forward areas and, to safeguard its interests and as a plausible deniability, the Soviet AAA gunners were issued Chinese documents before being inducted. In any case, the Soviet AAA troops were used only at airfields within Manchuria.[33] One AAA gunners Nikolay Melteshinov recalls:

> Our division was deployed next to a small Korean village near Andun. We were always happy when we shot down an American plane. However, our headquarters required evidence of downed planes. Therefore, the Koreans created special units, which were engaged in searches for evidence. During the first nine months of service, our division brought down 52 Sabres. Only once our joy was darkened: One of the Korean pilots flew a MiG to Seoul, defecting to the enemy.[34]

According to Soviet sources, the losses of the air corps during three years of war amounted to 335 aircraft, at least 120 pilots and sixty-eight gunners whereas the enemy's losses, according to the (inflated) data from the same sources, amounted to 1,250 aircraft, of which 1,100 were destroyed by the fighters and 150 by anti-aircraft artillery.

The Chinese AAA complement was four AAA divisions. The PVA Third and Nineteenth Armies, under orders from Chairman Mao Zedong, began to enter Korea in February 1951, alongside four field artillery divisions, two long-range artillery divisions, four anti-aircraft divisions, one multiple rocket launcher division and four tank regiments, marking the first time the Chinese had deployed such weapons in the war.[35]

The North Korean AAA, which was primarily used along supply routes and with the forward troops, was not so well equipped. At its zenith in early 1953 the North Korean Army had only 786 heavy and 1,672 light AA guns.[36]

A mixed deployment of AAA resources and a lack of a centralized control and co-ordination system obviously resulted in a number of fratricide cases, as mentioned earlier. It was not that the Communists did not have a radar network or lacked ground control interception (GCI) facilities to guide and control movement of their own aircraft. It was only that the three air forces operated in a vacuum, without any real co-ordination.

Even this un-coordinated air defence system was lethal enough. During the later stages of the war, the increasingly efficient communist radar defences threatened USAF strategic air operations. The numbers and sophistication of the Sino-Soviet radar net increased significantly. By December 1951, thirteen RUS II or DUMBO radars operated in the Sinuiju to Sariwon area alone.[37] In addition, a new type of high-frequency GCI radar, nicknamed TOKEN, appeared. The TOKEN radar operated in the S-band frequency around 3,000 megacycles. First detected in Moscow in 1951, it could direct several fighters simultaneously at ranges up to seventy miles away and was the most advanced GCI radar of its time. By June 1952 Sino-Soviet radar sites were guiding their night fighters to intercept FEAF bomber formations. During the latter half of 1952, the Communists co-ordinated anti-aircraft artillery (AAA) gun-laying radar with searchlights to illuminate bombers as an aid for both night fighters and AAA.

As a result, FEAF Bomber Command lost six B-29s and four crews during the month of December alone. Fortunately, the communists lacked a good night-fighter which was the only saving grace as the MiG-15s could not effectively close for the final kill. On 30 January 1953, Brigadier General W.R. Fisher, Commander of the Far East Air Force's Bomber Command wrote to the SAC Director of Operations about the marked improvement in the North Korean air defences and warned that if they(the North Koreans) develop an all-weather capability, 'the B-29 business is really going to get rough'.[38]

The effect of the co-ordinated air defence can also be gauged by the fact that the USAF was being forced to use more aircraft for diminishing results as the following illustrates:

> On a single mission, as many as forty B–29s hit a bridge, a mission that formerly might have been assigned to eight of the bombers; and fighter-bombers lavished 500 or more bombs on a single length of track. This kind of work from both Air Force and Marine squadrons, impressive though it was in terms of effort, could maintain no more than six cuts on North Korea's main rail lines, too few to do more than inconvenience the enemy.[39]

Failure or success of the interdiction missions is another debated topic. While the USAF maintains that its operations were successful and that it was even accepted by the Communists,

> During his meeting with Mao, Peng complained that the fighting capability of his troops had been weakened severely due to mounting casualties and too little supplies during the past few months of offensives. For Peng, the principal cause was that the CPV had no air cover or adequate anti-aircraft artillery to protect communication and supply lines, thus only 'sixty to seventy per cent of supplies' could reach the CPV's soldiers at the front.[40]

The USAF claim of effectively interdicting the Communist armies is, however, belied by an acknowledgement by the US Army that the North Koreans were better supplied, fed, and equipped in January 1953 than at any previous time. The interdiction did disrupt the North Korean's daylight movements and reduced their daily supplies by a substantial margin. Yet the isolation of the battlefield was never achieved. The study concluded[41]

> Notwithstanding the heavy damage inflicted by UN airpower, the overall air interdiction campaign in Korea had only partial success. The destruction did not succeed in significantly restricting the flow of the enemy's supplies to the frontlines, or in achieving interdiction of the battlefield.

Since the Chinese and North Koreans neither mounted nor were forced to repel large-scale attacks, they could adjust their supply effort to take advantage of the main weakness of Operation STRANGLE, an inability to conduct sustained attacks by night or in bad weather. Traffic moved with near impunity through darkness or rain, for aircrews had to rely on flares or moonlight to locate targets. Damaged roads and bridges were quickly repaired or bypassed, and the damage inflicted from the sky was not as severe as hoped because intense anti-aircraft fire reduced bombing accuracy in daylight. Nevertheless, interdiction continued, although against a broader range of targets, at times accompanied by great fanfare and arousing unrealistic expectations.

The US strategic reconnaissance missions were hit badly by the Communist air defence, almost as much as the bombing missions. The reconnaissance aircraft had to be accompanied by escort aircraft; at times two RF-80s were escorted by as many as forty F-86 fighters. The slow RB-29s had been stopped from operating in north-western Korea without fighter escort in June 1951, and the Communists eventually denied the MiG Alley to RB-29s during the day.[42]

While the Communist anti-aircraft artillery did admirably well against a technologically advanced air force, the US anti-aircraft artillery was hardly tested during the course of the war notwithstanding the fact that the first shots fire by US troops during the Korean War were by the anti-aircraft artillery.[43]

During the course of the war, a total of thirty-two anti-aircraft artillery units served in Korea, under the 216th Anti-Aircraft Artillery Group and 22nd Anti-Aircraft Artillery Group Headquarters. The US Air Force-led

UN forces effectively controlled the skies over Korea all throughout the war,. There was little for anti-aircraft artillery in terms of countering the Communist air threat and the anti-aircraft artillery units mostly functioned in the ground support role thereafter.

The 90mm gun battalions functioned largely as field artillery, supplementing the 155mm howitzer battalions. In one case, a 90mm battalion even served as divisional artillery. Automatic weapons battalions also served, very conspicuously, in the ground role.[44]

One of the battles where anti-aircraft artillery was used effectively in the ground role was during the retreat from the Chosin Reservoir.

> As the leading Chinese infantry came within range of the Americans, the US 57th Field Artillery Battalion used its 40mm anti-aircraft guns in an anti-personnel role. The heavy rounds tore through the densely packed Chinese ranks and some shells struck the rocky terrain, adding to the shrapnel effect and increasing the number of casualties. Both advancing and retreating Chinese units were cut to pieces by this gunfire. Only 600 of the division's men survived, but the PVA commanders were still eager to resume the offensive and deployed wings to work their way around the Americans' flanks.[45]

It was not that the US Air Force did not establish an air defence system in Korea. The air threat from North Korean Air Force had been effectively neutralized in the early weeks but, with the CPV joining the war, the threat from Communist air forces was real and credible. MiG-15s represented the top of the line Soviet aircraft and were more than a match to the best of US aircraft in service at that time. The Fifth Air Force had been given authority by the Far Eastern Air Force for the air defence in Korea. The threat of reprisal attacks and keeping the Communist air bases neutralized had worked initially and was enough for all the air defence UN forces required. Things changed with the Chinese Air Force getting involved directly in the war and there was always a risk that the Chinese with their air divisions in place could go for an all-out air war and take out targets in UN controlled areas. The other factor weighing in was the move of Fifth Air Force scheduled for autumn 1951. With a limited number of bases to operate from, the massed deployment of air assets presented a lucrative target to the Communists, making it imperative for the establishment of a formal air defence system.

The air defence system was formally established on 25 July 1951 with the Tactical Air Direction Centre of 605 Tactical Control Squadron assuming responsibility for air defence control over South Korea. The entire region was divided into four air defence sectors with the control being exercised by tactical air direction centres manned by 606 Aircraft Control and Warning Squadron at Kimpo airfield, 607 Aircraft Control and Warning Squadron at Yoju airfield, 6132 Aircraft Control and Warning Squadron at Taegu airfield and 1st Marine Air Wing's Ground Control Interception Squadron at Pusan. The system was beset by problems from the very outset. The main drawback was the limited range of the radars. Moreover, the Identification Friend or Foe (IFF) Mark III which equipped the Far Eastern Air Force aircraft could not be used and relied upon as the same IFF was also in service with the Soviet Union as it had been given to the Reds during the Second World War. A system of air corridors was then relied upon to identify friendlies – not that there was much need for the same, with the Communist air keeping a safe distance. The following is illustrative of the restrictions imposed by the Soviet Union on use of air force against targets in the South.

> Kim Il Sung wanted both the Chinese and Soviets to take a more active role in the air war and even take on offensive missions against the South but while acceding the need to strengthen the air defence system, Stalin in particular was emphatic that 'the air force belongs to the state and that the Chinese Volunteers should not use state planes'[46]

China was thus forced to carry out air defence missions only. Faced with the relentless air operations by the US Air Force, North Korea again appealed for offensive missions in autumn 1952. But all China agreed to was to allow North Korea to carry out 'heckler' missions with Po-2 biplanes.[47]

These restrictions on the use of air force were obviously not known to the USAF while planning and laying out their air defences. The Eighth Army's anti-aircraft artillery assets deployed in Korea, not including the anti-aircraft artillery units organic to field formations, totalled only ten automatic weapon batteries and two gun battalions. The 90mm gun batteries were deployed at Pusan, Inchon and Seoul for defence against high level attacks; 40mm automatic-weapon batteries were deployed at airfields and port installation for protection against low-level attacks. These anti-aircraft artillery units were not considered adequate and the Fifth Air Force, in June 1951, stated a minimum requirement of three gun battalions and twenty automatic weapon batteries which was increased to five gun battalions and thirty-six automatic-weapon batteries. These anti- aircraft units were simply not available and Fifth Air Force had to do with whatever was available. Things improved by the end of 1951 when the anti-aircraft artillery strength in Korea increased to four gun battalions and four automatic-weapon battalions (sixteen batteries).

The inadequacies of the US air defences were repeatedly exposed by North Korean Air Force lying PO-2 *hecklers*. The slow-flying aircraft were routinely picked up by the radars but the US Air Force found it difficult to shoot them down due to the speed differential between the intruders and the US interceptors. It was not that Communist *hecklers* always managed to get through unscathed, but such successes were rare. During a raid on Kimpo airfield on 23 September 1951, the PO-2 was detected but the automatic weapons failed to hit the raider. The Tactical Air Defence Centre 'Dentist' then scrambled an F-7F which intercepted and shot down the PO-2 north of Seoul.[48] In another incident involving 'Dentist', it was the anti-aircraft automatic-weapon battery which shot down a PO-2 over Inchon on 2 October. Such kills were rare, however, and on most of the occasions the Communist *hecklers* managed to raid the targets and get back without any loss.

The frequent raids by the Communists using slow, low-flying aircraft repeatedly exposed the chinks in the US air defence system. Though they hardly caused any damage, these raids were a huge embarrassment and frustrating. The limitations of US air defence in countering the limited air threat are best enumerated by the Director of Operations of Fifth Air Force:

'Shortages in anti-aircraft artillery weapons, deficiencies in available radar equipment, limitations in the number of aircraft and aircrew detailed to air defence duties, lack of sufficient dispersal space at our overcrowded air bases, the incompleteness of the Mark X IFF program, and the normal passive resistance to defensive measures after prolonged freedom from enemy attack, find both the Air Force and other installations vulnerable to enemy air attack.[49]

To add to the frustration, most of the raids were staged from partially operational airfields and even open fields as the light planes were not tied down to fully operational bases. The light aircraft could, and did, use any open field as their base and carried out the night raids. The effectiveness of the raids may be debatable but the harassment caused by the raids cannot be denied.

The Electronic Warfare Battles

During the war, most of the radars used by the North Korea were of Japanese origin, having been captured after the Second World War. Later, the Chinese PLAAF set up an integrated early-warning network with radars located at Vladivostok, Antung and Pyongyang and the three ground-controlled intercept (GCI) radars deployed along the Yalu. These radars were the German 'Freya' early warning and the 'Wurzburg' searchlight and anti-aircraft-control radars, also captured during the Second World War.

To counter these radars however, the US did not have the required wherewithal. Not only was there a lack of electronic warfare (EW) equipment but it lacked even the basic Electronic Intelligence (ELINT) about the North Korean air defences. The US had only two ELINT-configured RB-29s when the war broke out and, by early 1951, were left with only one.

Whatever data could be collected was hardly used due to organizational blocks. As the bombing operations continued to be intercepted and harassed, a rethink of the US EW policy was carried out which relaxed the norms for spot-jamming operations although barrage jamming, use of chaff, or communications jamming continued to be prohibited without specific approval from Far Eastern Air Force. One reason for not allowing the use of chaff was a misplaced fear that the Soviets would gain intelligence about a US capability which could be later used against the US.

With such restrictive guidelines, the first electronic counter-measures (ECM) operation was carried out on 10 April 1951 when B-29s jammed enemy gun-laying radars near Pyongyang. The efficacy of ECM was difficult to evaluate although intelligence specialists did note that the Chinese were making observable changes to their radar procedures and that anti-aircraft fire was 'extremely inaccurate' on cloudy days or at night. The US Air Force losses continued, however, and, following the loss of all eight bombers to communist interceptors in the Battle of Namsi on 23 October 1951, daytime operations by US Air Force were halted.

To improve the efficacy of bombing missions and escort tactics, a form of electronic triangulation called SHORAN (SHort RAnge Navigation) was introduced and soon it became the primary method of operation after November 1951 although it was not without problems, the main one being mutual interference between SHORAN and the ECM equipment.

Even as the US Air Force was trying out new tactics, North Korean defensive tactics were also evolving in response to Bomber Command's switch to night operations. Until the use of SHORAN, the ECM operator's primary focus was on jamming enemy anti-aircraft control radars. Now the primary threat to the B-29s came from a system which the Luftwaffe had called *Helle Nachtjagd*, or illuminated night-fighting, in which radar-controlled searchlights illuminated a bomber and GCI-guided fighters then attacked it visually. North Koreans used small groups of six to eight radar-controlled searchlights as guides for twelve to fifteen manually-controlled ones, and with many searchlights guarding key targets the threat posed by North Korean anti-aircraft fire was very credible. As the B-29s could only use a limited number of approaches due to limitations of SHORAN, the anti-aircraft was quite potent in select areas.

In the autumn of 1951 a vastly improved Soviet radar, nicknamed 'TOKEN' made its debut which further enhanced North Korean air defences.[50] Faced with such co-ordinated defences, the US Air Force feared that there would not be any 'safe' places left for the B-29s to operate, even at night. The fears came true over Kwaksan on the night of

10/11 June 1952 when the air defences claimed three B-29s. Alarmed by these developments, the commander of the Far East Air Forces Bomber Command noted:

> Without wishing to appear unduly alarmed, the whole feeling here is that these guys are beginning to develop a real overall air defense team which is making our margin of security in operations slimmer all the time. If they ever crack that last link and get an all-weather capability of pressing an accurate firing attack, the B-29 business is really going to get rough.[51]

This marked the end of the safe phase of nighttime B-29 operations. To counter the improved North Korean air defences, the USAF took on new measures of which the first was to carry out extensive ELINT missions building up the North Korean electronic order of battle. By June 1953 the USAF had identified twenty-eight confirmed North Korean early warning and twenty GCI radars along with thirty searchlight radar locations.

While stepping up EW measures, the USAF took some defensive measures to negate North Korean air defences. Firstly, it started avoiding altitudes where contrails could be formed, preventing the air defences from picking up the bombers. Secondly, no raids were planned during bright, moonlit nights. As cloud cover could not be controlled, US Air Force bombers had their undersides painted jet black to reduce the reflection in case they were caught by searchlights. Finally, the US Air Force compressed the length of the bomber stream by reducing the intervals between aircraft, which thus reduced the amount of time the entire formation was exposed to anti-aircraft fire. Reducing the interval between aircraft from three minutes to one reduced the period of vulnerability by 66 per cent.

Next was focusing on the three critical parts of the North Korean defensive system: the radars themselves, the searchlights, and the MIGs. US Air Force Bomber Command prioritized which radars should be jammed first, starting with the searchlight control units, then GCI radars, and, finally, early warning sites. The searchlight control radars were the most critical link as the entire defensive effort rested on illuminating the bomber so that the MiGs could carry out an 'observed' attack. September 1952 also saw the introduction of two more counter-measures – direct attacks on the searchlights and the use of chaff. While efforts to suppress searchlights were not successful, chaff was by far the most effective counter-measure employed.

The value of electronic counter-measures can be understood by the simple fact that the use of jamming and chaff by the bombers caused the searchlights to lose contact in more than 75 per cent of the cases, thus breaking the critical link in the defensive system. This left the MiGs blinded and not able to intercept the bombers. After January 1953, no more B-29s were lost. A study done by FEAF found that, after the switch to night operations in November 1951, losses and damage would have been three times greater if the bombers had not been able to employ electronic jamming and chaff.

While the use of electronic warfare tactics was beneficial, the official USAF history of the war admits that Air Force personnel 'had forgotten much of what they had learned ... about ECM' and they had to re-learn the techniques, not only wasting precious man hours but endangering the lives of countless airmen by not following standard procedures. This was highlighted by a FEAF *Report on the Korean War*, which noted in a searching and honest self-evaluation:

> An astounding facet of the Korean War was the number of old lessons that had to be relearned. Personnel, from the very highest staff officer to the lowest supervisor in the smallest unit, sometimes demonstrated a profound lack of knowledge of basic procedures and techniques learned in past operations and conflicts. We must conclude that these lessons were ignored, forgotten, couldn't be located, or were never documented – or if documented, were never disseminated.[52]

No matter what the reasons, the end result was that the Air Force had to relearn about electronic warfare, and it had to pay for those lessons in the same currency which all military forces must use to relearn forgotten lessons: reduced mission effectiveness, damaged and destroyed equipment, and the lives of brave men.

Forgotten lessons and losses due to the same are bad enough but incidents of fratricide are far worse. Nothing is more demoralizing than the air force attacking its own troops and claiming it as enemy kills. In one of such incidents, a B-26 bomber mistakenly struck a South Korean motor pool five times, killing four Republic of Korea (RoK) soldiers and damaging two jeeps.[53] Returning to base, the US crew claimed six *enemy* trucks destroyed. In another incident, UN anti-aircraft artillery destroyed two 315th C-119s while the aircraft were attempting a re-supply airdrop in June 1951. This fratricidal incident led to the adoption of new procedures for Identification, Friend or Foe during air-drop operations.[54]

Another issue brought to focus due to fratricide incidents was the need to check and verify the claims made by the US Air Force. Heightened scepticism within the Air Force over the validity of claims led to a test in August 1952 whereby B-26s bombed derelict trucks at night. Despite the rigged conditions, the bombers damaged slightly fewer than two trucks for every 100 bombs dropped – a far cry from the average of .97 enemy vehicles per sortie that the airmen advanced in their after-action reports.[55] On the other hand, there was a tendency to downplay own losses.

UNAF Losses	
Combat losses	1,041
Non-combat losses	945
Total losses	1,986
Losses to AAA	816
Air to Air Losses	147
Other causes	78
Total	1,041

Notwithstanding the claims of respective air forces, it is generally accepted that the UN Air Forces lost a total of 1,986 aircraft during the Korean War. Of these, 1,466 belonged to the Far East Air Force. If the non-combat related losses are excluded, the total losses were 1,041, with 816 aircraft falling to the anti-aircraft 'flak' and only 147 aircraft being lost in air-to-air combat.

Considering the losses to anti-aircraft weapons, light flak accounted for 79 per cent of the downed aircraft and 45 per cent of the damaged aircraft while heavy flak accounted for 14 per cent of downed aircraft and 3 per cent of the damaged aircraft, with small arms accounting for the rest.[56] More aircraft were lost during the tactical air operations, i.e. the close air support and interdiction missions, rather than during the strategic bombing operations, as revealed by a comparison of losses of F-80 Shooting Stars and B-29 Superfortresses. The F-80 flew 98,500 combat missions over Korea in which 277 aircraft were lost – a 150 in operational accidents, 113 shot down by anti-aircraft fire and fourteen in air-to-air combat.[57] On the other hand, B-29s flew over 21,000 sorties and only thirty-four B-29s were lost in combat, including four to flak.[58]

The flak effectiveness was marginal at best when viewed in terms of overall attrition rate. The total American (Air Force, Marine Corps, and Navy) combat losses of 1,230 aircraft were from 736,439 sorties which translates into an attrition rate of only 0.17 per cent. Although ground fire claimed all but 143 of the 1,230 aircraft, it still reflects a very low attrition rate by anti-aircraft artillery.

Not only was the attrition rate for the US Air Force low, it declined from 0.18 per cent per sortie in 1950 to 0.07 per cent in 1953 in spite of an increase in the North Korean anti-aircraft inventory during the same period although a major reason for the decline in loss rate was a shift from tactical to strategic air operations wherein aircraft like the B-29s flew beyond the effective ceiling of ground air defence weapons.

The overall loss of US aircraft may seem *negligible* when viewed in terms of attrition rate but the effort required to sustain the prolonged air campaign, and maintain a low loss rate, was a drain on the US economy. When weighed against the gains claimed by the US forces, it is debatable if the loss of over a thousand aircraft and aircrew can still be termed as negligible. Malcom Muir, a US Navy pilot who served in Korea, carried out an analysis of the gains of the US interdiction campaign and, considering the fact that US Navy alone lost seventy-four aircraft, each costing an average of $250,000, he was of the opinion that the air campaign may have been more costly for the US rather than North Korea and its allies.

> It is doubtful whether the interdiction campaign in Korea has been as costly to the enemy as to the US. The enemy has lost many vehicles, much rolling stock and supplies and has suffered heavy

physical destruction of property, but it is doubtful whether this has placed a greater strain on the economies of North Korea, China and the USSR than upon the economy of the United States. The cost of maintaining interdiction forces in and near Korea, the cost of the hundreds of aircraft lost and the thousands of tons of munitions and supplies consumed, and the expenditure of national resources have been keenly felt. Certainly the value of the United Nations aircraft lost alone is greater than that of all the enemy's vehicles, rolling stock and supplies destroyed. While the cost of the war assumes fantastic proportions to the United States, the enemy largely offsets our efforts by the use of his cheapest and most useful asset, mass manpower.[59]

Korea was the first of the many wars that USA was to fight post the Second World War in which an increasing reliance was placed on air power to achieve the stated goals. As the US Air Force remains technologically superior to all its adversaries, it has always aimed at achieving air supremacy over the battlefield and has routinely been successful in doing so. If anything has prevented a total domination of air space by US Air Forces, it has been the enemy air defence artillery rather than the opposing air force(s). The same was seen in Korea also. Although the US Air Force appeared to have had an upper hand over anti-aircraft, it failed to achieve its stated aims. This was the singular achievement of anti-aircraft artillery.

Chapter 2

Vietnam

The First Vietnam War began in December 1946 as the French attempted to disarm the Viet Minh Self Defence Forces in Hanoi and fullscale fighting broke out.[1] By early 1947 the French had driven the Viet Minh out of the major cities throughout the country but the communists controlled the countryside in the north with a growing army of some 50,000 men capable of standing up to the best the professional French Army and Navy could throw at them.[2] The war settled down to a deadly affair of guerrilla warfare, ambush and counter-ambush as Vietnamese and French forces fought for control of Vietnam and the population. By 1954 'Giap and the Chinese had built a tough, well-equipped, experienced, and dedicated army – a tool awaiting a great task and a master craftsman.'[3] The great task would be the decisive battle of Dien Bien Phu in western Vietnam, near Laos, a battle that would end the First Vietnam War and the French presence in Indochina.

French Operations

The initial French operations in Vietnam did not have to face any hostile Vietnamese AAA as the communists fielded their first anti-aircraft opposition only in January 1950.[4] The first three years did not see any worthwhile contribution by the AAA and it was only in November 1953 that it started affecting French Air operations in a significant manner when forty-five of fifty-one French aircraft were hit and two downed during air attacks on communist supply lines.[5]

It was during the battle of Dien Bien Phu that the AAA played a major role, helping the communists achieve a decisive victory over the French, leading to the end of the First Vietnam War and French presence in Indochina.

The battle was planned as a set-piece encounter by the French to insert forces in a stronghold, supported by air, to draw out the Vietnamese and destroy them with superior firepower. However, the communists turned the tables during the battle which occurred between March and May 1954. The French had carried out a similar operation at Na San in 1953 and hoped to repeat the same success, but the air turned out to be the weak link. To support the battle, the French had a total of 107 Second World War vintage combat aircraft. Having learnt their lessons, the communist had beefed up their artillery and had mustered eighty anti-aircraft guns – sixteen Viet Minh and sixty-four Chinese.

The battle started on 10 March 1954 with the communist artillery subjecting Dien Bien Phu to a direct artillery assault that closed down the airstrips within four days of the battle beginning.

The commander of Battalion 681, an air defence unit, recollects:

> The unit's troops had to operate round the clock to control the battlefield. The anti-aircraft guns and artillery pieces were disassembled to parts and carried by troops to regrouping places, and then re-assembled. Because the battalion's position was on a high mountain, troops had to dig long fortifications and build more than 200 footsteps for moving weapons, ammunition and wounded soldiers. Meanwhile, the enemy frenziedly bombarded these places to push back our operations and weapons transport for the Dien Bien Phu campaign. Some days, our troops had to work on empty stomachs because the enemy's bombs had hit the logistics team.
>
> During this campaign, Vietnam's air defence units shot down 62 enemy aircraft. Battalion 681 alone downed three enemy aircraft, contributing to the final victory of the Dien Bien Phu Campaign.[6]

A number of French aircraft were lost in the artillery assault. More importantly, the intense AA fire forced the French aircraft to fly higher, affecting the accuracy of both weapons and supply delivery. It was not long before the French garrison was choked – starved of its supplies and, as the garrison shrank with the Viet Minh closing in every day, French aircraft attempting to drop supplies became more and more vulnerable to anti-aircraft fire.[7]

The airdrops were a harrowing experience in that narrow valley, which permitted only straight approaches. According to one estimate, over half of French air drops fell in the communist areas.[8] In this seemingly one-sided battle, one of the rare occasions when the French achieved some success was on 28 March 1954 when, in an operation against the anti-aircraft artillery of the Viet Minh, legionnaires from *1er Bataillon Étranger de Parachutistes* (BEP) and *2e Régiment Étranger d'Infanterie* (REI), alongside French troops, destroyed one of the Viet Minh's anti-aircraft regiments. The communist anti-aircraft artillery otherwise took a heavy toll on the French aircraft. Quoting Barnard Fall:

> Communist anti-aircraft artillery played havoc among the lumbering transport planes as they slowly disgorged their loads. A few figures tell how murderous the air war around Dien Bien Phu was: of the 420 aircraft available in all of Indochina then, 62 were lost in connection with Dien Bien Phu and 167 sustained hits. Some of the American civilian pilots who flew the run said that Viet Minh flak was as dense as anything encountered during World War II over the Ruhr River.[9]

More than the direct losses caused to the French aircraft, the anti-aircraft fire helped in cutting off the garrison, leading to its eventual fall. More importantly, they cut off the fortress from the outside and neutralized one of its most potent weapons. Starved of its supplies, the garrison could no longer hold.[10]

What had happened at Dien Bien Phu was the failure of a momentous gamble that had been attempted by the French High Command and one of the major reasons for this failure was the anti-aircraft artillery. The French were routed at Dien Bien Phu, leading to their withdrawal from Vietnam.[11]

Second Indochina War

While the Gulf of Tonkin marks the formal US involvement in Indochina, the American had begun despatching advisers and equipment in the 1950s. The Viet Cong (VC) were a formidable opponent, although lacking air power. However, their anti-aircraft forces more than made up for the absence of an air force and gave stiff opposition to US air forces. The United States suffered its first combat aircraft loss on 2 February

1962 when a Fairchild C-123 Provider flying a low-level training mission failed to return. The United States lost eleven aircraft to hostile causes in 1962 and twenty-three in 1963. Even the tactical advantage that the South Vietnamese had by way of American helicopters was negated to a large extent by the VC using the hardy .50-calibre machine guns to bring down the rotary blades. The battle of Ap Bac fought on 2 January 1963 was one such example.

The battle was important for several reasons, least of all that for the first time the Viet Cong had achieved a victory over a numerically superior force.[12] They stood their ground, although outnumbered by more than five to one, and successfully stopped the well-equipped South Vietnamese army, supported by a combination of artillery and armoured units as well as by thirteen warplanes and five UH-1 helicopter gunships.

The Viet Cong displayed tactical acumen and a high standard of training when they held their fire as the reconnaissance aircraft flew over, lest they give away their positions. As the ten Plascecki CH-21 Shawnee helicopters carrying troops, escorted by the UH-1 Huey gunships, came in to land, the Viet Cong engaged them with machine-gun and small-arms fire and, within a few hours, downed five helicopters. The five heavily-armed Hueys failed to suppress the enemy fire. The Viet Cong anti-aircraft fire hit all five Hueys – one crashed as its rotor blades were knocked off. The intense groundfire shot down four of the troop-carrying CH-21s.[13]

Of the fifteen American helicopters, only one escaped undamaged, and five were either downed or destroyed.[14] Not only had the VC achieved a great tactical victory, the manner in which the anti-aircraft fire had played a role in doing so was something that could not be ignored for long, more so as the air was central to all operations in heavily forested terrain. The one advantage that South Vietnam had was air support and even that was now under threat.

The growing efficacy of Viet Cong anti-aircraft fire was specifically mentioned in the Central Intelligence Agency (CIA) Intelligence Report for November 1963.

> Perhaps even more disturbing than the VC's continued offensive abilities is evidence of a growing defensive capability against air-

supported assault by government forces. A government operation on 24–25 November in reaction to a VC attack in An Xuyen Province encountered heavy fire from what is believed to have been a VC anti-aircraft company prepositioned in anticipation with the result that a number of aircraft were damaged or destroyed. The anti-aircraft fire also helped prevent the operation, once the troops landed, from developing the momentum necessary to close off the VC defenders' avenues of escape.[15]

The growing AA capability, as the CIA report put it, was an acknowledgement of the tactical acumen by which the Viet Cong used their meagre resources for they had only light anti-aircraft weapons for the most of 1963. They had one anti-aircraft regiment, equipped almost entirely with weapons provided by China between 1950 and 1954.[16] Hanoi had been improving its air defences over the years but in 1963 it was still incapable of taking on a modern air force. To improve its air defence system, North Vietnam integrated the ground-based anti-aircraft systems and the North Vietnamese Air Force into one Air Defence Command on 23 October 1963.

Even with the infusion of new weapons, the force level was still modest as the air defence forces had only twenty-two search radars and a single Wurzburg fire-direction radar that China had supplied in 1954. These controlled sixteen batteries of Second World War era German 88mm anti-aircraft guns, supplied by the Soviets, although some sources mention that the North Vietnamese air defences had only four fire-control radars in the country, with only a tiny fraction of anti-aircraft weapons being radar-guided.

The 600 light anti-aircraft guns with the Viet Cong had no radar fire control. The radars were unreliable, short-range and almost useless during the frequent heavy rains; the primary early warning system was a network of forty visual look-out posts that reported hostile air activity to Hanoi and then on to each district headquarters that controlled anti-aircraft weapons. The transmission method was telephone or Morse code.[17]

Realizing the need to have an efficient warning and gun-control system in place, North Vietnam prioritized the raising of radar units. This was all the more required as the Vietnam People's Air Force (VPAF) had less than a hundred aircraft, none of them fighters, and the entire responsibility of air defence rested on ground-based anti-aircraft artillery. Moreover, US efforts had been to harass the coastal radars and degrade whatever little early warning capability Hanoi had. Starting with the Chinese supplied radars, North Vietnam built up three VPAF radar regiments (of the total eleven regiments), having eighteen radar companies. They held forty-four radars in 1964, sixty by February 1965 and about 100 by May 1965.

To exploit the limited resources to their optimal capability, an anti-aircraft training centre was established in Quang Ngai Province to impart instructions on aircraft recognition, techniques of fire, calculation of firing leads, preparation of anti-aircraft sites, drills in the use of these sites and basic tactics, the emphasis at this stage being to counter the South Vietnamese heliborne operations. The main challenge remained the paucity of resources which was partly met by autumn 1963 when Hanoi started receiving newer anti-aircraft weapons like the 12.7mm Soviet DSHK and .50-calibre machine guns. A limited number of 20mm cannon and 13.2mm machine guns and a few 35mm anti-aircraft guns were also provided by China during the year.

The new weapons soon made their presence felt as the Viet Cong anti-aircraft artillery, in a repeat of the battle of Ap Bac, hit twenty-five aircraft and downed five in An Xuyen province on 24 November 1963.[18] The more capable and effective 37mm guns and the 40mm anti-aircraft guns were received the next year, in April. For the first time, the Viet Cong had radar-capable AA weapons which could fire up to an altitude of more than 10,000 feet. These new weapons were to pose a serious threat to air operations, marking a sharp increase in US aircraft losses. From average monthly losses well below fifty until September 1963, losses rose to about a hundred from October 1963 onwards and, with the arrival of the new anti-aircraft weapons, US losses in aircraft climbed up to 180 in April 1964 and peaked at nearly 400 in September 1964. The correlation between increased attrition and the new AA weapons with the VC was obvious.

The war in the air took a turn following the Gulf of Tonkin incident in August 1964 when the US launched Operation PIERCE ARROW in retaliation for the purported attack on its Signals Intelligence (SIGINT) ship the USS *Maddox*.[18] This was the first air strike against North Vietnam, with the US Navy carrying out sixty-four strike sorties from the aircraft carriers USS *Ticonderoga* and *Constellation* against four torpedo-boat bases and an oil-storage facility. The US lost two of the sixty-four aircraft to anti-aircraft fire, with one pilot killed and another taken prisoner.[19]

This incident galvanized the North Vietnamese air defences as they carried out the mobilization and formation of large numbers of militia air defence cells. With not many anti-aircraft weapons to equip the militia, the majority were issued with rifles; only some cells were equipped with 12.7mm machine guns. All adults armed with rifles were told that it was their duty to shoot at US aircraft. This resulted in a unique phenomenon when, at the sound of air raid sirens, 'even waitresses would run outside and start firing, using weapons from 7.62 rifles to WWII Browning M-2 .50 calibre machine gun'. This was the 'Hanoi Habit'.

The military aid from the Soviet Union and China accelerated after Operation PIERCE ARROW. Anti-aircraft guns and ammunition constituted the bulk of the early Chinese and Soviet air defence assistance, a mixture of heavy (85 to 130mm), medium (57mm) and light (23mm) artillery with associated search and fire-control radars. It was not only weapons that China provided as assistance: it moved a large number of air and anti-aircraft units along the Chinese-Vietnamese border. On 12 August the headquarters of the Chinese People's Liberation Army (PLA) Air Force's Seventh Army was moved from Guangdong to Nanning, so that it would be able to take charge of possible operations in Guangxi and in areas adjacent to the Tonkin Gulf.[21] Four air divisions and one anti-aircraft artillery division were moved into areas adjacent to Vietnam and were ordered to maintain combat readiness. In the following months, two new airfields were constructed in Guangxi to serve the need of these forces. Beijing also designated eight other air force divisions in nearby regions as second-line units.[20]

Meanwhile, to augment the air defence forces, Ho Chi Minh requested Chinese anti-aircraft units during a meeting with Mao in May 1965 to help defend the capital, Hanoi, and the transportation network to include rail lines and bridges.[21] As Chinese forces began moving into North

Vietnam in July 1965 the 67th Anti-Aircraft Artillery Division was one of the first formations to move in and was used for operations in the western area of North Vietnam.[22] It was followed by the 61st and 63rd Anti-Aircraft Artillery Divisions, which entered Vietnam on 1 August 1965 from Yunnan and Guangxi respectively. The 61st Division had just arrived in Yen Bay on 5 August when, four days later, it was put into action against American McDonnell F-4 Phantom fighter-bombers for the first time. Using 37mm and 85mm anti-aircraft guns, they shot down one F-4, which was the first American aircraft to be shot down by Chinese anti-aircraft units. The troops of the 63rd Division entered the Kep area and engaged in their first battle with the Americans on 23 August. They shot down one American plane and damaged another.[23]

From early August 1965 to March 1969, a total of sixteen divisions (sixty-three regiments) of Chinese anti-aircraft artillery, with a total strength of over 150,000 men was deployed to defend strategically important targets, such as critical railway bridges on the Hanoi-Youyiguan and Hanoi-Lao Cai lines, and to cover Chinese engineering troops. There is no evidence that any of these units were engaged in operations south of Hanoi or in the defence of the Ho Chi Minh Trail. The last unit of Chinese anti-aircraft artillery forces left Vietnam in mid-March 1969. The Chinese claim that these troops had fought a total of 2,154 battles, and were responsible for shooting down 1,707 American planes and damaging another 1,608.[24]

It is interesting that the Chinese Air Force was never directly engaged in operations over Vietnamese territory while Chinese anti-aircraft artillery troops were sent there, although there was evidence that this had been discussed by Chinese and Vietnamese leaders in the spring and summer of 1965. The Chinese combat troops were not to be used south of the 21st Parallel in North Vietnam; however, the presence of those units secured the North's rear, turning the nation into the most heavily defended area in the world, and allowing the DRV to use resources in South Vietnam and elsewhere that would have been devoted to homeland defence.[25] In effect, the US would not be able to open a second front over the skies of North Vietnam, as it had been able to so successfully over Germany in the Second World War, due to these Chinese divisions.

The arrival of new and better anti-aircraft weapons was not the only problem facing US forces as they faced difficulty in mustering up adequate support elements for the air campaign. American signals intelligence coverage, particularly electronic intelligence, was limited to a handful of Air Force Douglas EB-66B Destroyer light bombers, the Marines' EF-10 Skyknight fighters and the Navy's EA-1 Skyraider attack aircraft and EA-3 Skywarrior bombers. The only American radar coverage of North Vietnamese air space for most of ROLLING THUNDER's first year came from Monkey Mountain just outside Da Nang, Navy ships and carrier-based Grumman E-1 Tracer airborne-early-warning (AEW) aircraft. Monkey Mountain's radar and signals-intelligence coverage was limited to about eighty miles north of the Demilitarized Zone. The Navy's radars, designed for detecting targets over water, were not effective in tracking low-flying targets that were moving over jungle or had mountainous terrain in the background. The radar coverage reliably penetrated only about thirty-five miles inland. Lacking a sophisticated radar cover, US Navy and Air Force planes operating over North Vietnam had to rely on visual detection of the enemy, be it on the ground or in the air. They were practically on their own.[26]

As a result of the limiting factors, the US air campaign took off in fits and starts as it mustered adequate resources for a sustained operation. After limiting itself to armed reconnaissance and fixed-target strikes in Laos in December 1964, the US carried out limited reprisal strikes on North Vietnam in February 1965, but the full-scale bombing campaign started only in March 1965. Codenamed ROLLING THUNDER, the first mission was launched on 2 March against an ammunition storage area near Xom Bang. The first ROLLING THUNDER mission was scheduled for 20 February, but was pushed back due to intervention by the American Embassy in Saigon.[27] Scaling up from reprisal attacks, the operation aimed to persuade North Vietnam to cease its support for the communist insurgency in South Vietnam, interdict communist supplies, destroy North Vietnam's industrial base, transportation system and air defences, and also boost the sagging morale of the Saigon regime while demonstrating American will. Relying primarily on air power, the foundation of the US strategy was summed up as 'if air strikes could destroy enough supplies to impede the flow of men and weapons coming south, [they] could help save American and South Vietnamese lives'.[28]

The manner in which the operation was planned, i.e. 'a program of measured and limited air action ... against selected targets in the DRV [Democratic Republic of Vietnam]', which would target North Vietnamese roads and railways south of the 20th Parallel and overall strategy revolving around preventing Soviet or Chinese intervention which was goal equal in importance to that of establishing South Vietnamese independence, was counter-productive.[29] Using air power with restrictions imposed on it was never going to yield the desired results and was to prove a costly affair, the signs of which were visible from the start of the campaign. And the anti-aircraft network had apparently not been factored in realistically. The complete operation went through five phases with Phase I, from March to June 1965, aimed at persuading North Vietnam to negotiate for peace and going in for selective targets only. The air strikes served little purpose, other than to harden the resolve of North Vietnam and leading to the creation of the world's most complex and lethal air defence networks.

At the start of ROLLING THUNDER, North Vietnam's anti-aircraft inventory had expanded from an estimated 1,000 guns to 2,000 which were assessed to be deployed at about 400 AA sites by the year's end. The primary anti-aircraft weapons were the 37mm and 57mm AA guns, although there were also a few 85mm and 100mm guns. The biggest threat, however, remained smaller calibre anti-aircraft weapons which were spread all over the countryside.

Starting in April 1965, as ROLLING THUNDER progressed, the North Vietnam air defence system underwent another massive expansion as it grew from twelve regiments with fourteen battalions to twenty-one regiments with forty-one battalions, including eight mobile battalions. The large numbers of guns were tactically dispersed to defend critical installations and population centres. North Vietnamese Army personnel had been undergoing training in the Soviet Union on the SA-2 missile system and, on their return, two regiments of SA-2s were raised and inducted into the air defence forces. Even the VPAF was expanded from one regiment of MiG-15/17 aircraft to three regiments while additionally introducing the MiG-21 Fishbed front-line fighter into the inventory. Continuing with the expansion of AD forces, North Vietnam increased the numbers of early-warning and fire-control radars, thereby enhancing the lethality of the AAA. In this, two more radar regiments were raised, bringing the total to four. This was to pose a serious challenge to the US air campaign in the future.

On 2 March, the first day of ROLLING THUNDER, nineteen A-1 Skyraiders struck the Quang Khe naval base. Six of the US aircraft were shot down during the mission.[30] This brought the total number of aircraft shot down since Operation PIERCE ARROW to eleven (five Air Force, four Navy, and two VNAF) with an additional forty-one damaged (seven Navy and thirty-four VNAF) during the various air strikes.[31] Lacking a modern air force to take on the combined US and South Vietnam Air Forces, North Vietnam had no intention of giving a free run to the opponents and its AAA was going to exact a heavy toll.

The initial air strikes had been limited to enemy radar and bridges between the 17th and 19th Parallels and were later extended to other military targets below the 20th Parallel, the first being the Quang Soui barracks which was attacked on 22 May 1965. The number of areas authorized to be attacked was gradually extended.

This was one major factor against the operation – the 'stop-go' manner of its conduct making it more of a series of isolated actions and not a continuous programme of sustained reprisals. The second mission was not launched until nearly two weeks after the first. Moreover, the routeing of US aircraft was fixed, with strict orders to follow the same route, time and again. This graduated extension of target areas, and the manner in which they were addressed, repeatedly, from the same route was going to be exploited by the North Vietnamese air defences to their advantage. Once a target was attacked, the North Vietnamese could expect the same target or types of targets to continue to be attacked for some time. This afforded them the opportunity to concentrate their defences on the predicted targets and routes. The route restrictions meant that aircraft would fly on predictable routes. The North Vietnamese simply had to concentrate large volumes of barrage fire along the likely avenues of approach that the aircraft would have to fly through. There was no need to aim at the aircraft, but simply fire into a predetermined area in space. As one US Navy pilot described it:

> Gunners didn't have to track a jet. All they had to do was draw a straight line between the airplane's roll-in point and its target, then

fill that portion of the sky with as much steel as possible. Regardless of its speed, the jet had to fly through that box. At that point probability theory takes over. It becomes a crapshoot.

The other problem of target selection was of a more serious concern. Airstrikes were strictly forbidden within sixty kilometres of Hanoi and within twenty kilometres of the port of Haiphong. A buffer zone along the China-Vietnam border was off limits as well. The geographical areas, called 'route packages', were demarcated and specific responsibility given to the USAF or the US Navy.

USAF aircraft were restricted to Route Packages I, V and VIA, while Navy aircraft were to attack targets in Route Packages II, III, IV and VIB. Not only was the target list approved by Washington, but restrictions were imposed which undermined the operations. According to one assessment:

> Targeting bore little resemblance to reality in that the sequence of attacks was unco-ordinated and the targets were approved randomly – even illogically. The North's airfields, which, according to any rational targeting policy, should have been hit first in the campaign, were also off-limits.[32]

The increase in anti-aircraft fire was affecting US air operations and there was mounting concern among air commanders over the cost of the constricted ROLLING THUNDER programme. In order to expand the air operations, Phase II of ROLLING THUNDER was launched in July 1965 and was to last until January 1966. It was primarily an interdiction campaign aimed at roads, bridges, boats and railways. The campaign met with stiff resistance from the North Vietnamese air defences which had grown not only in numbers but had become more effective.

Increase in Conventional Anti-Aircraft Weaponry[33]
5 July–30 September 1965

	Light Guns	Medium Guns	Auto Weapons	Total
5 July	920	1,386	639	2,945
30 Sep	1,183	1,747	1,229	4,159

The efficacy of anti-aircraft artillery can be assessed by the fact that in the last three weeks of August the Viet Cong shot down nineteen aircraft while, in September, they downed twenty-one more aircraft, taking the total US aircraft lost over the north to 114, and the surface-to-air missiles (SAMs) were yet to be fully unleashed against US aircraft. One major lapse on the part of the US air forces was to underestimate the anti-aircraft artillery, not only the sheer numbers fielded by Viet Cong but also their impact. In early 1965 the North Vietnamese manned about 1,200 anti-aircraft guns, which had increased to almost 3,000 guns within six months and over 4,000 by September 1965. Yet a study by the USAF estimated that the North Vietnamese had about 700 light and 900 medium guns, but made no estimate of the number of smaller automatic weapons.[34]

Most anti-aircraft guns were concentrated around important towns and cities, industrial sites, rail and road bridges, and transportation points. Mobility was an important tenet for using anti-aircraft artillery with as many as four alternative anti-aircraft battery sites prepared around a vital target area. Integrated with the anti-aircraft guns were the small arms which were used against all aircraft within range and regardless of speed. The Viet Cong would keep firing at an aircraft until it was out of sight, with a trained platoon shooting up to 1,000 rounds at a high-speed jet in three to five seconds. Barrage fire was another tactic employed by the Viet Cong with the guns kept heavily concentrated around select targets. Defending the important towns of Hanoi and Haiphong, the towns of Vinh, Thai Nguyen, Thanh Hoa and Yen Bai were an estimated 60 per cent of the 57mm and 85mm guns. This forced the US aircraft to operate in missions of two, three, or four aircraft.

To concentrate the fire and improve effectiveness, the Viet Cong deployed the anti-aircraft guns in formations of triangles, diamonds, and pentagons. Use of 'dummy sites' and moving the guns around to confuse the pilots, concentrating the fire on selected aircraft yielded good results for the anti-aircraft gunners. Along the Ho Chi Minh Trail, the anti-aircraft guns were emplaced on high ground, triangulated to cover the most likely approaches to the landing zones.[35] This increased their efficacy and, coupled with high standards of training and fire discipline, made it difficult for the USAF to operate, especially at low level. The Viet Cong were firing for effect as the following incident illustrates.

They made each bullet count. On December 22, 1972 a Vietnamese anti-aircraft unit using a single-barrel 14.7mm gun shot down an F-111 supersonic fighter-bomber. What was remarkable was the anti-aircraft gun had only 19 shells left when they spotted the American aircraft.[36]

Effective it may have been, but the Viet Cong anti-aircraft strength was yet to peak in numbers. By 1967 there were an estimated 9,000 anti-aircraft guns in North Vietnam. However, it was not the numbers that ultimately made the difference but the way they were employed that made the real impact.

The Soviet SA-2 Guideline surface-to-air missile system, which was to go on to alter the tactical air situation and the way the air war was conducted not only in South East Asia but in all subsequent wars, would prove to be the real game changer. The decision to supply SA-2 to North Vietnam had been taken in late 1964, after which training on the system was imparted to selected North Vietnamese personnel. Initially the SA-2 in North Vietnam was manned by Soviet personnel only and it was only later that they were handed over to the VC. The first SA-2 was detected by a Strategic Air Command (SAC) U-2 aircraft about fifteen miles south-east of Hanoi on 5 April 1965.[37] Earlier, a US Navy RF-8A Crusader had brought back photographs of the first positively identified SAM, but attacks to destroy the SAM sites were not ordered as a view within the US establishment was that the SAMs would not be used. The US Department of Defence believed that the sole purpose of the Soviet Union in placing missiles around Hanoi was to bolster the sagging morale of the North Vietnamese, not to fire them against aircraft. John T. McNaughton, the assistant secretary of defence for international security affairs, made clear the US belief of that time, saying, 'You don't think the North Vietnamese are going to use them. Putting them in is just a political ploy by the Russians to appease Hanoi.'[38]

This assumption was proved wrong on 23 July 1965 when the first missiles downed a USAF F-4C Phantom and a drone was shot down two days later.[39] Until that day there had been no incident of a SAM having been fired at US aircraft. It was a routine MiG combat air patrol (CAP) over North Vietnam for the 'Leopard' and 'Panther' flights on

24 July 1965, to cover the ingress and egress of a strike force of F-105D Thunderbirds attacking ground targets. Little resistance was expected as only a few MiGs had been sighted until then and no anti-aircraft fire was expected at 23,000 feet. Suddenly, the RB-66 electronic support aircraft accompanying the strike force called out 'Bluebells ringing, bluebells ringing', indicating that a Fan Song radar of an SA-2 had been found transmitting, but no SAM was sighted by the CAP. Five minutes later, the RB-66 again called out 'Bluebells ringing, bluebells ringing'. It was then that the pilot of Leopard 4 saw a missile climbing up towards the F-4s. The missile detonated less than a second later, flipping Leopard 2 upside down. Both crew members ejected just before the aircraft disintegrated. Three more F-4s were damaged. The SA-2 had struck.[40]

On July 23, American electronic warfare aircraft intercepted emissions from the Fan Song radars associated with SA-2 missiles. Early the next morning, the radar came up again. At this moment, several F-105 Thunderchiefs were about to hit an explosives plant at Lang Tai.

Flying cover above them, at about twenty thousand feet, were four F-4Cs under Lt Col William A. Alden. The EA-66B Destroyer that had recorded the radar signals flashed a warning, but it was too late. Alden looked down and discovered two or three missiles rising toward his Phantoms. One exploded just beneath his wingman. The F-4C caught fire, rolled away, then spiralled downwards. Its pilot, Capt. Richard P. Keirn, almost did not make it. He ejected successfully, but had to use the secondary system as flames surged through the cockpit. Keirn suffered a shrapnel wound in the leg, burns, and a bruised shoulder.

Capt. Keirn joined the ranks of prisoners of war, of whom, at 41, he became one of the oldest. He also gained the unfortunate distinction of being captive a second time: as a young pilot Keirn had been shot down by the Germans in the last months of World War II. Keirn's radar intercept officer, Capt. Roscoe H. Fobair, died in the attack. The other Phantoms also were damaged by near-misses, but safely returned to their base. On July 25, SA-2 missiles reacted again, this time to a reconnaissance drone, which they hit at 59,000 feet.

The SA-2 that shot down the RF-4C was fired by a Soviet training crew as the Vietnamese crew had not yet been fully trained. But Keirn's aircraft was not the only one hit by a SAM that day as all four RF-4Cs in the flight were severely damaged by close proximity fuse detonations. An account of the firing, as given by the Soviet personnel, mentions shooting down two F-4s:

> Everything began to change abruptly in July 1965. In North Vietnam began to deploy two battalions of air defence, equipped with our (Soviet) mobile anti-aircraft missile systems (SAM), S-75 'Dvina'. The support staff included Soviet soldiers and officers.
>
> On July 24, 1965 the SAM held their baptism by fire. At 14.00 hours, two major objectives were detected on the radar screens which were four 'Phantom' aircraft, flying in pairs. At 14:25 hours, Senior Lieutenant Konstantinov pressed the 'Start' (Launch) button. The first missile shot down the aircraft and the second missile hit same aircraft as it fell. Second Division had shot down two 'Phantom' aircraft.[41]

Starting in 1965 Soviets manned the SAMs and nearly all the forty-eight US aircraft shot down by SAMs were by Soviet personnel. One Russian SAM operator, Lieutenant Vadim Petrovich Shcherbakov, is credited with having destroyed twelve US aircraft from twenty engagements.[42] It was not that only Soviets manned the SAMs. The Viet Cong also did so, after undergoing training in the Soviet Union for six to nine months. Almost 1,000 Viet Cong underwent SAM training, of whom Nguyen Van Pheit was one. *The Missile Men of Vietnam* recounts his experience[43]

> Nguyen Van Pheit joined the North Vietnamese military in 1960. Five years later, as a young lieutenant, he was sent to the Soviet Union along with about 1,000 of his countrymen for SA-2 training. For nine months, they studied and drilled 14 hours a day, seven days a week, learning enough Russian that many became conversant with their instructors. The Soviets regularly served them bacon. Used to a Vietnamese diet rich in rice and vegetables, Phiet initially found the meat unappetizing, but he eventually got used to it. The

culmination of his training was launching SA-2s at two unmanned aircraft. Phiet and his crew nailed both of the targets and toasted their hits with champagne.

After graduating from missile school, Phiet was deployed to Hoa Binh Province, south-west of Hanoi, to work on the city's outer ring of air defence. Like the other SA-2s deployed to defend the North, the six missiles assigned to Phiet were arrayed in a rough circle on mobile, truck-towed launchers, with each missile positioned about a mile from its control and support vehicles.

A typical SA-2 battery relied on a truck-mounted Spoon Rest acquisition radar unit, which provided target location data to a rudimentary computer, and Fan Song guidance radar, which aided in missile guidance as well as target acquisition. To operate each SA-2, a minimum of five primary crewmen, in addition to maintenance and other support personnel, were required: three radar operators, one controller, and a battery commander.

On the afternoon of October 22, 1966, with his Soviet advisers looking on, Phiet received a report from headquarters in Hanoi that approximately two dozen US warplanes were inbound from Thailand. When the formation was within about 37 miles of his position, says Phiet, he ordered his radar operators to turn on their scopes, then reported back to his superiors that he'd electronically acquired the enemy formation. He was instructed to fire one missile when ready. His SA-2 roared off its launch rail. Though he was confident in his training and abilities, Phiet says he was nonetheless surprised when it hit its intended target, a US Air Force F-105 Thunderchief.

US records show that no F-105s were lost on that day over North Vietnam. The day before, however, a 'Thud' assigned to the 469th Tactical Fighter Squadron, based in Thailand, was seen exploding in a fireball on a bombing mission south of Hanoi. The pilot, Captain David J. Earll of Dallas, Texas, was initially reported missing in action. Twenty years later, his remains were located.

'The whole aircraft exploded,' Phiet remembers, gazing placidly into space.

Like other SA-2 crewmen, Phiet and his soldiers rarely got a day off or were granted leave. When they weren't on alert, they dozed inside their trucks or slept on the ground outside. The army supplied them with rice and other rations, which were often augmented with fresh meat and produce that North Vietnamese civilians living nearby provided.[43]

The real import of this incident was that the ability to enter North Vietnam at medium altitude and only face visually directed anti-aircraft and automatic weapons in the final 3,000 feet of roll-in on a target was now denied to US aircraft. The US Air Force tactical fighters had no protection in the form of onboard jammers and were vulnerable to radar-guided SAMs. It was only the strategic bombers, viz. B-52s, which had that capability, as did the US Navy. Nevertheless, by deploying the SAMs, the initiative was now with North Vietnam. In order to wrest back the initiative, the US decided to carry out retaliatory strikes against SAM sites. Launched on 27 July, the initial missions were a failure. Forty-six F-105s, supported by fifty-eight other aircraft, attacked the SAM site in the first such mission but, not only were six aircraft lost to AAA, the targets attacked were dummy sites.

On July 27, under the code name Spring High, General Moore sent forty-six F-105s, carrying napalm and CBUs, supported by fifty-eight other aircraft (three EB-66s, six Marine EF-10Bs, two EC-121s, eight F-105s, eight F-104s, four RF-101s, twelve F-4Cs, and fifteen KC-135s) to the offending missile installations. Eleven Thunderchiefs struck site 6 and twelve struck site 7. At the same time, twenty-three aircraft hit barracks areas suspected of housing SAM air defence personnel at nearby Cam Doi and Phu Nieu. In their bombing runs, pilots flew 50 to 100 feet above the terrain, four abreast, to deliver their napalm and CBU ordnance. The attack was very costly. The North Vietnamese had ringed the sites with 37mm, 57mm, and 85mm anti-aircraft guns, and aircraft flying into and out of the target areas faced intense groundfire for seven and a half minutes. Enemy gunners damaged one F-105 striking site 6. During the approach to Udorn with an escort, the damaged aircraft rammed its escort and both planes and pilots were lost. Two more Thunderchiefs were shot down with their pilots while attacking site 7. A fifth F–105 and pilot were lost in an associated strike on the Cam Doi barracks. A sixth was downed after hitting the barracks at Phu Nieu, but the pilot was rescued, the sole survivor of the anti-aircraft barrage. The heavy attrition was even more distressing in light of electronic evidence that Fan Song radars were emitting before, during, and after the air strikes and that bomb damage assessment photos disclosed that there was a dummy missile in site 6, placed there as a trap, and that site 7 was empty.

Although all but one of the aircraft losses were caused directly or indirectly by conventional antiaircraft fire, air commanders were most concerned about the proliferating SAM sites.

During the next two days, the Navy flew 124 missions, with an outcome not unlike the Air Force's first anti-SAM effort on July 27: high cost and no verifiable results. Intense groundfire downed five Navy aircraft and damaged seven. Two pilots were lost. Once again, North Vietnam's air defence cadres had camouflaged the sites, positioned many anti-aircraft weapons in the surrounding area, and dispersed their missile equipment prior to the Navy's search. The downing of a second U.S. aircraft by a SA-2 missile and the Navy's five losses during its retaliatory search sent shock waves throughout the JCS and the services.[44]

The USAF having failed to find and destroy any SAM sites, the US Navy decided to carry out anti-SAM missions of their own. On 12 August, Operation IRON HAND was launched by the US Navy while the USAF was asked to stand down. A total of 124 US Navy aircraft undertook a massive search for the SAM sites in North Vietnam over two days, but fared no better than the USAF attempts. The result was the same as for the first anti-SAM mission of 27 July – the US Navy failed to locate any SAM site and in less than forty-five minutes during the second day of the operation, they had lost seven aircraft to intense AAA.[45]

The US Navy continued with the IRON HAND missions to try and reduce the effectiveness of North Vietnam's SAM and anti-aircraft threat. Centred on the AGM-45 Shrike, these missions were mostly flown in support of 'Alpha strikes' or any other mission in which a major SAM threat was recognized. They were considered some of the most terrifying and costliest missions flown. Even with IRON HAND, the Alpha strikes suffered heavy losses due to the lack of self-protecting jammers which necessitated the use of low-level tactics, exposing them to AAA. It was not uncommon for more than 50 per cent of aircraft on each Alpha strike to receive combat damage.[46]

One reason the initial anti-SAM strikes failed to hit a real site and were taken in by North Vietnamese deception measures was because the North Vietnamese took great pains to conceal the SAM sites, readily abandoning built-up sites to build new ones, using a 'launch and move' tactic. A large number of these sites were equipped with dummy missiles to deceive USAF crews.[47] Another measure adopted was to deploy the SAMs in a more spread out and non-uniform pattern, unlike the standard Soviet clover pattern. However, the traditional deployment pattern was retained for some sites and camouflage was used extensively on the mobile launchers; some missiles were even stood upright and covered up to look like trees while still being ready to fire in under two minutes.

By now, the North Vietnamese had five SA-2 missile sites in place, roughly in a circle within twenty nautical miles of Hanoi and were sufficiently trained to man the SAMs on their own. They were able to carry out a full engagement on their own a month later, on 24 August 1965. By the end of the year, they would have fifty-six such sites ready. Although the initial attempts had been disastrous, the US continued with anti-SAM strikes, finally achieving success on 17 October 1965 when, for the first time, a SAM site was claimed to have been destroyed by an air strike.[48]

> Five Navy Iron Hand aircraft, accompanying a joint Air Force and Navy Rolling Thunder mission against the Bac Can and Thai Nguyen bridges on the north-east rail line, prepared to strike a missile site near Kep airfield, not far from the rail line. The missile installation, assigned number 32, had been detected two days earlier by a drone. As the Rolling Thunder mission neared the target, the Iron Hand aircraft, consisting of one A-6A Intruder and four A-4E Skyhawks, all from the carrier *Independence*, broke off, popped up to

8,000 feet, and attacked the missile and associated equipment from two directions. As the lead aircraft, the A-6A strung eighteen Mark V 500-pound bombs across a missile transporter park, each of the A-4Es dropped 500-pound and 1,000-pound bombs from about 4,500 feet on the revetments. One missile was destroyed by a bomb, and the second missile, after snaking on the ground, burned itself out. The attack also destroyed ten missile transporter vehicles, damaged four others, and left three vans in flames. All five aircraft returned safely to the *Independence*. This was the first confirmed destruction of missiles and related equipment since the Air Force conducted an initial authorized strike on a missile site on July 27, 1965.

The IRON HAND repeated the successful strike on 7 November 1965, when the SAM sites south of Nam Dinh, of 236th Missile Regiment, were attacked and two of the regiment's four missile battalions and the regimental technical support battalion were claimed to have been destroyed.[49] The USAF had started its own anti-SAM programme in August 1965 and, after tests in continental USA, the first Wild Weasel team with four modified F-100Fs arrived in Vietnam in mid-November to carry out further field tests from 28 November 1965 to 26 January 1966. During these, it lost an F-100F to AA fire on 20 December, hit by a 37mm shell in the afterburner of the aircraft. The first success for the Wild Weasel programme came soon after on 22 December, when a SAM site was taken out in the railyard at Yen Bai, some seventy-five miles north-west of Hanoi. According to one source, all but one of the F-100s were lost during the year and were replaced by three more F-100s in February of 1966.[50]

The early warning radars that provided cueing for the North Vietnamese anti-aircraft artillery were also stuck repeatedly during the year but proved hard to destroy due to their mobility and ease of repair. At the time of the Christmas ceasefire in 1965, the US had lost a total of 163 aircraft during the first eleven months of ROLLING THUNDER, including FLAMING DART and had failed to bring North Vietnam to the bargaining table. The figures for aircraft losses, however, need elaboration. During the year, a total of 55,560 sorties was flown by US and South Vietnam Air Force aircraft during which a total of 481 aircraft, both fixed-wing (311) and rotary (170), were lost over South Asia to include North Vietnam, South Vietnam and Laos. Over North Vietnam, the US lost a total of 185 aircraft – 153 to anti-aircraft fire, eleven to SAMs and four to MiGs while seventeen were operational losses. Over 82 per cent of aircraft shot down over North Vietnam were to anti-aircraft fire alone.[51]

When the air operations resumed in 1966, the US continued its efforts to expand its efforts in the air, adding new categories of targets and expanding the targeted areas. Phase III of ROLLING THUNDER, from January to October 1966, focused on North Vietnam's petroleum, oil and lubricant (POL) resources. Industrial and POL targets were struck for the first time inside the prohibited areas surrounding Hanoi and Haiphong. April saw the initiation of attacks against the chokepoints along the lines of communications. The first use of B-52s in North Vietnam occurred on 11 April, with thirty B-52s dropping nearly 1,400 750lb and 1,000lb bombs on Mu Gia Pass. With the experience gained during the latter half of 1965, electronic counter-measures were employed only when operationally necessary to avoid undue exposure of US capabilities to North Vietnamese SAM and radar operators.

While the USAF and Navy were refining tactics and procedures, North Vietnam had used the long ceasefire from December 1965 to January 1966 to further consolidate its air defences as it spread from Hanoi and Haiphong to Thanh Hoa and to Ha Tinh. New SAM sites were built, an increase by one-third in just one month and anti-aircraft artillery deployments were extended to cover the vulnerable lines of communications. The VPAF added new MiGs. Command and control procedures were refined, as was the surveillance cover. The result of these measures was the first night intercept of a US F-4B flight by MiG-17s on the night of 3 February 1966.

In February 1966, an RB-66C Destroyer was shot down by a North Vietnamese SA-2.[52] What made this incident important was that the RB-66 was an aircraft specifically modified to detect and jam the SA-2 but it had been shot down by the very SAM it was supposed to detect and jam. North Vietnamese SA-2 operators had used multiple radars to detect the RB-66, then adopted frequency agility to get on to a frequency not being jammed by the RB-66, and then carried out a delayed target engagement to defeat the counter-measures employed by the RB-66C. These measures also reduced the time the SAM site was actually vulnerable to detection and possible destruction. This engagement showed the high degree of technical proficiency of the North Vietnamese SAM operators, and revealed the vulnerability of US aircraft in spite of all the electronic counter-measures being used by them.

For all the tactical aircraft, with detection and counter-measure equipment inferior to the RB-66C, the only possibility of countering the SAM was visual detection of the missile and the violent 'SAM break' manoeuvre to defeat the missile guidance.[53] One major limitation of this approach was the impracticability of using it with an overcast sky when clouds could hide the missiles in flight, reducing the reaction time available to the pilot.

By August 1966 the North Vietnamese air defence system had sixty-five fighter aircraft, twenty-five battalions of SA-2s, 271 radars and 4,400 pieces of anti-aircraft artillery. The light anti-aircraft guns had been increased fourfold to set up a concentrated anti-aircraft network covering the airspace below 13,000 feet. The improvement in the air defences, both qualitatively and quantitatively, had an immediate impact on the air operations with both the USAF and US Navy experiencing an upward trend in losses in 1966. This was evident by the increase of air losses in 1966 to 280 from 163 the year before. The less than full implementation of the strategy for ROLLING THUNDER had only worsened the situation and the low-level tactics previously employed by US aircraft were no longer viable due to improved AAA defences. The US Navy, from using an approach to the target at 3,500 to 5,000 feet, was forced to use a high-speed approach to the target between 7,000 and 12,000 feet, with varying altitudes and heading. This change in tactics was a result of the increased SAM threat although it resulted in the need for flying through the heart of the SA-2 envelope, resulting in extremely high loss rates. Between January 1965 and December 1966, 384 aircraft were shot down by anti-aircraft fire and thrice that number suffered battle damage due to flak. Of this, 53 per cent of hits were found to have occurred below 4,500 feet altitude and only 6 per cent between 4,500 and 5,000 feet. The anti-aircraft fire at low level was still the single biggest threat to US aircraft[54].

The loss of the initiative forced the United States to make a concerted effort to innovate not only tactics but also develop new technological support systems. The QRC-160 jamming pod introduced in September 1966 was one such measure. Normally carried by F-105s, the use of QRC-160 was initially found to be effective in deceiving the SAMs but they were never available in adequate numbers to make a real difference.[55] Moreover, the North Vietnamese SAM operators soon refined their drills to counter the new challenge and came up with SAM ambush tactics. The use of multiple radars to track and identify RB-66s had already been demonstrated by them. Now they used a MiG to lure the US fighters into an engagement zone covered by multiple radars and having overlapping engagement circles, from a number of SAM sites. Once the US fighters were lured into the circle, the SAM operators fired six SA-2 missiles, from different sites, followed by an attack by four MiG fighters. Although no US fighters were shot down, this had shown the technological and tactical acumen of North Vietnamese SAM operators, and that the SAM threat could not be countered or suppressed just by jammers and electronic measures. The SAM tactics adopted by North Vietnam underwent another change in December 1966, when they used the SAM barrage for the first time. Rather than firing SAMs in ones and twos, the SAM operators fired larger number of SAMs from multiple sites. This was to negate the effects of self-protection jammers. The use of stand-off jammers was in any case getting restricted as the proliferation of SAM sites was forcing back the protective orbits of the stand-off jammers like the EB-66C and EKA-3B, greatly reducing their jamming effectiveness. With the effectiveness of jammers being reduced, it resulted in the highest losses to the SA-2 for the entire year.[56]

As with the other attempts like QRC-160 and RB-66, Project Shoehorn of the US Navy never really succeeded. In this, the US Navy tactical fighters were equipped with the ALQ-51 deception jammer which sent a false return signal to the SAM or AAA radar, with the aim of presenting a false target to the radar operator so that he would not be able to figure out which target to fire on. Initially the deception jammer worked out fine and the loss rate to SAMs fell to one plane per fifty missiles fired, compared to one plane per ten missiles with no ALQ-51.[57] With repeated exposure to the ALQ-51, the North Vietnamese missile crews soon developed a technique to differentiate the false returns presented by the deception jammer. The ALQ-51 was no longer a guarantee that the aircraft would not be fired upon by the SA-2. It proved to be just another attempt by the US to use technology to defeat the SAMs but had yet again it had not succeeded. The losses to SAMs continued to rise. The one weapon that seemed to have succeeded in countering the SAMs was the AGM-45 Shrike missile which had been first used on 18 April 1966. It was designed to guide itself to the targeted radar by homing on to its emissions. Widely used in IRON HAND strikes, this was one weapon whose counter had not yet been developed by North Vietnam and they, for now at least, were forced to switch off the radars and cease any active engagement. The one drawback of Shrike was the small 150lb fragmentation warhead, designed to perforate radar antennae which did not cause much damage to the radar. Still, the switching-off of the radars and cessation of engagement by the SAMs was no mean achievement.[58] The upward trend in losses to SAMs was also related to an increase in overall air operations. From 54,860 sorties in 1965, the US carried out 147,020 sorties during 1966, an increase of almost 170 per cent. Of greater interest was an increase in attack sorties – and a decrease in number of support sorties during the year. While the attack sorties increased to 81,360 sorties (an increase of over 200 per cent over the previous year), the support sorties decreased to only 65,660, i.e there was a lesser number of support sorties. The losses on the other hand increased to a total of 814, including 495 fixed-wing aircraft and 319 rotary wings. The losses over North Vietnam were 316, of which 240 were to anti-aircraft fire, thirty-one to SAMs and twelve to MiGs with thirty-three operational losses.

A realistic assessment of ROLLING THUNDER operations in 1966 showed that the scaled-up air operations against North Vietnam had not delivered the promised results and whatever the damage had been caused it was not so severe so as to hamper North Vietnam's operations. On the other hand, North Vietnam had demonstrated a tremendous ability to repair and recover from the damage it had suffered. Militarily it had improved its capabilities, especially of its air defences. ROLLING THUNDER, at the end of 1966, had failed in its objectives.[59]

1967 saw air operations peak during ROLLING THUNDER as a total of 191,120 sorties was launched by the US, of which 106,940 were attack sorties. The US also fielded newer weapons and tried out newer tactics. In 1967 the Bullpup was augmented by the AGM-62 Walleye. A glide bomb, it used a television camera in the nose to lock on to targets of high contrast and, once released, flew to the point of impact without the need for constant control by the pilot. It was first used on 11 March by the US Navy against the Than Hoa bridge. Although all three bombs hit the bridge, the spans could not be brought down due to the limited amount of HE the weapons carried – the 1,000lb weapons contained only 450 pounds of explosives; it simply lacked the firepower to bring down the spans. They were, however, used successfully against other targets like the MiG bases at Phuc Yen and other pinpoint targets in the Hanoi and Haiphong areas, including the Paul Doumer Bridge. The main impact of using precision-guided munitions was the reduction in sorties required to attack a target, thereby bringing down exposure to hostile anti-aircraft fire and controlling attrition.[60] Interestingly, the overall loss rate rose during the year, even as more and more PGMs were used by the US during the year. This was a clear sign of the better air defence network that had come to cover almost the entire North although the focus of air defences remained the defence of Hanoi.

By June 1967 Hanoi was protected by one of the most lethal air defence networks ever assembled. In addition to the 361st Air Defence Division, it now had the 365th and 367th Air Defence Divisions augmenting the defences. The Air Defence Command had by now committed ten anti-aircraft regiments and five SAM regiments, totalling 60 per cent of North Vietnam's available anti-aircraft artillery batteries and 52 per cent of its SAM battalions, along with the entire North Vietnamese Air Force to the defence of Hanoi.[61] In the face of this, the US continued air operations and paid a heavy price for doing so. This was especially true for the US Navy which continued to fly missions over North Vietnam in the heart of the SA-2 envelope, without knowing that the North Vietnamese had discovered a way to defeat their jammers. While the Air Force loss rate to SAMs fell over the period, Navy losses steadily increased. Throughout 1967, SAMs accounted for one-half of the Navy's losses. By 1967 the North Vietnam SAM operators had became so proficient against the US Navy's jammers that, on 31 August 1967, two A-4 Skyhawks from the USS *Oriskany* were destroyed by a single SA-2 missile.[62]

The attempts to put down the SAMs were not yielding results as the US lost sixty-one aircraft to SA-2s during the year, its highest ever loss to the SAMs. On the other hand, the attack sorties against SAM facilities – approximately 1,600 attack sorties were carried out in a eighteen month period alone between July 1966 and the end of 1967 – had apparently not reduced either the total number of active SAM battalions or the available firing sites. There were now up to thirty active battalions which could use about 230 prepared or pre-surveyed sites. The claims of reduced effectiveness of SAMs, repeatedly made by US aviators, also did not stand up to scrutiny as the losses kept mounting. It was not only the SAMs that had not been suppressed. The USAF and Navy could conduct strikes against only two of the five targeted radars in the fourth quarter of 1967 and the damage they caused was insignificant. From a total of 149 radars at fifty sites in 1966, North Vietnam had built up a radar network of 195 operational early warning and ground-control intercept radars at ninety-five sites by 1967. Similarly, the attempts to isolate Hanoi from Haiphong, and both cities from the remainder of the country, as well as the destruction of remaining industrial infrastructure, which was the stated aim of Phase V, the final phase of ROLLING THUNDER, was nowhere close to being achieved. And the US was paying a heavy price for its attempts to target Hanoi and Haiphong. During the last six months of 1967 sorties within Route Package VI, i.e. the zones including Hanoi and Haiphong, were only 25 per cent of all ROLLING THUNDER sorties but losses suffered were more than 50 per cent of total losses. Attrition rate for the Route Package was 4.5, almost three times the overall average for other route packages.

The high loss rate is understandable considering the fact that US pilots confronted the most comprehensive air defence network in the world with the North Vietnamese Air Defences firing over 25,000 tons of AAA ammunition from 10,000 anti-aircraft guns and hundreds of missiles from over twenty-five SAM battalions during any given month of 1967.

The high attrition is summed up in the table below:

Period	Attack Sorties	Combat Losses	Rate
Apr–June 1967	800	21	2.62
Jul–Sep 1967	685	8	1.17
Oct–Dec 1967	810	12	1.48
Total	2,295	41	1.79

Loss rate during attack sorties within ten nautical miles of Hanoi and Haiphong in 1967

Overall, the US losses were highest in 1967. It lost a total of 1,213 aircraft over South-East Asia, 581 fixed-wing aircraft and 680 helicopters. There was almost a doubling of rotary-wing losses, up from 319 the previous year. Over North Vietnam the increase was a manageable 15 per cent as a total of 366 aircraft were lost over the North. While the losses to AAA were almost the same, 241 as compared to 240 in 1966, losses to SAMs and MiGs had shown an upward trend. Both were almost double the losses in 1966. The US lost sixty-one aircraft to SAMs over North Vietnam in 1967, up from thirty-one in 1966 and twenty-four to MiGs, up from just twelve in 1966.[63]

As the US losses were mounting, so was the cost of inflicting damage. From an $6.68 operational cost in 1965 to inflict one dollar's worth of damage, the operational cost went up to $10.98 in 1966 before it came down to $7.05 in 1967. Even then, it was proving to be drain on US resources to keep up the pressure on North Vietnam. And this was when the full extent of ROLLING THUNDER's power was never brought to bear out of fear of the Union of Soviet Socialist Republics and China entering the conflict. The failure to completely close the port of Haiphong allowed the North Vietnamese to be supplied continuously with more weapons, munitions and foodstuffs. Without closure of this key centre of gravity, all the damage and disruption caused by air power was coming to naught. The weather was, as was wont in the region, making it difficult to continue with uninterrupted air strikes. The first quarter of 1968 only saw four days of clear weather.

In January, the North Vietnamese Army and the Viet Cong launched a major offensive over the Tet lunar new year holiday. Faced with mounting protests and no results to show, US President Johnson ordered a partial halt to the bombing of North Vietnam in March 1968 and a complete stop on 1 November. The last day of ROLLING THUNDER was 31

October, almost three years and eight months after it had begun, a sad end to an operation which failed by all accounts. An assessment made a year after the conclusion of the bombing campaign found that:

> Operation Rolling Thunder actually improved North Vietnam's war making capacity by forcing them to create more supply networks and removing choke points. The report stated that Rolling Thunder had 'no measurable effect on Hanoi's ability to mount and support military operations in the south'.[64]

The hundreds of thousands of sorties, more specifically the 153,784 attack sorties flown against North Vietnam by the US Air Force between March 1965 and November 1968, plus an additional 152,399 by the Navy and Marine Corps during which 864,000 tons of ordnance was dropped on North Vietnam, could not achieve the intended aim.[65] This does not consider the 506 US Air Force, 397 Navy, and nineteen Marine Corps aircraft lost over or near North Vietnam.[66]

North Vietnam, on the other hand, lost an average 1,000 casualties per week, 90,000 in the forty-four months, of whom 72,000 were civilians but the will of the people was still not broken. On the other hand, 'the enemy AAA grew to be more lethal than anything ever encountered by allied aircrews over Germany in [the Second] World War.'[67]

By the end of ROLLING THUNDER in 1968, it was estimated that North Vietnam possessed 8,050 anti-aircraft guns of all calibres, thirty-two MiG-21s and fifteen MiG-15/17s in country, with another 108 in southern China. The North Vietnamese also fielded thirty-five to forty SA-2 battalions, with six missile launchers each, and the requisite complement of Fan Song tracking radars. Additionally, 400 radars of various types and functions were spread across the country. By the middle of 1968 the airspace above North Vietnam was recognized as perhaps one of the most complex electromagnetic defence threats ever to be combatted by USAF tactical forces.

After the 1968 Tet offensive, with the American troop levels in Vietnam capped and no bombing of North Vietnam above 20 degrees north latitude, the war in Vietnam took a turn. The new President, Richard Nixon, went a step further and the burden of war began to be handed over more to South Vietnam. With no more bombing raids, there was an expected drop in American aircraft losses. This state of lowered military activity continued until March 1972 when North Vietnam launched the Operation NGUYEN HUE, better known as the 'Eastertide Offensive', the coup de grace expected to completely defeat South Vietnam.

From the guerrilla war fought until then, North Vietnam, confident of its military prowess, had graduated to full conventional invasion using weapons not employed before; amongst them was the shoulder-fired man-portable surface-to-air missile SA-7. Unlike the fixed SA-2 missile used until then, the SA-7 gave the foot soldiers a potent weapon against aircraft. The American air forces had a new threat to contend with. The threat on the ground was no less potent. The US had scaled down its forces and had to rebuild them to stop the push back the North Vietnamese. American and Republic of Vietnam Air Force (VNAF) were already carrying out operations to support the ground troops but bad weather hampered most of the missions.

By April, the USA had built up its B-52 fleet available to support the war in Vietnam to 209. In addition, 176 F-4 Phantoms had been moved to the war zone. The big change, however, was the resumption of bombing missions north of the 20th Parallel, cleared by President Nixon on 5 April. On 10 April, the US launched the first largescale raid with twelve B-52s against the petroleum storage facilities around Vinh. During this mission, an SA-2 hit one of the B-52s, severely damaging it, although the aircraft managed to reach Da Nang air base in South Vietnam.[68] The fact that SA-2s posed a serious threat to the B-52s was beyond doubt now. This mission was followed by bombing missions against widespread targets, including bridges, rail lines, logistic installations and, more importantly, both Hanoi and Haiphong.

On 10 May, the day Operation LINEBACKER began, the USAF and Navy flew a total of 414 sorties. During the day, the US forces claimed eleven North Vietnamese MiGs, while two Air Force F-4s were shot down. In addition, the US Navy lost two more aircraft to anti-aircraft fire. As part of its campaign to target bridges, the US aircraft destroyed the Paul Doumer and Thanh Hóa bridges using laser-guided bombs for the first time. This was on 13 May, when USAF F-4s hit the bridge with twenty-six laser- guided bombs, several of them heavy 3,000-pounders.

Repeated attempts using conventional bombs and missiles had hitherto failed to destroy these bridges. Against the Thanh Hoa bridge alone, the Air Force and the Navy had sent 871 sorties until 1972, losing eleven aircraft but failing to knock out the bridge.[69] Over seventeen bridges had been destroyed by the end of the month along the rail lines and between Hanoi and Haiphong. The targets were then switched over to oil and logistic installations and airfields. This had an effect on the battlefield as the North Vietnamese forces were facing a shortage of supplies, including ammunition. By one estimate, between May and June only 30 per cent of supplies called for actually reached the front-line units.[70]

By mid-May the entire North was cleared for air operations and the US air forces had flown 18,000 sorties against North Vietnam anti-aircraft defences alone in the two months between 1 May and 30 June for the loss of twenty-nine aircraft.[71] By June, the relentless strike and bomber operations first helped stem the North Vietnam offensive, and then push it back. The grand plan of Giap had failed to achieve its aim. On 23 October 1972, the US halted Operation LINEBACKER when it was appreciated that North Vietnam could be brought back to the negotiating table.

During these operations, North Vietnamese Air Defences had been a prime target with US air forces using a combination of active and passive measures to try and degrade, if not completely destroy, the North's air defence. This was strongly contested by the North, including the North Vietnamese Air Force. Unlike the Korean War when the US air forces had a far better kill ratio, the US Air Force could muster a 1:1 kill ratio only during the first two months of the campaign while the US Navy, with its better training and tactics, fared better with a kill ratio of 6:1 in its favour. In fact, USAF lost seven aircraft, of its total loss of twenty-four aircraft in air-to-air combat during the entire LINEBACKER campaign, in the twelve-day period between 24 June and 5 July without any corresponding North Vietnamese loss.[72] Only by August could the USAF improve its performance to a more favourable 4:1 kill ratio as the North Vietnamese ground control interception capabilities were degraded and the USAF pilots gained combat experience.[73]

Even as the USAF was improving its kill ratio, the North Vietnamese Air Defences were also undergoing a change. Before Operation NGUYEN

HUE, the SA-2s covering the demilitarized zone had shot down only three F-4s in February using eighty-one missiles, a rather dismal record. Once LINEBACKER I started, they were able to shoot down three aircraft in March and the next month were used against B-52s for the first time as the bombers attacked Vinh, the twenty-three SA-2s fired on 21 and 23 April claiming a B-52, the first loss of B-52s to SA-2s.[74]

During the entire operation, North Vietnamese Air Defences reportedly fired a total of 2,750 SA-2s downing forty-six planes.[75] The other surface-to-air missile, the man-portable SA-7, was used in combat for the first time during LINEBACKER. A first generation heat-seeking missile, the SA-7 was slow and vulnerable to even simple counter-measures like flares. The most effective counter-measure was for the pilots to just increase their speed. For all its limitations, SA-7s forced the aircraft to fly higher, thus decreasing their effectiveness, and downed a number of low-flying slower aircraft and helicopters. One estimate suggests that seventeen fixed-wing aircraft and nine helicopters were downed by the 315 SA-7s fired between 29 April and 1 September.[76]

The introduction of the guided munition and improved ECM equipment were to play an important part in reducing the vulnerability of strike aircraft to ground-based air defences. Such was the accuracy of the guided munition that they were considered to be 100 times more effective than dumb bombs against bridges and 100 to 200 times better against hard targets. Besides greater accuracy, reduced exposure and fewer losses to enemy anti-aircraft fire was the big pay-off of using guided munition although a 1968 study presented a contrarian view and suggested that the aircraft using smart munitions were hit more than the aircraft using dumb bombs.[77]

There are, however, no contrarian views about the use of chaff. Chaff dispensers like the ALE-38 and chaff bombs were a major factor in reducing attrition, as was the change in anti-SAM tactics. From the use of anti-radiation missiles (ARM) only, the US air forces started using a combination of aircraft armed with ARM and cluster bomb units (CBUs) which increased the efficacy of the Wild Weasels. In spite of all these, or, as some may say, because of these measures, the US lost a total of 134 aircraft during LINEBACKER I[78] although some other sources put the loss at 111 with an equal proportion claimed by anti-aircraft artillery, MiGs and SAMs.[79]

The US Air Force alone carried out 9,315 sorties during the operation and the attrition rate of 1.4 per cent seems manageable, well within acceptable limits, but it needs to be remembered that the war had seen the use of support aircraft in large numbers to protect, guide and support the bombing missions. Of the total 9,315 sorties, only 2,346 were directed against enemy installations; almost 7,000 were in support of attack missions.[80] The ratio of support aircraft was even higher than these numbers indicate (3.4:1), as they do not include tanker and reconnaissance aircraft. The support aircraft did not necessarily come in harm's way and were thus not so vulnerable to air defences.

A better method to understand the efficacy of *enemy* air defences and the attrition inflicted on the US Air Forces would be to consider only the strike sorties, in which case the attrition rate goes up to 4.7 per cent. It is for this reason that air forces in general calculate attrition rate using total number of sorties and 'window dress' the attrition rate.

The requirement for large numbers of support aircraft tied down valuable resources, denying their use for other offensive missions. In a manner of speaking this was *virtual attrition* of the air effort and was rather frustrating for, in spite of all the effort, the US did not get the agreement at the end of Operation LINEBACKER that they were so desperate to force on to North Vietnam.

If General Giap's offensive failed to achieve its aim, so did LINEBACKER I.

After another round of 'now on, now off' operations, and negotiations, the USA renewed its efforts to have an agreement in place before the year was over. On 14 December it gave North Vietnam an ultimatum to get back to the negotiating table within seventy-two hours 'or else'; an air offensive against the North was ordered that very day. The three-day bombing offensive was extended for an indefinite period on 19 November, codenamed Operation LINEBACKER II. This was intended to be a 'maximum effort' bombing campaign to 'destroy major target complexes' in the Hanoi and Haiphong areas and was to be almost exclusively carried out by B-52s although the bombers were still to be supported by other aircraft to suppress enemy air defences.

The USA resumed the bomber offensive on the night of 18 December using 129 bombers in three waves, supported by F-4 fighter escorts, F-105 Wild Weasel SAM-suppression missions EB-66 and EA-6 radar-jamming aircraft, chaff drops, KC-135 refuelling capability, and search and rescue aircraft. These were preceded by F-111s attacking the airfields to keep the MiGs down. Each wave of B-52s comprised twenty-one to fifty-one B-52s supported by thirty-one to forty-one other aircraft flying the same pattern, the same heading from the west and, after a sharp turn following bombing, the same exit heading to the west. The first wave struck the airfields at Kép, Phúc Yên and Hòa Lạc while the second and third waves struck targets around Hanoi itself. Three B-52s were shot down by the sixty-eight SAMs launched by North Vietnamese batteries[81] while two more suffered heavy damage although they managed to return to U-Tapao.[82] These were not the only losses that day as an F-111 Aardvark was shot down over Hanoi.[83] The second night, the air defences were not so fortunate as none of the twenty SA-2s launched destroyed any B-52s although a number were damaged.

The North Vietnamese struck on the third night. The first wave lost three B-52s to SAMs, resulting in the second wave being aborted, but SAC ordered the third wave to go through – using the same times, routes, altitudes and targets as the previous nights. This was to prove a costly error: the North Vietnamese had anticipated the strike pattern and were ready. Three B-52s were shot down by SA-2s while a fourth crashed in Laos after being damaged by an SA-2.[84]

This was very high attrition. The first wave was of thirty-three B-52s and the loss of three was an attrition rate of almost 10 per cent – more if the figure of four B-52s shot down is considered. The third wave had fared even worse as it was only of twelve B-52s and three B-52s had been shot down by the SA-2s. The North Vietnamese Air Defences had used thirty-four SA-2s, fired in salvos, making it five missiles to a 'kill'. This was worse than the anticipated loss of 3 per cent. The bombings may have rocked Hanoi but the aftershocks were felt more by SAC. After the reported dismal performance of SA-2s in LINEBACKER I, the USAF, especially SAC, had never anticipated such high losses. In the first three days, the US had lost twelve aircraft, ten of them B-52s, the primary strategic bomber of the USAF. Crunching numbers, it was a loss rate of 3 per cent on sortie rate which was alarming, but manageable. Taken in absolute terms, the loss was almost 5 per cent of total number of B-52s in South East Asia and 2 per cent of the entire B-52 fleet in US service.[85]

The reason for the high attrition was not that the North Vietnamese Air Defences had suddenly become more efficient. The spurt in losses was more to do with the tactical and technical lapses by the US forces – and the North Vietnamese Air Defence exploiting these to their advantage. The US aircraft used the same flight paths, altitudes, formations, even the same timings (gaps between waves and within the wave, between flights), making it all very predictable for the SAM operators. The North Vietnamese are reported to have even fired unguided missiles aimed at the anticipated location of the aircraft and switched on the radars only at the last stage, for only the last five to ten seconds of intercept, to guide the missiles on to the target.[86] Such controlled transmission by the radars made its (radars') jamming difficult.

On the night of 20/21 November, SAC forced the third wave to go through even though the first wave had suffered heavy losses (four of thirty-three B-52s were shot down) and that, too, using same flight path. It was an unwarranted lapse which cost the USAF dearly. SAC also mandated a 'press-on' procedure, which dictated that bombers continue their missions despite the loss of engines, computers and, most critically, ECM equipment. Although this policy was later changed, it did contribute to initial losses. As the bombers and support aircraft were controlled by two separate headquarters, there were co-ordination problems between them. At least couple of incidents of the B-52s firing on the escort aircraft occurred during LINEBACKER II.[87] Other problems related to lack of compatibility between the electronic equipment used by various aircraft. The EB-66 ECM aircraft jammed the US radio communications while the B-52 ECM severely degraded friendly radar.[88]

Besides the compatibility problems, the way the electronic equipment was handled by the USAF also enabled the People's Army of Vietnam (PAVN) electronic and air defence forces to detect B-52 strike groups in time, provide target acquisition data to the ADMF and prepare the necessary initial firing data.[89] The major lapse related to the jammers being turned on in the entire wave range before the B-52s approached the radar's surveillance zones. This followed the standard operating procedure (SOP) for the B-52 electronic warfare officers (EWOs) who were required to turn on and test all jammers at a pre-set in-flight point prior to entering the threat zone, then turn them off until they entered enemy airspace. This *test* lit up the radar screens, in a way announcing the imminent arrival of the bomber strike groups. The second mistake that the EWOs committed was to turn on the jammers prematurely, at frequencies pre-set and regardless of the operating frequency of the missile-guidance systems. The EWOs cannot be faulted for this, as it was all according to the SOPs, but such simple lapses proved to be costly as the strike groups may well have suffered additional losses due to these.

The one counter-measure that worked well was the chaff although it was not without its problems, mainly the dispersion due to wind. In case of wind pattern differing in direction and speed from the forecast, the number of B-52s given the chaff protection dropped, leaving them exposed. On 20 December, only four of twenty-seven B-52 cells received chaff protection at the bomb-release line, and all of the B-52s downed were five to ten miles from chaff cover. This was corrected in subsequent missions when the USAF dropped more chaff, trying to create a chaff blanket and not just a chaff corridor.[90] The other measure taken to increase survivability was to have only one wave of thirty B-52s attacking the targets with varied timing, headings and altitudes from 21 December onwards. The USAF tried using hunter-killer teams on 23 December to suppress the SAMs but not with much luck, mainly due to bad weather.

While the USAF was taking various measures to increase the efficacy of its strike groups, and keep its aircraft safe from the PAVN air defence, North Vietnam was stepping up its own efforts to inflict maximum losses on the raiding aircraft. The SAM units of the PAVN Army were central to this. At the beginning of LINEBACKER II, PAVN had thirty-six air defence missile battalions armed with the Soviet- manufactured SA-75 M 'Dvina' (SA-2 'Guideline') missile system. They were supported by nine technical battalions. The battalions were organized into nine air defence missile regiments and these were further organized into four air defence divisions. The divisions were assigned to three air defence groups – Hanoi, Haiphong and the 4th Combat Zone.[91]

The Soviet report on LINEBACKER II reports that the Vietnamese People's Army conducted over 180 engagements, two-thirds of which were against B-52s. In all, they destroyed 54 aircraft (31 B-52s, 13 F4s, and 10 A- 6s or A-7s) with the expenditure of 244 missiles against the B-52s, i.e. an average of 7.9 missiles were expended for every B-52 aircraft shot down. If the tactical and carrier-based aircraft are singled out, then 3.3 rockets were expended for every aircraft shot down.[92]

These claims are understandably at variance with the figures given out by US sources. Werrell mentions the loss of only twenty-seven aircraft, including fifteen B-52s, although he also mentions that North Vietnam claimed eighty-one aircraft.[93] Even the figures for the number of missiles expended is disputed by the US and North Vietnam/Soviet Union. While the US claims that North Vietnam fired 1,285 SAMs and downed only eighteen aircraft – fifteen B-52s lost and three others – the Soviet report claims an expenditure of only 322 missiles, 266 against the bomber missions and fifty-six against tactical and carrier-borne aircraft. The number of aircraft shot down claimed is thirty-six of the bomber strike groups, thirty-one of which are B-52s, and eighteen tactical and carrier-borne aircraft. The average missile expenditure per kill is 7.9 for B-52s and only 3.3 for tactical aircraft.[94]

This is a much better performance than what is generally presented by Western sources. While there may be some exaggeration in the Soviet claims, it is equally true that the US did not reveal the actual losses that would have occurred during LINEBACKER II. There have been repeated attempts to put down the performance of SAMs and project the B-52 losses as within manageable limits. Taking the total sortie rate and considering the loss rate as under 2 per cent may present a rosy picture but when the actual losses of (say) thirty B-52s of the total 200 used during the operation are considered, in real terms it is a loss of 15 per cent. The presentation of the same figures in more presentable terms has always been resorted to by all air forces and LINEBACKER was no exception.

The North Vietnamese Air Force (NVNAF) did not perform as well as the ground-based air defence. The NVNAF had four fighter aviation regiments with a total of 187 fighters. Of these, only forty-seven aircraft (thirty-one MiG-21s and sixteen MiG-17s) could be used for combat – 26 per cent of the military aircraft. The MiG-19s were made in China and were not used in combat. The NVNAF launched thirty-one air sorties, twenty-seven by MiG-21s and four by MiG-17s. They claimed to have shot down two B-52s, four F-4s and one RA-5C for the loss of three MiG-21s.[95] US sources, however, claim to have shot down six MiG-21s for the loss of two F-4s.[96] Only three tactical aircraft were lost to Vietnamese anti-aircraft fire.

The suppression of enemy air defence (SEAD) missions launched against SAM sites were not very effective either. Besides the SAM sites, the storage facilities were also targeted by both the B-52s and F-111s. SAM sites were not targeted for the first five days and only on 23 December was the first one targeted. Continued strikes by US aircraft, however, only partly damaged two SAM sites. Eight sites were targeted but did not suffer any damage. The US claims to have degraded SAM sites and missile re-supply so much that North Vietnam had run out of SAMs. The truth of the matter is that the re-supply was affected by the naval blockade and not the air campaign; thus giving credit to LINEBACKER for throttling North Vietnamese Air Defences is misplaced and incorrect.

The overall efficacy of LINEBACKER can also be viewed with varying perspective. North Vietnam returned to the negotiating table. This makes LINEBACKER a successful air campaign – a validation of air power. However, the air campaign did not achieve the decisive end. The terms agreed to, after LINEBACKER II, were the same as agreed to *before* the campaign. The only change was that North Vietnam agreed to the peace talks. Moreover, within two years of LINEBACKER II, US forces had all returned home, North had overrun South Vietnam and a Communist government ruled a unified Vietnam. The strategic bombing campaign had achieved only tactical gains and certainly failed to achieve the strategic goals.

US Air Defences

The North Vietnamese Air Force threat was marginal at best and was never serious enough to warrant deployment of massive ADA resources which otherwise would have been necessary, keeping in mind the vast deployment of US resources. The reported supply of Il-28 light bombers by the Soviet Union to North Vietnam, however, changed the threat perception as the North now had the capability to strike deep down, as far south as Saigon. The 929th Bomber Squadron was reported to have been raised in May 1965 and there now was a critical need to deploy US ADA units.[97]

The 1st Light Anti-aircraft Missile (LAAM) Battalion, United States Marine Corps (USMC) was the first US AD unit to be deployed in

Vietnam, one of the first US units to be deployed as part of the build-up. It arrived in Vietnam in February 1965 and was deployed at the Da Nang Air Base.[98]

US Army AD artillery units in Vietnam were used more for base defence and providing direct fire support and convoy protection than air defence against the PVAF. The ADA units deployed in Vietnam were a mix of Duster 40mm gun, Quad 50s and Vulcan units along with HAWK battalions. The first ADA unit to be deployed in Vietnam was the 1st Battalion, 44th Artillery, a M42A1 Duster unit, which arrived in November 1966, followed by 5th Battalion, 2nd Air Defense Artillery the same month and 4th Battalion, 60th Air Defense Artillery a year later; both were Duster battalions.[99]

Each Duster battalion had a headquarters and four line batteries with each line battery having two platoons; further organized in to four sections, each with a pair of M42A1 Dusters. The Duster battalions also had a battery each of M55 .050 calibre quad and searchlights attached to them. The Duster largely operated in pairs while jeep-mounted Quads normally operated singly but were often used in support of a Duster section.

All throughout the war, the North Vietnamese air threat was almost non-existent. The only time it could be considered serious was in February 1968 when four Il-28s and thirteen MiGs penetrated the DMZ where they loitered for about an hour without incident. Later, in December 1967, some unidentified aircraft were reported to have penetrated the South Vietnamese air but nothing materialized thereafter.

Overall, the USAF lost 2,254 fixed-wing aircraft from February 1962 to October 1973 in the South-east Asia theatre of operations. Some 1,737 fixed wing aircraft were combat losses, and another 517 aircraft went down in related non-combat operations. Losses occurred nearly every day. It was rare for a week to pass without an aircraft being lost in combat operations. The Air Force lost 40 per cent of its total production of F-105s to combat in Vietnam. Approximately one out of every eight F-4s ever built by McDonnell Douglas, for all services, was destroyed in Vietnam.

The North Vietnamese Air Force (VPAF) had between sixty and seventy-five aircraft in service at most points during the war. Yet the

MiG-17s, MiG-19s and MiG-21s shot down sixty-seven USAF aircraft against a loss of 137 of their own, leaving the US Air Force with barely a two-to-one exchange ratio over the course of the war.

Air operations peaked with ground operations from 1966 to 1968. The Air Force flew a total of 101,089 combat and combat support sorties in 1967 alone. SA-2s were supposed to be the wonder weapons, feared the most, but, ultimately, more than 83 per cent of the USAF's total combat losses were to ground fire – mostly anti-aircraft guns.[100] However, SAMs were central to the increased effectiveness of North Vietnam's anti-aircraft branch. The mere presence of the SA-2 forced a fundamental change in American tactics. While the number of aircraft lost to SAMs was never more than a small proportion of the total lost, the very existence of the missile threat forced American commanders to change their tactics. Once launched, SAMs disrupted American formations and drove aircraft to lower altitudes. At those lower altitudes, small arms and radar-controlled anti-aircraft artillery took an excessive toll. Before the SA-2 was introduced, American aircraft could remain at altitude, above the effective range of even the largest guns. Faced with intense anti-aircraft fire, as strike aircraft moved to higher altitudes, they became better targets for the SA-2. There was a proportional increase in losses to the SA-2 in 1972, climbing from 20 per cent to 29 per cent of the total losses, a 9 per cent increase. Similarly, losses to enemy MiGs climbed precipitously, from 7 per cent in 1967 to 26 per cent in 1972. Even though jamming pod technology had improved, such as the new, more powerful QRC-335, these pods required rigid adherence to flight formations to be effective. Disrupting MiG attacks scattered these formations, and the protective electronic phalanx was broken. Additionally, several aircraft were lost performing IRON HAND, or suppression and destruction of the very weapons that shot them down. The North Vietnamese Air Force had nearly doubled the aircraft it had between ROLLING THUNDER and LINEBACKER, and laid a great deal of emphasis on pilot tactical training. Additionally, introduction of the SA-2F, with its optical tracking capability, and the retrofit of every other SA-2 with this capability in the summer of 1972, meant that the systems were virtually immune to jamming, as well as reducing the warning given to American pilots from radar warning receiver (RWR) sensors. All these factors led to greater efficacy of SA-2s in the later years.

All these factors were a result of the North Vietnamese General Staff taking immediate action to correct any deficiencies and giving the highest priority to the defence of Hanoi and Haiphong. Each time the US enforced a bombing halt, the Air Defence Command would re-deploy anti-aircraft guns and SAMs to cover gaps exposed during the most recent round of raids. The Air Defence Command was pro-active all throughout and that made all the difference.

Chapter 3

India Pakistan War 1965

At 3:30 hours on 1 September 1965, Pakistan launched Operation GRAND SLAM, with the objective of capturing the vital town of Akhnoor in Jammu and sever communications to Kashmir. The Akhnoor sector was lightly defended by four Indian infantry battalions and a squadron of tanks. Against a militarily stronger and larger Pakistani thrust, the Indian forces could not hold on to the defences and called on its air force to blunt the Pakistani attack. The first Indian aircraft took off within an hour of the go ahead.

When the first four Indian Air Force Vampires came overhead, in a case of mistaken identities, they attacked their own troops causing considerable damage – all artillery ammunition vehicles, three AMX-13 tanks, one armoured recovery vehicle and one tank ammunition lorry were destroyed. The Vampires then turned their attention to Pakistani armour. As the Indian aircraft started their run over the Pakistani tanks, the anti-aircraft guns of 111 LAA Battery/29 LAA Regiment opened up, knocking off the lead Vampire. Pakistan's anti-aircraft artillery had scored its first kill in the very first engagement.[1]

Soon after partition in 1947, India and Pakistan had gone to war in 1948 when Pakistan invaded Kashmir in an attempt to annex it. Its plans thwarted after a bloody nose, Pakistan bade its time and, after the Sino-India war of 1962, thought the time to be opportune to again try and annex Kashmir. That it had a military junta in power was another factor that emboldened Pakistan. The conflict had started in April 1965 when the Pakistan Army had launched Operation DESERT HAWK in the desolate region of Rann of Kutch. It was the first of a four-phase plan to annex Kashmir.

The Rann is a poorly connected area with hardly any roads or tracks on the Indian side AND with no air base nearby. Pakistan, however, had an advantage of a having a major air base, Badin, located just thirty kilometres from the international border. After a month of minor tactical skirmishes, Pakistan launched an attack on forward Indian posts on 9 April and, while the two armies fought it out, the C-in-C, Pakistan Air Force rang up his Indian counterpart on 14 April and offered that the two Air Forces stay away from the conflict in the Rann.[2] The Indian Air Force (IAF) Chief agreed to this. An opportunity to test the operational readiness of both the air forces and air defences was lost.

The Pakistan Air Force had meanwhile moved its combat aircraft to Mauripur and regularly carried out combat air patrols and missions in support of its ground troops. An air defence exercise was carried out in the sector by Pakistan on 15 April with all operational aircraft at the two largest bases, Mauripur and Sargodha, ordered to operate from wartime dispersals in combat readiness, and the operations rooms were to be manned round the clock.[3] With both sides continuing to carry out extensive patrolling and exchange of artillery fire, the Pakistan Air Force had increased its activities by mid-April. Armed combat air patrols and reconnaissance sorties by F-86F Sabres from Mauripur, reinforced by two F-104A Starfighters on detachment from Sargodha, were a routine activity. During one of these sorties on 19 April, a two F-86 mission of No. 17 Squadron, PAF, was covering the move of Pakistan Army when they were engaged by Indian anti-aircraft fire, hitting one of them. The F-86 was being piloted by Flying Officer Waleed Ehsanul Karim who managed to bring his Sabre back to Badin where it was patched up and repaired. Karim carried out another sortie in the evening, a reconnaissance mission, when his aircraft developed engine trouble and plunged into the Arabian Sea about ten to fifteen miles off the south coast of Karachi. Although the immediate reason of the crash was engine failure, the loss was undoubtedly due to the hit by anti-aircraft fire. This makes it the first loss of a combat aircraft attributable to anti-aircraft fire in the sub-continent.[4]

Events in the Rann flared up in the early hours of 24 April when an Indian post was attacked and overrun by Pakistani armour and mechanized infantry. This was followed by an attack two days later on a post by a company of infantry. As the two sides had agreed to keep the air forces at bay, the only support given by the Indian Air Force was in carrying out reconnaissance missions. While the ground operations carried on, there was mounting international pressure on both India and Pakistan to cease the hostilities. A ceasefire, brokered by the United Kingdom, was agreed on 1 May.

Pakistan considered the operation to be a success and soon thereafter launched the second phase of its war plan – Operation GIBRALTAR. Aimed to cause an uprising in the local population of Kashmir, it failed in its aim as the locals remained firmly behind India.

On 1 September 1965 Pakistan launched phase three, Operation GRAND SLAM, with the aim of capturing Akhnoor on the road linking Kashmir with mainland India so as to cut off Kashmir. The area was selected so that Pakistan's superiority in armour, fire power and mobility could be fully exploited. Facing the Pakistanis' offensive was only one Indian infantry brigade, spread thin in the sector. Unable to hold the defences, the brigade commander asked for air support and, within an hour of the request being cleared by the Indian Defence Minister (neither Pakistan nor India had formally declared war as yet), the Indian Air Force responded. The four-ship Mystère flight was engaged first by Pakistani anti-aircraft fire which shot down a Mystère, making this the first loss of an Indian aircraft to Pakistani anti-aircraft fire.[5] Meanwhile, two Pakistan Air Force F-86s had been vectored in to intercept the Indian Mystères. The remaining three Mystères did not stand a chance against the more agile Sabres and all three were shot down. The Indian Air Force put in a total of twenty-eight sorties that day to support the hard pressed infantry brigade and managed to help stem the Pakistani advance, but at a heavy cost of four Mystères.

This was the first war in which anti-aircraft artillery (AAA) of both countries were taking active part. In 1948 Pakistani AAA had been used in a limited manner and that too in the direct firing role. Indian AAA had taken part in the Sino-India War of 1962 but, as the Chinese Air Force had kept away, had not been tested in battle.

Comparing the two armies, Indian AAA had a numerical advantage – with twenty-one regiments – but, with a larger area and requirement to cater for a two-front war, the seeming advantage dissipated. With a large number of assets to be defended, the AAA was spread thin. The other drawback was of having only one type of AA gun; that, too, was of 1930s vintage, viz. the Bofors 40mm L/60 AA gun. Pakistani anti-aircraft artillery, although numerically smaller, concentrated on fewer assets, giving them a heavier concentration of anti-aircraft cover. Pakistan also had a better range of weapons with the M42 Duster tracked double-barrelled AA gun system for armoured columns, 40mm L/60 AA guns for static tasks and 20mm quad AA guns to beef up anti-aircraft defences. Pakistan also had a PAF Regiment equipped with 20mm AA guns for base defence.

The 40mm L/60 AA guns, a legacy of the Second World War, often referred to simply as the Bofors gun, was an anti-aircraft gun designed in the 1930s by the Swedish arms manufacturer AB Bofors. It was one of the most popular medium-weight anti-aircraft systems during the war, used by most of the countries and, even after seven decades, remains in service and saw action as late as the Gulf War. Both India and Pakistan got these as 'hand me downs' from the British.

India had two independent air defence brigades deployed in the west and one in the east. One of the brigades, 22 (Independent) Air Defence Brigade, was responsible for Delhi, Rajasthan and Gujarat, while Punjab and Jammu & Kashmir was the responsibility of 33 (Independent) AD Brigade. The air defence regiments were primarily deployed for protection of air bases, bridges, radar stations and strategic assets with the Territorial Army regiments being deployed on static tasks. None of the infantry divisions had any integral AD regiments, which had been the practice until 1962. Air Force bases took most of the resources, leaving just a couple of regiments for the field army.

The air defence regiments were organized and equipped on the lines of the British Army in that a regiment had three batteries, with three troops each with six AD guns in a troop, making a total of 54 40mm L/60 guns in the regiment. The regiment with 40mm L/70 guns also had three batteries but not all had the new L/70 guns as the regiment was still in the process of receiving them from the ordnance factory. More likely that it had about a battery worth of L/70 guns (about twelve to eighteen guns in all).

Pakistan had eight AD regiments, of which one was deployed in East Pakistan. Pakistan had raised its first AD formation in 1954 and had also been following the practice of allotment of AD regiments/batteries to its field formations. The co-ordination of these was done by 3 (I) AD Brigade and IV Corps Artillery Brigade, the former responsible for strategic assets and the latter for the field formations.[6]

The mainstay of Pakistani anti-aircraft artillery was also the 40mm L/60 AA gun although the Pakistan Army had one LAA regiment equipped with M42 Dusters – 19 LAA Regiment (SP), a battery of which (111 LAA Battery) was orbatted with the Pakistan Army's infantry brigade which initiated the offensive against Chhamb on 1 September 1965 and has to its credit shooting down the very first aircraft lost in combat during the twenty-two-day war.

While there was not much to choose from in the number of regiments and batteries in the Western Sector, what made the difference between India and Pakistan was the respective control and reporting system, the nerve centre which controlled the AD resources.

As part of the Soviet aid package, India had received P-30 (M) Radar and SA-2 surface-to-air missiles. While the SA-2 did not have a spectacular debut, the P-30 (M) radar deployed at Amritsar was the only radar on the western borders with a GCI facility.[7] Given the codename *Fishoil* by the Pakistan Air Force, it had a major role to play in the air war and was repeatedly subjected to air raids. In addition to the radar at Amritsar, India had a number of low power radars all along the border, but their limited coverage made them almost useless because of the very limited reaction time and coverage they provided. 1 Air Defence Direction Centre (ADDC), then called the Air Defence Area Headquarters, was located at Delhi and was responsible for co-ordinating all AD operations on the western borders.[8] The situation in the east was worse as there was no high power radar in the entire sector. At Rampurhat, 411 Signal Unit provided some rudimentary GCI capability while 55 Signal Unit at Kalaikunda with a Second World War vintage radar was the only other early warning radar. No. 2 Air Defence Area Headquarters located at Jaffarpore, about four kilometres from Barrackpore on the outskirts of Calcutta, was responsible for air defence operations in the Eastern Sector.[8]

Pakistan had a far better and efficient control and reporting system and radar set up as compared to India. The radars were backed up efficiently, not only by a well-integrated communication network but also by a robust mobile observation units (MOU) grid. There were gaps in the cover, but not so critical as compared to India. The efficiency can also be judged by the fact that the first information about the Indian offensive was given by an MOU. The main surveillance radars were at Sakesar in the north and at Badin in the south.

After the high octane drama on Day One (1 September), when India lost four aircraft in the air, the second day hardly saw any action with both sides restraining themselves in the air. Action resumed on 3 September with the Indian Air Force and the anti-aircraft artillery drawing first blood.[9] Official records show that Indian anti-aircraft guns, deployed to defend a strategically important bridge at Akhnoor, shot down a Pakistani F-86. The bridge was strafed by a pair of PAF F-86 Sabres when they were engaged by the AA troop deployed there, with the detachment led by Havildar Perumal C shooting down the Sabre. *The Hindu*, a prominent national daily, reported the incident.

> Two Pakistani F-86 Sabre jets were shot down in the last 24 hours in the Chhamb area. One of the Sabre jets was brought down by the Indian Air Force, Gnat fighters (manufactured in India) in an air battle in the area. The second Sabre jet was destroyed by the ground forces which also went into action against the intruding Pakistani aircraft. The aircraft crashed in Indian territory.[10]

With limited air operations by Pakistan against ground targets, the anti-aircraft troop had to wait another day for its second kill when Haviladar Tata Pothu Raju of 27 AD Regiment shot down an F-86 while defending the Tawi Bridge on 5 September. Potha Raj, the detachment commander, recalls:

> We were posted on a hill to protect the bridge. I was in-charge of an L-60 gun with a capacity to fire 120 rounds from 7,000 ft. It was quite early in the morning when I noticed a couple of fighter jets swooping down on the bridge.
>
> I was trained to recognize aircraft and I knew they were Sabre Jets from their wide mouths. After getting the nod from my commanding officer, I aimed at the target and fired. I hit the target. The aircraft came down in a hail of smoke and fire and the pilot was killed.[11]

The war until then was limited to the Akhnoor sector where Pakistan had made headway. To relieve the pressure on its defences, India decided to take the offensive into Pakistan and on 6 September the Indian Army's XI Corps crossed the border in the Lahore-Kasur sector on three thrust lines. Each thrust was by an infantry division, supported by armour and artillery. What was remarkable about the offensive was an almost total disregard for ensuring air defence for the ground troops. On the Northern thrust to Lahore, 15th Infantry Division did not have any anti-aircraft component when it crossed the international border as the air defence complement earmarked had not yet arrived.[12] The leading Indian infantry battalion captured the first two objectives by 0658 hours when the Pakistan Air Force struck with impunity, destroying several ammunition vehicles which kept on burning for hours, blocking the main axis and forcing the advancing troops to take the tracks through slushy rice fields. There was just no opposition to the Pakistan Air Force in absence of the Indian Air Force and the army's anti-aircraft complement. Ironically, the Pakistani I Corps was responsible for defence in the sector and, unlike the Indian Army XI Corps, had two AD regiments and two AAA batteries. These were not tested as the IAF strangely enough kept away.

The main obstacle on the main Indian thrust line, the Ichogil Canal, was crossed by the leading infantry Battalion (3rd Battalion of the Jat Regiment) but had to withdraw following a strong counter-attack by the Pakistani armour. One of the reasons that the battalion could not hold on to its gains was that it had lost its anti-tank guns to an air raid early in the day. Not catering for air defence for the formation had proved to be a costly mistake. In spite of the setback, 15th Infantry Division had reached the outskirts of Lahore by the end of the day where the offensive stalled. The Pakistan Air Force could claim partial credit for checking the Indian advance towards Lahore.

On 6 September the Pakistan Air Force also executed its *Air War Plan No 6*[13], hitting Indian air bases and radar stations at dusk. The plan had been prepared in June 1965 and was aimed to strike at Indian air bases in the event of an all-out war. It called for simultaneous raids on the Indian bases by eight F-86s attacking each air base, to be followed by night raids by the B-57s. In addition, the radars located at Amritsar and Ferozepur were to be attacked.

As the plan was put into action, it severely tested the Indian air defence set-up. Keeping in mind the need to maintain a balanced posture, the PAF had allocated the following resources for the pre-emptive strikes

Take off Base	Aircraft	Target
Sargodha	8 x F-86F Sabres	Adampur
Sargodha	8 x F-86F Sabres	Halwara
Sargodha	4 x T-33	Ferozepur Radar
Sargodha	6 x F-86F Sabres 1 x RB-57	Amritsar Radar
Peshawar	8 x F-86F Sabres	Pathankot
Mauripur	4 x T-33s	Porbandar Radar
Mauripur	12 x B-57	Jamnagar

As Sargodha did not have the required complement of aircraft to carry out simultaneous raids against four IAF bases, the PAF had planned to shift twelve F-86 Sabres and six T-33s from Mauripur. The move of these aircraft was delayed so as not to have too many aircraft out in the open on the tarmac but this delay proved costly as four of the twelve Sabres from Mauripur developed defects and had to be put down for repairs. Air effort earmarked for Pathankot was not reduced as it was the most important target and this left only six F-86 Sabres for three targets – Adampur, Halwara and Amritsar radar.

The first Indian base to be attacked was Pathankot. The radar at Amritsar picked up the strike formation and passed on the warning to Pathankot base operations room but, strangely enough, no action was taken and the Pakistanis had a free run as they went on to destroy ten aircraft and damage three more. The anti-aircraft guns deployed, in absence of any warning, could only react once the Pakistani F-86s were overhead and failed to hit any aircraft. This was the worst loss suffered by either air force in the war during a single raid.[14] The intense anti-aircraft fire at other bases meant that the Pakistan Air Force could not replicate the success it achieved at Pathankot although it managed to shoot down two Indian aircraft in air-to-air combat and destroy three more on the ground during the day. Overall, the IAF lost a total of thirteen aircraft, eleven on the ground and two in the air while seven aircraft were damaged.

Pakistan lost two F-86s to the Indian Air Force in aerial combat and one B-57 was shot down by Indian AAA at Jamnagar.[15]

Except for the failure at Pathankot, the Indian anti-aircraft artillery did well to safeguard the air bases and installations at which it was deployed. Though it shot down only one B-57 during the day, it ensured that no harm was done to any of the bases or the radar stations. The Pakistan Air Force had earlier denied that it lost any aircraft to anti-aircraft fire, insisting that the loss was due to pilot fatigue. It was only decades later that it accepted that the B-57 was indeed shot down by the anti-aircraft artillery.[16]

Although no aircraft was shot down by anti-aircraft fire over Amritsar, an RB-57B was badly damaged by the flak and was almost written off. Pakistan had two RB-57Bs, operated by its No. 24 Squadron, which were meant for high altitude surveillance of Soviet missile test ranges but were routinely used by Pakistan to monitor Indian radars. One RB-57B was to accompany the F-86 strike mission against the Amritsar radar on 6 September. The raid against Amritsar radar was launched at dusk by four F-86Fs led by Wing Commander Mohammad Shamim and they took off at 17:40 hours. Accompanying the Sabres was an RB-57B flown by Squadron Leader Rashid. The RB-57B was to home on to the radar and lead the Sabres. However, the onboard electronic equipment of the RB-57B developed a technical snag and the mission had to be aborted. Luckily, the second RB-57B was airborne at that time and it was decided to use this second RB-57B for the strike mission. The F-86Fs, low on fuel, refuelled at Sargodha and rendezvoused with the electronic intelligence (ELINT) aircraft. The RB-57B led the F-86s to the radar and, as it overflew the site, the anti-aircraft gunners opened up, knocking off one of the engines of the RB-57B with their intense fire, forcing it to abort the mission. Unable to locate the radar without the ELINT aircraft, and literally left facing the flak, the Sabres aborted the mission.

Although the pilot nursed his stricken aircraft back to Peshawar with one engine, it was so badly damaged that the aircraft had to be sent to the USA for repairs.

Next day was a continuation of the counter air operations but this time around it was the Indian Air Force that was on the offensive. The main focus of the Indian Air Force was to strike Sargodha, the base for almost half the Pakistani Air Force, but it was a half-hearted effort with only thirty-one sorties throughout the day. The notable achievement for India was the shooting down of an F-104, the front-line Pakistani aircraft, by a Mystère. India claimed to have destroyed one aircraft (an F-86) on the ground also, but this was denied by Pakistan. One of the reasons for this dismal performance was the Pakistani anti-aircraft batteries deployed at Sargodha – five batteries with over 100 ack-ack guns, making it the most densely defended target in Pakistan. In addition, one PAF regiment equipped with 20mm guns was also located at the air base. The ack-ack shot down at least four aircraft – a Mystère in the first raid itself and a Hunter in a later raid. On the way back, another Hunter, fast losing fuel, flamed out. It had also been hit by the ack-ack fire, damaging it and making the aircraft lose fuel. In addition, at least one aircraft was claimed to have been hit by the PAF regiment. These claims were disputed by the Indian Air Force which classifies the loss of two aircraft as 'technical loss'.[17] One Pakistan Air Force account mentions the events of the day as follows:

> At 0538 hours Sargodha was reported under attack by six Mystères. The F-104 had already been positioned in the general area of Sargodha; it made visual contact as the enemy were exiting from the attack at low level and, piloted by Flt Lt Amjad, it attacked two Mystères and destroyed them. As there were many aircraft in the area, the pilot decided to keep up his speed, and while he was attacking the second Mystère, the enemy aircraft blew up in front of him. The pilot flew through debris of the exploded Mystère and damaged the stabilizer of his own aircraft; he ejected from 300 feet after having lost control of his aircraft. Two other enemy aircraft were shot down by anti-aircraft guns at Sargodha while exiting after their attack.[18]

The Indian Air Force had flown thirty-one sorties against Sargodha during the day with a loss of five aircraft and it claimed fifteen PAF aircraft while the PAF admitted the loss of only two aircraft – one Starfighter shot down in air-to-air combat over Sargodha and one Sabre lost on the ground. As with the B-57 shot down at Jamnagar, India had not claimed the F-104 Starfighter initially and only later would it acknowledge the first kill.

> The action was short and swift. As the Indian Air Force (IAF) Mystères exited after a low strafing pass over Sargodha airbase, a lurking Pakistan Air Force (PAF) Starfighter on Combat Air Patrol latched on to their tail. With the Indians short of fuel and endurance, the Pakistani was looking for easy pickings. He found the first Mystère and fired a Sidewinder, the deadliest weapon in that air war. But the Mystère surprised him with swift evasive action, sending the missile harmlessly into the ground. The Pakistani closed in, gave the Mystère a burst from his six-barrelled Vulcan cannon and climbed jauntily for more kills. He knew the stodgy old Mystère had no chance against his nimble Starfighter.
>
> Little did he realise that the doughty Indian he had shot was neither down nor out, but pursuing him, nursing his wounded aircraft. The Starfighter tried desperately to break free but the Mystère pressed on and scored several hits with its 30mm gun. In the smoke-filled Starfighter cockpit, a shaken Flight Lieutenant Amjad Hussain struggled with [the] controls but finally managed to eject. Devayya had waited too long for his aircraft's aged ejection seat to save his own life, and perished on Pakistani soil. And there lay, buried with him, the tale of his supreme sacrifice.
>
> The action was over in less than two minutes and it took the world 23 years to establish that it did, indeed, take place.[19]

In addition to the raids on Sargodha, there were other raids. No. 3 Squadron, IAF, raided a Pakistani radar at Gujranwala. While the radar was claimed to have been destroyed, one of the four Mystères in the raid was hit by AAA, making it go out of control and plough headlong into the ground leaving no time for the pilot to eject.[20]

The PAF, too, carried out raids on Indian bases on 7 September but all they achieved was a DC-3 Dakota and a DHC Caribou at Srinagar airfield.

Having suffered heavy losses, the Indian Air Force shied away from carrying out further counter air operations and instead got down to engaging interdiction targets and providing limited support to the army. Even the Pakistan Air Force, after its success at Pathankot, did not take any further chance and focused instead on carrying out close support missions. As there were only limited anti-aircraft resources with the Indian ground troops, no damage was caused to Pakistani aircraft as they inflicted *considerable damage to logistic vehicles supporting the Indian offensive.*[21] In another incident, an Indian cavalry regiment claimed to have destroyed a PAF F-86 Sabre, using .50 AA machine-gun fire.[22] As with other losses to Indian ground fire, Pakistan put the loss of the F-86 Sabre down to fratricide as it claimed that Flight Lieutenant Sadruddin's aircraft was instead hit by Pakistani anti-aircraft fire.[23] While Indian flak with the field army was yet to get a kill, the anti-aircraft guns deployed at rear areas were more successful as they claimed one F-86 at Jammu and a second at Amritsar.

The night of 8/9 September saw the first reported use of the SA-2 surface-to-air missile by the Indian Air Force as it claimed to have engaged and destroyed a Pakistani C-130 on a bombing run over Delhi. Reports stated that SA-2 missiles were fired from an air force base near Delhi and a loud explosion was heard, indicating that the missile had indeed hit the target, but no debris was found.[24] Interestingly, some Pakistani accounts claim that it was a case of fratricide since it was an Indian An-12 which had been engaged and shot down. Neither the IAF nor the PAF accounts have ever been verified.

On 9 September, while carrying out a close support mission along the Ferozepur-Lahore axis, the Indian Air Force lost two Hunter aircraft at Kasur to Pakistan flak while two more aircraft were damaged. The next day India lost a Mystère to anti-aircraft fire in the same area. Indian anti-aircraft shot down an F-86 Sabre over Wagah, near Amritsar, and a Martin B-57 at Halwara. This was the second PAF B-57 to have been shot down by Indian anti-aircraft artillery; the first was at Jamnagar. Incidentally, Pakistan lost four B-57s during the war and all four were shot down by anti-aircraft guns. No B-57 was lost by Pakistan to the Indian Air Force.

Meanwhile, the Indian offensive formations were being continuously harassed by the Pakistani Air Force. India's main offensive formation, 1st Armoured Division, had an integral air defence regiment equipped with truck-mounted L/60 AA guns, but it was not able to put up an effective challenge with its antiquated guns. The Pakistani Air Force had a relatively free run, forcing the commanding general of 1st Armoured Division to personally request the corps commander for air support for at least the next three days.

On 11 September there were mixed fortunes for both sides claimed to have shot down adversaries. Indian aircraft engaged Pakistani Army targets and destroyed eighteen tanks for the loss of one Mystère to Pakistani anti-aircraft fire. In turn the PAF again attacked the main Indian radar at Amritsar and claimed to have destroyed it for the loss of one Sabre.[25]

For the attack on 11 September, 4 Sabres plus a top cover of 2 F-104s were to be led by OC 33 Wing Commander Anwar Shamim with Flight Lieutenant Bhatti as his No. 3 and F/L Cecil Chawdery as No. 4. Enquiries as to the whereabouts of the wing leader's No. 2 were answered by Squadron Leader Munir, who arrived at the briefing in a freshly starched uniform, and announced that Flight Lieutenant Seraj had been kind enough to stand down so that the ops officer could come along in his place. Resignedly, Shamim completed the briefing, and the 4 Sabres set off at low level at 0800 hours on the half hour flight to Amritsar.

Despite poor visibility from the usual dust haze Bhatti, who was responsible for the navigation of this mission, brought the 4 Sabres out at low level precisely on track to Amritsar. Some help in identifying the target was in fact received from the Indian ack-ack fire, which began even before the Sabres started their pull-up to attack. As planned, Bhatti and Choudhry began climbing to about 7,000 ft as top cover to draw some of the ack-ack fire, while the two F-104s, flown by Squadron Leader Jamal and Flight Lieutenant Amjad, orbited even higher to guard against interference from IAF fighters.

As the first pair of Sabres started their climb, Bhatti called on the radio 'Target at 3 o'clock', and Shamim replied 'Lead and No. 2 pulling up.'

As the first pair of Sabres started their climb, Bhatti called on the radio 'Target at 3 o'clock,' and Shamim replied 'Lead and No.

2 pulling up.' By this time the target area was a veritable inferno of light and medium flak and within a few seconds there came another call, 'Two is hit.' Bhatti, when later describing the mission, recalled it in these words:

'No. 2 of course, was Munir but his voice on the radio was calm and unhurried. As I looked down, however, I saw three balls of flame tumbling through the air where his Sabre had already exploded. He must have taken a direct hit from a heavy ack-ack shell and never had a chance to eject. The flaming wreckage fell on the eastern outskirts of Amritsar town, and Munir was reported that evening by the Indians to have been found dead in the debris.'

In their exuberance the Pakistanis had claimed to have destroyed the radar but, except for a short period, the radar remained operational throughout the war and was even subjected to raids by the Pakistan Air Force later during the war.

That was also the day when Pakistan had its worst incident of fratricide with an RB-57B aircraft being shot down by its own anti-aircraft guns at Rahwali.[26] Frustrated by the repeated failure to locate and target the Amritsar radar, Squadron Leader Muhammad Iqbal, Officer Commanding No. 24 ELINT Squadron, along with his navigator Saifullah Lodhi, decided to carry out a practice 'homing' mission using the Pakistani radar unit near Rahwali as the target. As the radar had not been allotted any army anti-aircraft guns for its air defence, it was considered a safe target on which to practise. However, the radar commander at Rahwali had liaised with the nearby army air defence unit and got some guns for its protection.

As Muhammad Iqbal and his navigator, Saifullah Lodhi, were busy making a low dive-bombing practice run on the radar station, the army ack-ack unit deployed around the radar system opened fire on the diving RB-57B and shot it down, killing both pilot and navigator. It was a case of mistaken identity, but a costly one as Pakistan had now lost both its RB-57B aircraft to anti-aircraft fire and, tragically enough, one was to its own guns.

In another incident, during the battle of Phillora, an Indian cavalry regiment shot down a Pakistani army helicopter using the tank's main gun, the first such instance of a tank shooting down a helicopter. In the same area, the anti-aircraft guns with the Indian armoured formation put up an effective barrage of fire, shooting down the PAF strike leader's aircraft and forcing the others to abort the mission. This was probably the first such instance when the PAF had to abort a mission in the tactical battle area in the face of anti-aircraft fire.[27] Indian ack-ack scored again on 13 September as a Pakistani F-86 Sabre was shot down while attacking the railway station at Gurdaspur.[28] The IAF was not so lucky as it lost a Mystère to Pakistani AAA in the Kasur sector and another in the Sialkot area.

After a slow start, Indian anti-aircraft gunners with the field formations came to grips with the task and were soon enough giving stiff opposition to Pakistani aircraft over the battle area. The Pakistani close support missions flown over Phillaura and Chawinda faced intense anti-aircraft fire and most of the PAF Sabres were hit and damaged, a fact even acknowledged by Pakistan which mentions that almost fifty F-86 Sabres were hit by ground fire while carrying out the close support missions. Continuing to perform its deterrent role, Indian flak shot down an F-86 Sabre on 18 September and three more in the Khem Karan sector on 20 September. The war had been reduced to a slugfest with the Indian offensive losing its steam and both sides trying to make tactical gains. On 22 September, the last day of the war, the IAF lost a Mystère aircraft to its own ground fire in a case of mistaken identity in the Lahore sector. As on the first day, the IAF had wrongly attacked Indian ground positions on the last day of the war. This time the error proved to be costly.

While defending the air bases it was a mixed performance by the Indian ack-ack. Adampur, a front-line IAF base, faced its worst air raid of the war on 13 September as the PAF B-57 bombers carried out three raids during the night, all by a solitary B-57, admiringly referred to as '8 Pass Charlie' as it would come over the target every night, make eight passes in each raid and drop just one bomb in each pass on the selected target. The pilot would try to pick out different targets for each pass, and then try to carry out an effective drop each time. Paddy Earle (an Indian Air Force fighter pilot during the 1965 war) thus paid tribute to the unknown Pakistani pilot:

> I have the utmost respect for the Pakistani Canberra bloke who loved to ruin the equanimity of our dreary lives! 8-Pass Charlie was

an ace, but he had this nasty habit of turning up about 30 min. after moonrise, just as we were downing our first drink! Seriously, he was a cool dude and a professional of the highest order. To disguise the direction of his run, he used to cut throttles before entering a dive and by the time the ack-ack opened up he was beneath the umbrella of fire. After dropping his load he'd apply full throttle and climb out above the umbrella.

Even as '8-Pass Charlie' flew along at almost a leisurely pace, the anti-aircraft guns did not get any hits. This was all the more surprising as the newer radar-controlled L-70 AA guns were deployed at Adampur. As it was suspected that the tracking radars were being tampered with making them ineffective, all the radars were re-calibrated and rechecked after the raid.[29] Next day, as two PAF B-57s raided Adampur, the story would be different. The anti-aircraft gunners were ready and waiting for the Pakistani bombers. Both bombers survived the first run but, as they were on their second run, the anti-aircraft guns hit one of the B-57s. The badly stricken B-57 hastily dropped its bomb load in an open area nearby and managed to fly a short distance before plunging to the ground.

On the other hand, Indian anti-aircraft gunners were not so efficient at Halwara, another IAF base. No Pakistani aircraft were shot down by the Indian ack-ack during the entire war even as the Indian Air Force suffered a loss of lost six aircraft on the ground with a further seven damaged. The frustration of seeing almost a daily bombing run by B-57s and the ineffectiveness of the ack-ack was best summed up by Squadron Leader A.S. Lamba, an Indian pilot based at Halwara: 'We used to pull out our service pistols and take pot shots at the aircraft, more out of frustration than with any hope of hitting it.'[30]

In a late attempt, PAF B-57s escorted by two F-86 Sabres attacked Amritsar at 1615 hours even though a ceasefire had been declared at 0330 hours in the morning. It was a foolhardy mission, launched hours after the declaration of the ceasefire and more so as Pakistan lost both F-86 Sabres to anti-aircraft fire.[31] The next day, Pakistan used the last of its RB-57s. It was the RB-57F *Droopy* this time, to carry out a post-war reconnaissance mission. The RB-57F reportedly overflew Delhi and, as it was descending on its way back, was picked up and fired upon by the SA-2s deployed near Ambala. Three SA-2 Guideline missiles were fired which exploded in close proximity to the aircraft, causing some damage to one of its engines. The RB-57F was nursed back to its base at Peshawar, but the aircraft suffered more damage when the nose wheel did not extract and the aircraft skidded along the runway. This was the end of the last of the four modified RB-57s with Pakistan.

So ended the war of September 1965 in the Western theatre.

The Eastern Theatre

The two sides were unevenly matched in the East as Pakistan had only one squadron (No. 14) and one air defence regiment facing the much stronger Indian presence. For air defence, India had fourteen regiments in the theatre although some were deployed to cater for a possible threat from China.

The lone Pakistani squadron, called the *Tail Choppers*, was located at Tejgaon near Dacca, but its exact location was not known to Indian Intelligence.

The first six days of the war saw no action in the theatre as both adversaries waited for the events to unfold in the West. After the Indian counter-offensive was launched on 6 September, the Indian Air Force carried out some missions to try and put down the Pakistani airfields at Tezgaon and Chittagong, including a raid on the morning of the 7th, but without success. The Pakistan Air Force retaliated soon after, striking Kalaikunda, located south-east of Calcutta. It was one of the major Indian air bases in the East and housed two squadrons, one each of Canberras (No. 16, *The Rattlers*) and Hunters (No. 14). Initially, no ack-ack guns were deployed at Kalaikunda and a battery had been moved in on the 6th but was still in the process of settling down and all its guns would not be deployed until the morning of the 7th. For early warning, the air base had a Second World War vintage radar.

On 7 September at 0640 hours, just after the Canberras had returned from Chittagong and a failed mission, six Pakistani F-86 Sabres struck the air base, catching the defences off guard, claiming six aircraft – two Canberras and four Vampires.[32] This was followed by a second raid by four F-86s at 1030 hours. This time around, the Indian Air Force was ready with a combat air patrol (CAP) by two Hunters, as was the ack-ack.

The two Hunters took on the incoming raiders, shooting down an F-86 each and claiming one more. The ack-ack deployed at the air base also shot down an F-86 Sabre.

Though India had a much larger presence in the sector, it did not carry out any offensive missions thereafter and restricted itself to air defence sorties. Pakistan, however, continued to carry out sporadic raids, during which it not only lost three more aircraft on ground, but also lost two more F-86 Sabres to ack-ack.[33]

With no further operations by either side, the AAA there had not much to do.

Participating in a war for the first time, both Indian and Pakistani anti-aircraft artillery performed creditably against all odds. Equipped with Second World War weapons with no radar cover, hopelessly inadequate in numbers, taking on modern jets for which the guns were not designed, the ack-ack of both countries did well. According to the *Official History of Indo-Pak War 1965* Indian anti-aircraft artillery shot down twenty-five of forty-three Pakistani aircraft lost in the air,[34] that is 58 per cent of Pakistani losses in air were due to Indian ground-based air defences. Moreover, all the four B-57s lost by Pakistan during the war were to ack-ack. Considering the serious limitations of 40mm L/60 guns, which had very limited capability while operating at night, this performance is indeed creditable.

Indian Losses

Aircraft	In Air	On Ground	Accidents	Total
Vampire	4	6	–	10
Mystère	7	9	3	19
Hunter	10	3	4	17
Gnat	2	2	3	7
Canberra	1	4	–	5
MiG-21	–	3	–	3
Packet	–	3	–	3
Dakota	–	5	–	5
Auster	1	–	1	2
Sea Hawk	–	–	1	1
Civilian aircraft	1	2	–	3
Total	26	37	12	75

Indian Air Force Losses by cause
Losses in Air to Air Combat 15
Losses to AAA 10
Technical causes 2
Accidents 8

The Indian losses are listed as fifty-nine, of which twenty-four were in the air, including ten to ground fire, and thirty-five on the ground due to enemy action. A number of losses are shown as 'technical loss' or as 'accidents' even though there is credible evidence to show that the aircraft was hit by ack-ack fire. It is as if the air forces are hesitant in giving credit to anti-aircraft artillery.

Pakistan Air Force Losses
Official figures of PAF Losses
Air to Air Combat 7
Losses to AAA 6
Destroyed on ground 1
Accidents 3
Unknown causes 2
IAF Claims
Shot down in Air 14
Destroyed on ground 9

Losses as per Official History of India Pakistan War 1965

Aircraft	By Air Action	By AAA	Total
F-86	15	19	34
B-57	–	4	4
F-104	1	–	1
Others	2	2	4
Total	18	25	43

The performance of both the ack-acks was good but, if the number of aircraft hit or damaged is also considered, a more realistic assessment can be made. Indian anti-aircraft guns deployed at Amritsar were able to hit and damage 90 per cent of Pakistani aircraft attacking the Amritsar radar. Similarly, No. 19 Squadron PAF, based at Sargodha, is reported to have suffered hits on twenty of its aircraft from Indian ground fire. While the Pakistan Air Force officially claims that 'it lost no F-86 Sabre while undertaking 500 close support sorties' or that it lost no aircraft to ground fire, it does admit that fifty-eight of its F-86 Sabres were hit by ground fire. With so many contradictory reports and claims, the exact number of aircraft shot down by anti-aircraft artillery may never be known.

If the performance of the opposing AAA is seen, India AAA fared reasonably well. The number of aircraft lost by India on the ground was more because of the poor planning on part of Indian Air Force – keeping them parked out in the open – rather than only a failure of anti-aircraft artillery. The continued deployment of Indian anti-aircraft artillery in the East was counter-productive and the regiments could have better served their purpose in the West. Similarly, the anti-aircraft guns were spread too thin – as if trying to cover all assets, whereas they could have been better used in a concentrated manner to defend the more important and critical assets. Keeping the field formations denuded of air defences was another costly lapse.

Pakistani anti-aircraft artillery, with limited resources, defended well and made the Indian Air Force pay whenever it tried attacking the Pakistani bases. Over the battle area also, Pakistani anti-aircraft artillery performed well. By the later stage of the war, the Indian anti-aircraft artillery had made its presence felt and made it difficult for Pakistan Air Force to carry out support missions for its army.

On balance, there was not much to differentiate between the two armies' anti-aircraft artillery.

Chapter 4

The Six Day War

At 8:45a.m. (local time) on 5 June 1967, the Israeli Air Force (IAF) attacked eleven Egyptian air bases in a pre-emptive strike. The Israeli Air Force, in the first wave of the attack, which lasted two hours, destroyed 197 Egyptian aircraft on the ground and shut down six air bases. The Egyptian air defences had been caught off guard and offered minimal resistance. At the end of the first wave of air attacks, Israel launched its ground offensive and invaded Sinai.

The Six Day War had started.

The IAF carried out two more waves of strikes on Arab air bases destroying almost 400 enemy aircraft for the loss of nineteen of its own, all but three to anti-aircraft artillery.[1] By the end of the day, Arab air forces had been destroyed, leaving the skies free to the Israeli Air Force. In one of the shortest wars of the twentieth century, Israel went on to rout the Arab forces, achieving a spectacular victory and capturing territory three times its own size.

The Six Day War, as it came to be called, is considered to be the first war won by air power. The common perception is that it was a war in which the air defences failed totally. This statement, however, hides more than it reveals about the performance of anti-aircraft artillery and the air forces and calls for a more detailed study. The pre-emptive strikes carried out on 5 June 1967 were not without precedent in the Middle East, having been carried out during the Suez Crisis of 1956 – only it was the combined Anglo-French forces that had attacked Egyptian air bases on 31 October 1956. The Egyptians should have been aware of the possibility that such an operation could be launched by Israel and prepared for it.

Going back to 1956, the war was a result of an attempt on the part of Israel, the UK and France to seize control of the Suez Canal. While Israel launched Operation KADESH in the Sinai, it used its air force for close support, as also for para-dropping and transport support for the Israeli Defence Forces (Army).

The Egyptian Air Force carried out strikes against the Israeli army using de Havilland Vampire and Gloster Meteor jets, losing seven to nine aircraft in air combat while shooting down just one Israeli aircraft. As the British and French forces attacked Egypt, the Egyptian Air Force moved back its aircraft to southern Egypt leaving the Israeli Air Force free to operate over Sinai.

Meanwhile, the combined Anglo-French forces launched Operation MUSKETEER as Egypt rejected the ultimatum presented by Britain and France and its closure of the Suez Canal. Twelve Egyptian airfields in the Canal Zone and the Nile Delta were attacked on 30 October by English Electric Canberra and Vickers Valiant bombers – the first time that an element of the 'V-force' had been used operationally.[2]

On the first day itself, 260 Egyptian planes were destroyed on the ground.[3] Over the next three days, attacks on Egyptian military airfields continued, with strikes by de Havilland Venom FB4s of the Royal Air Force, Westland Wyverns, Hawker Sea Hawks and de Havilland Sea Venoms of the Fleet Air Arm, Republic F-84F Thunderstreaks of the Armée de l'air, and Chance Vought Corsairs of the Aéronavale. Egypt lost 400 of 500 combat aircraft on its inventory. The near-absolute destruction of the Egyptian Air Force gave the British and French air supremacy, clearing the way for the invasion of the northern Suez Canal.

During the air campaign, the Egyptians hardly opposed their adversaries although Anglo-French forces lost ten aircraft to various causes. The performance of Valiants came in for criticism as their performance was disappointing – only three of the seven airfields they attacked were seriously damaged. The Egyptian Air Force had been effectively destroyed in a wider series of multinational attacks of which the Valiant bombing missions had been only a part.

During the war, Israel is believed to have lost ten to eighteen aircraft out of its total inventory of about 150 aircraft most of which were to ground fire[4] while the Egyptian Air Force lost twelve aircraft, eight of which were claimed by Israel in aerial combat.

The air operations during the 1956 war had a profound impact not only on the Israeli Air Force but also on all the branches of the Israel air defence forces. While the Israeli Air Force has always been in the limelight, the Israelis had never neglected their air defence forces and had paid equal attention to them, away from public glare. Keeping in mind, the lack of strategic depth, such an attention was understandable. The first Israeli anti-aircraft guns were the Swiss-made 20m cannon received in 1948 during the Passover holiday, smuggled into Israel hidden among sacks of potatoes. Using the services of Second World War veterans who had served with the British Army, Israel established an air defence school at Herzlia. By January 1950, the Air Defence Forces, although part of the Artillery Corps, were formally organized directly under the Israel Defence Forces vice commander and, by 1956, the Air Defence Forces had one battalion of twelve radar-directed 3.7-inch heavy AA guns, plus about 300 single-barrel 20mm and 30mm manually controlled AA cannon.[5]

Following the Suez crisis, as the Soviet Union provided large-scale military aid to the Arab air forces, including modern aircraft like the Tu-16 and Il-28 bombers and MiG-19 and MiG-21 combat fighters, Israel could no longer ignore the increasing air threat and took efforts to upgrade its air defences. In a departure from its earlier practice of relying on aircraft for interception and ensuring air defence, Israel decided to introduce surface-to-air missiles (SAMs). The trigger for this decision was the threat to the Dimona reactor from low-altitude, hit-and-run incursions from Egyptian airfields in Sinai. It was assessed that it would be impossible for the Israeli Air Force to prevent such an attack solely through aerial interception of the MiGs, and even while the intruders could be intercepted it was economically not possible to ensure constant defensive air patrols. The following assessment by the Israel General Staff brought out the need to introduce air defence missiles as a viable counter to the emerging air threat:

> The worst-case scenario for the defense establishment is an attack from the air instigated by the enemy on our airfields and population centres. There is no way to completely hold back such an attack with aircraft only.... Surface-to-air missiles are a better defensive means against faster aircraft than interceptors.[6]

Israel decided to introduce the HAWK (Homing All the Way Killer) surface-to-air missiles of which five batteries were acquired for $30 million. Initially, the Air Force had opposed the acquisition of HAWK as, in its view, it would have been better to increase the size of its fighter jet force and construct more airfields (Israel had only three airfields at that time). Improving air defence capabilities was a low priority for the Air Force as it sought to build up its offensive arm. Major General Ezer Weizman, the IAF commander, felt that the introduction of a good air defence system would result in a defensive approach and would strengthen arguments against a preventive air strike.

> I feared that when the senior leadership would need to approve an air offensive the presence in Israel of Hawk missiles would actually block a fast-affirmative decision [to strike first].[7]

Budgetary consideration was another factor in opposing the HAWK deal as the Israeli Air Force wanted the scarce resources to be provided instead for an additional Mirage squadron or be used to build a fourth airfield. Not that the USA was very keen to provide the HAWK missile system as it had apprehensions about the possible Soviet reaction. It was feared by Washington that equipping the Israeli Defence Forces with surface-to-air missiles would result in sale of advanced surface-to-surface missiles (SSMs) by the Soviet Union to Egypt, enhancing the threat to Israel. However, this concern was not considered relevant by Israel as it felt that it was the Soviets who were introducing advanced air and ground-based weapon systems into the Middle East, and Israel was only reacting, not leading the arms race.

After much ado, when the first HAWK missiles finally did arrive in 1965 over the objections of the Air Force, they led to another debate – the operational control of the missile systems. Having failed to prevent their acquisition, the Air Force at least prevailed in gaining control over the surface-to-air missiles and the HAWK batteries were placed directly under air force control.[8]

Meanwhile, to augment the air defence forces, Israel acquired about 200 power-operated 40mm L-70 AA guns and forty Super Fledermaus radar-fire-control systems from West Germany. With these Israel had a well co-ordinated air defence layout by June 1967, with multiple batteries of 40mm power-operated radar-directed AA guns augmented by 30mm manually-controlled AA guns and the HAWK SAM batteries. The missiles were used to protect the Dimona nuclear reactor, airfields and the radar stations.

While its strategic assets had a reasonably sound air defence, the Israeli ground troops had only a minimal air defence, not considering the organic 12.7mm and 7.62mm machine guns with the army units.[9]

Even as Israel was upgrading its air defences, the Arab air forces and the defence forces were being infused with new weapon systems from the Soviet Union. These weapon systems included eighteen to twenty-five batteries of SA-2 surface-to-air missiles provided to Egypt alone. It was not only material support that was provided by the Soviet Union and its allies – Egyptian Army personnel were trained by Soviet and Czech Army instructors on handling and operating the new weapons systems though, even after the intense training regime, there was much scope for improvement both in terms of equipment and training. According to Hussein Abdel-Razek, an Egyptian general who served during the 1967 war, Egypt had severe shortcomings at the time of the Six Day War

> All the armies were still building themselves. For example, Egypt was still building its forces, many of the main weapons weren't even available, for example the air defenses. Egypt's skies were open, we didn't have radar systems, enough to cover all of Egypt's skies. We didn't have air defense systems that were able to deal with the modern Israeli airplanes.[10]

Razek emphasises, 'We were not ready, our air defence was very weak.'

It was not that the Egyptian Army did not try to correct these shortcomings. Air Marshal Madkoor Aboul-Aez, who had served in the Egyptian Air Force as its deputy chief and was later a key figure in its reconstruction, had advocated for investment in more airstrips, hardened air shelters and bases to disperse Egypt's jet fighters and bombers so that the air power could defend Egyptian ground formations and naval assets from the Israeli Air Force. But, as was the case with Israel, there were not enough funds available and, when the allocation did happen, the

Egyptian Air Force lost out to the army which was given the lion's share to raise more divisions. When asked by Nasser about the Egyptian Air Force just days before the Six Day War, Aboul-Aez red-flagged several matters, the main ones being that Egypt was in no position to withstand a first aerial strike as the air bases were devoid of any anti-air missile cover and the fighters and bombers parked in the open would all be destroyed on the ground itself. He warned that '1956 will happen again, only this time around the Egyptian Army would be forced an even worse retreat in the Sinai'.[11]

Aboul-Aez was not the only one who was questioning the lack of preparedness, and the sabre-rattling by Nasser. Air force chief Sidqui Mahmoud warned of a repeat attack on Egyptian airfields like the 1956 Suez War and submitted a report to Nasser late in 1966, warning him and Field Marshal Amer that the air force would not be ready until 1970, highlighting the fact that in the preceding ten years, Egypt had spent only 17 million Egyptian pounds – approximately $45 million – on air defence, which was grossly inadequate. He even proposed positioning two Egyptian fighter wings in Syria as it would help disperse Egyptian aircraft and have the benefit of supporting an Arab state. To get better information on Israeli air activities, Sidqui asked for Egyptian ground controllers to be stationed in Syria. Drunk on the political victory of 1956, all these proposals were rejected by Nasser.

Other details that are now available of the Six Day War suggest that during a meeting of top Egyptian military commanders with Nasser on 2 June 1967, the head of Intelligence, General Sadek, proposed moving back a few jet fighters from the Sinai air bases into Egypt, like Beth Suef Air Base, but this was not accepted by the air chief as it would *appear like a withdrawal.* According to Sadek, Nasser ended the evening of 2 June convinced that Israel would not risk political damage with the United States by conducting a first strike.

Another report, however, refers to a meeting of 2 June itself in which Nasser reportedly warned of an Israeli first strike sometime after 5 June. But when Nasser himself was asked permission for an *Egyptian pre-emptive strike* he refused. During the meeting Sidqui, the air chief, again emphasized that the Israeli first strike would be deadly and Egypt would not be able to absorb it.

All the fears expressed by the Egyptian Air and Intelligence chiefs would come true just a couple of days later.

In the early hours of 5 June, at about 6:00 a.m. (local time), Egyptian Intelligence issued a warning that an Israeli air attack was imminent. The message arrived at the Air Force Central Command Cairo, where a junior officer received the message but, for some unknown reason, it was not passed on to Sidqui, the Air Force chief. This was a fatal decision that would seal the fate of the Egyptian Air Force as, just three hours later, the air chief was to take off with War Minister Badran, Field Marshal Amer, General Anwar Qadi (senior military operations officer), and Colonel Mohammed Ayoub (aide to Field Marshal Amer) to inspect the Egyptian defences in the Sinai. Ignorant about the warning received from their own Intelligence staff, the war minister with the air chief and the senior military operations officer took off from Cairo as planned. None of the top brass of the Egyptian armed forces was to be in Cairo that fateful morning when the Israeli Air Force launched Operation MOKED (FOCUS).[12]

Initially planned in the years following the Suez Crisis in 1956, Operation MOKED was designed to completely destroy the Egyptian Air Force on the ground. A product of the Chief of Israeli Air Force, Brigadier General Mordechai Hod, the plan called for a pre-emptive strike against the military forces of neighbouring Arab countries and the maintenance of aerial supremacy thereafter during the follow-up operations. It was an ambitious and audacious plan given the fact that Israel had only 196 front-line combat aircraft as opposed to nearly 700 aircraft operated by the three Arab nations. The balance was tilted even more against Israel as the combined Arab armies could muster about 328,000 men, 2,300 tanks, 1,800 APCs and 2,200 anti-aircraft emplacements (including SAM batteries).

The bulk of Arab weapons and equipment were of Soviet origin; that included MiG-17, -19 and -21 fighters, Tu-16 strategic bombers and Il-28 medium bombers, while the Israeli Air Force was entirely equipped with upgraded French aircraft: Sud Aviation light bombers, Dassault Ouragon fighter-bombers, Dassault Super Mystère fighters and Dassault Mirage IIICJ fighters.

Well aware of the odds they faced due to the numerical disadvantage, the Israeli Air Force developed a very intricate and detailed plan to make every aircraft and crew count. The air force had a 3:1 ratio for pilots to aircraft, i.e. three pilots for every aircraft, ensuring that rested pilots would be available to replace tired or wounded flyers and no aircraft was left idling for want of trained pilots. The air force built several airfields in the desert modelled after Egyptian bases which were used for practice attack runs and to familiarize the pilots with the layout of Egyptian air bases. In addition, the ground crew were trained to re-arm and re-fuel an aircraft quickly, to bring down the 'turn-around' time and ensure the aircraft could fly multiple missions every day. These practices ensured an availability rate of 90 per cent and turn-around time of just seven minutes. Israel had another ace up their sleeves – a runway penetrating bomb. It was a product of a joint French/Israeli anti-runway weapon programme developed to target the runways. It used a rocket to propel the bomb after release so that it penetrated the runway surface and dislodged the concrete slabs, causing damage that was far harder to repair than the shallow craters made by normal bombs. This bomb was used later by the French company Matra to develop the Durandal bombs which entered service in 1977.

Ensuring a very high rate of aircraft and crew availability was just one part of the overall plan. The primary objective of MOKED was the destruction of Egypt's Tu-16 and Il-28 bombers, followed by the destruction of Egypt's MiG-21 aircraft. While the two bombers, being the only ones with the range to reach and hit targets in Israel, were considered the main threat by Israel, the MiG-21 was on the very top of the list of targets to be destroyed as it was the most capable fighter aircraft with Egypt and the only one which could have put up a fight in the air. Secondary objectives included the destruction of the airfields and anti-aircraft defences, to keep the Egyptian Air Force grounded and minimize the risk from anti-aircraft fire.

To avoid being picked up by the *twenty odd* Egyptian radars strung all along the Sinai, the IAF planned to send the aircraft at extreme low level (less than sixty feet above ground level). This was also to stay below the lower ceiling of SA-2 as it was ineffective below 4,000 feet. Plus, Israel had identified the gaps in the radar cover and was to exploit that. This still left the IAF aircraft vulnerable to light flak guns but that was a risk the IAF had to take. Coupled with this was a ruse built up by the Israelis. For two years they followed the same routine, at the same time, taking off from their base in the Negev desert and sweeping out to the west across the Mediterranean Sea. The aircraft would dive to wavetop height and return home. This routine was noted and tracked by the Egyptian radars and, as a precaution, the Egyptian Air Force would carry out a regular dawn alert. The Egyptian practice of dawn combat air patrols was in turn tracked by Israeli Intelligence, noting the exact time and route of the combat air patrols along the Egyptian-Israeli frontier in the Sinai. It was a daily practice for both air forces and this would lead to a sense of a dull boring routine – and a sense of complacency in the Egyptians.

The 5 June attack was planned around the intelligence input that the 0740 dawn alert had been cancelled by Egypt as they were taking the morning sorties by Israel for routine training.[13]

To keep up with the deception of carrying out routine training sorties, sixteen Fouga Magister training aircraft took off at 0710 Israeli time, maintaining radio silence and using the same patrol patterns that were used by the Mirage fighters, to indicate that it was just another routine practice. The Magisters were picked up by the Egyptian and Jordanian radars but as they were following the route followed by the Mirages, the radar operators took them for the Mirages. The ruse had worked.

Just five minutes later, the first of 183 IAF combat aircraft started taking off for the strike on Egyptian bases, leaving only twelve fighters – eight were airborne on combat patrol and four on the ends of runways – to provide air defence.[14] The strike aircraft formed up in groups of four, maintaining a gap between themselves to ensure that when they reached the Egyptian air bases they would be able to maintain almost a constant presence when they reached the targets at 0845.

The Israeli planes were able to reach their targets, evading the Soviet-made Egyptian air defence systems not only by 'flying very close to the ground' but also by deploying sophisticated electronic warfare.[15] Two Israeli Vautour planes flew at high altitude through the Sinai carrying electronic counter-measure systems to suppress the radars of SA-2 missiles, creating corridors within the Egyptian air defene, through which Israeli planes transited in relative safety.[16] In addition, Israeli C-47s flying along the border dispensed chaff to confuse the radar operators;

this completely shut down the Egyptian radar system. Moreover, the initial flights had provoked the Egyptian radars to move to their main frequency. That action exposed the whole radar system to an effective blockage of the radar stations in that critical moment.

According to the Czech Republic's After Action Report, another measure adopted by the Israelis was deployment of rockets by its aircraft which used the radars' transmitted waves as a guiding signal to home in on the radars, as a result of which each aircraft looked like three objects on the radar screens. This further added to the confusion amongst the radar operators.[17]

The Egyptian accounts consider the use of electronic warfare by the Israelis as far more important than the altitude at which the Israeli planes were able to fly. It is also mentioned in some sources that the US intelligence ship USS *Liberty* helped the Israelis during their surprise attack, but the USS *Liberty* was not near Egypt on 5 June and the confusion is more likely due to the *earlier* US efforts to gather intelligence of Egyptian air defence using their airborne systems.[18] As the Israelis used electronic warfare equipment similar to the US, the confusion is understandable.

The massive Israeli Air Force strike force of almost 200 aircraft managed to evade the Egyptian radars but was picked up by the Jordanian radar at Ajloun. Jordan attempted to warn the Egyptians, but the latter had changed their radio codes the previous day and didn't understand the messages. However, another source refers to the air chief Sidqui's claim that the message was not only delivered to the War Minister, Badran, but that he read the encoded cable from the Ajloon station in Jordan, which read, 'ISRAELI PLANES OVER EGYPTIAN AIRBASES AT 0745 (Cairo Time)', and also a second cable that said '50 ISRAELI PLANES WILL ATTACK EGYPT BETWEEN 0835–0845 (Amman Time)'.[19]

As mentioned earlier, Egypt's senior military leadership was travelling onward to Sinai. They reportedly came to know of the Israeli strike while still airborne. An account of the reaction to the news of the attack mentions:

> While on the plane, they read of high levels of radar-jamming activity and a report of increased Israeli Air Force activity on bases in Southern Israel. The pilots got word first that Kibreet and Abu

Suweir air bases were under attack, and they decided to return to Cairo immediately. While crossing the Suez Canal Zone, Amer's plane was surrounded by Israeli fighter jets, the senior officers looked at their windows muttering, 'Impossible! Impossible!' Amer's aide, thinking this was a coup attempt, pulls out his pistol and the other generals all go for their guns. Air force General Sidqui yells at them, 'Put down your weapons, you fools, Israel is attacking us now!' They fly over Inchas airfield in Cairo, seeing it in flames, and they finally land at Cairo's civilian airport, as the military section is in ruins.[20]

It was in such state of confusion that the IAF delivered the first blow, attacking the Egyptian bases at El Arish, Gebel Libni, Bir Gifgafa and Bir Thamada in the Sinai Desert; Abu Sueir, Kabrit, and Fayid along the Suez Canal; Inchas, Cairo West, and Beni Sueif on the banks of the Nile river. Eight MiG-21 formations were destroyed while taxiing for take off, and twenty more Egyptian fighters were either shot down in air-to-air encounters or crashed while trying to land on damaged runways. Four Egyptian MiG-21s which managed to take off shot down two IAF aircraft before being shot down themselves.

The first wave of forty IAF aircraft carried on with the attack for approximately seven to ten minutes for an initial bombing run with 'concrete dibber' bombs, followed by three to four strafing runs. While the first wave was attacking the air bases, the second wave was already on its way and the third was getting airborne. Just three minutes after the first wave left, the second wave struck for seven minutes, followed by the third wave after a three minute interval. The eight waves were spread over just eighty minutes. If this was not enough, further strikes were carried out in three waves for another eighty minutes after a pause of ten minutes.

The concrete dibber bombs were very effective, leaving craters five metres wide and 1.6 metres deep. The IAF pilots dropped the bombs with precision – the first two aircraft dropping them at the beginning of the runway, the following two aircraft in the centre of the runway and the last two aircraft in the wave dropping them at the end of the runway. Within a couple of minutes, the whole runway was bombed and totally unusable. The runway could not be repaired as the delayed fuses used on the bombs continued exploding until long after the raids.

The Egyptian air bases were well protected by anti-aircraft artillery and surface-to-air missiles – Egypt had almost 100 anti-aircraft batteries with over 1,000 Soviet-built anti-aircraft guns (37mm, 57mm and 85mm) and about 150 SA-2 surface-to-air missiles deployed at twenty-seven sites. But when the Israeli Air Force struck, all anti-aircraft batteries and missile sites had been ordered not to fire as the Egyptians feared that the anti-aircraft fire could endanger the War Minister's aircraft which was still airborne.[21] This was a costly mistake for Egypt to make.

Only at Cairo did the anti-aircraft guns open fire and try to repel the IAF aircraft. As with other anti-aircraft sites, the battery at Cairo had been ordered not to open fire, but Major Sa'id Ahmad Rabi, the battery commander decided to disregard the orders and to open fire on the Israeli aircraft. Rabi claims to have downed several IAF jets.[22] Similarly, at Luxor air base, Egyptian anti-aircraft guns stood up to the challenge, taking on the striking Vautour aircraft of the first wave, hitting and severely damaging one. As the Vautour lurched to a side and lost altitude after being hit, the pilot intentionally flew his aircraft into a group of four neatly parked MiG-17s on the runway. However, such instances of the local anti-aircraft commanders taking the initiative and opening fire were rare and, as a result, Israel lost only six aircraft to anti-aircraft guns in the first wave. Compared to this, the Egyptian Air Force managed to shoot down only two Israeli aircraft in air-to-air combat.

As the first wave was still being executed, the war minister's aircraft landed at Cairo International Airport, one of the few air bases not yet attacked. As he reached Supreme Headquarters, he asked Iraq and Syria to launch Operation RASHID – the planned bombing of Israeli airfields. Both countries cited technical problems at first but later joined in when Jordan started its own offensive. At 10:00 a.m., Jordan's Hunter aircraft strafed the Israeli bases at Netanya, Kfar Sirkin and Kfar Saba, destroying a transport aircraft at Kfar Sirkin. This was followed by air strikes by Syria and Iraq. The Syrian Air Force, in its raids, carried out just before noon, damaged the Israeli oil refinery at Haifa and destroyed several dummy aircraft at the Megiddo airfield. Israel retaliated soon after, carrying out air raids on five Syrian air bases and destroying sixty of the 127 aircraft.[23] Hit badly with almost half its air force written off, Syria withdrew her air force from the front line. The last entrant of the air war, Iraq, raided the Israeli base at Ramat David at 1400 hours. While it could not do much damage, it lost at least ten aircraft on the ground in the retaliatory Israeli raid on its base of H-3. Jordan, with the smallest air force in the region, was hit worst with all twenty-one of its combat aircraft destroyed on the ground in the Israeli air strikes. Moreover, the air bases at Amman and Mafraq were heavily damaged, as was the radar station at Ajloun. The only consolation was that its anti-aircraft guns shot down an Israeli Mystère during the second wave of attacks on its air bases.[24]

The late entrants had paid heavily for their (mis)adventure. In an interesting incident at Mafraq, it was a Pakistan Air Force pilot, Flight Lieutenant Saifzul Alam, on loan to Jordan as part of a training contingent of sixteen PAF pilots, who shot down an IAF Mystère:[25]

> At 12:48 p.m. on June 5, four Israeli jets were descending on Jordan's Mafraq air base to smash the country's tiny air force, shortly after the entire Egyptian air force had been reduced to rubble.
>
> To intercept the incoming attack, Jordanian air force commanders deputized Flt Lt Saiful Azam, who was on loan as an advisor from Pakistan. Once airborne with other Jordanian pilots, Saiful Azam engaged the attacking aircrafts in an air-to-air combat, shooting down a Mystère commanded by Israeli pilot H. Boleh and shot and damaged another that crash-landed in Israeli territory.

Returning to Egypt, the Israeli Air Force, in the second wave, attacked all the bases once again, at the end of which the Egyptian Air Force had lost 293 aircraft including thirty long-range Tu-16 bombers at Beni Sueif and Luxor, twenty-seven Il-28 medium bombers, twelve Su-7 fighter-bombers, ninety MiG-21 fighters, twenty MiG-19 fighters and seventy-five MiG-17 fighters. In just 170 minutes since the first strike, the Israeli Air Force had struck at a total of nineteen Egyptian air bases – ten in the first wave and the nine in the second. The air bases hit in the second wave were Mansura, Helwan, El Minya, Almaza, Luxor, Deversoir, Hurghada, Ras Banas and Cairo International. Of these, two bases in mainland Egypt and four in the Sinai Peninsula had been completely destroyed.

The next targets for the Israeli Air Force were the Egyptian radar stations which were the targeted in the afternoon. The air raids completely destroyed twenty-three radars, including all sixteen radars in Sinai. Egyptian air defences were completely blind now and there were no means of getting early warning of Israeli air raids. In any case, Egypt was left with no air force to act on the warning! The Israeli air raids continued into the night causing further damage. Egyptian anti-aircraft guns, now free of the restrictions, fired at the Israeli aircraft without respite. So intense was the fire that *the guns fired until their barrels melted.*[26] But even such intense fire was not enough to halt the relentless Israeli air strikes.

By the end of Day One, the Egyptian Air Force was finished as a fighting force with only remnants scattered at its heavily damaged air bases. Jordan had lost all its combat aircraft while the Iraqi and Syrian air forces had been badly crippled. It was a spectacular performance by Israel which had started the war with only 193 combat aircraft. It had generated 490 sorties against Egypt alone with an average turn-around time of seven and a half minutes. It had lost nineteen aircraft on the first day against Egypt, thirteen of them to anti-aircraft guns and only two in air-to-air combat.

The surface-to-air missiles had been blinded by lack of radar cover and were ineffective although a dozen of them were fired at the IAF aircraft. As the aircraft were flying too low for the missiles to be effective, none of the missiles hit any aircraft and could cause no damage. It was only the anti-aircraft guns that proved to be of some deterrence, but even they could not make the Israeli Air Force stop in its tracks. Had the orders not been issued by the Supreme Headquarters to hold their fire, the anti-aircraft guns would have caused far more damage, but it was not to be so.

The Egyptian Air Force put up a token air resistance, but it proved to be suicidal engagements with Israeli jet fighters. To compound the problems, as almost all the bases had been neutralized by the Israelis, the Egyptian aircraft that did manage to take off to take on the Israelis had no runway to return to and, as they landed on damaged runways, suffered irreparable damage. The Egyptian engineering crews tried to repair the damaged runways, knowing that planes needed to have a place to land, and they did it under fire and while fighting the heat and explosions around them but the delayed action fuzes used on concrete dibber bombs made it difficult to locate the bombs and clear them – making the runway repairs an impossible task. In the end, it was all in vain as the Arab air forces were so severely damaged that they could not undertake any meaningful operations, leaving the skies free for Israel to operate at will.

At the end of 5 June Israel had lost nineteen aircraft against Egypt, of which thirteen were to anti-aircraft artillery and only two in air-to-air combat. But they had claimed to have destroyed almost all of the Arab air forces.

As the ground operations carried on, Egypt compounded its tactical errors by ordering a general withdrawal on the second day. At that time, Egypt still had ten of its fourteen brigades in reasonably fit state to fight but, as the senior leadership wilted under pressure, the army retreated in a disorderly manner, giving Israel a victory it may not have dreamt of.

It was all the more tragic that the Egyptian army did not put up a fight as all its formations were well equipped to take on the Israeli Air Force and could have made a difference if only they had been employed.

Trained and equipped on the Soviet model, all its formations and battalions had an integral complement of anti-aircraft artillery. The infantry division had an integral battery of twelve 85mm, or 100mm, dual-purpose anti-aircraft guns while the tank division had a battalion of thirty-four anti-aircraft guns and the mechanized infantry division a battalion of thirty-six 100mm anti-aircraft guns. All these guns were dual purpose and could be used in anti-tank and anti-aircraft roles. Even an infantry brigade was given an artillery detachment which included a battalion of eighteen 57mm anti-aircraft guns. Similarly, the machine-gun company of the infantry battalion had twelve 12.7mm heavy machine guns and six 37mm anti-aircraft cannon.

The Egyptian Army had a total of ten infantry brigades in Sinai at the beginning of the war and, had these resources been used, they would have put up a formidable defence against the Israeli Air Force. Sadly, the Egyptian Army just capitulated, offering no resistance and none of the anti-aircraft weapons were ever used or tested.

The war ended in just six days but the hostilities did not. No peace prevailed thereafter and the war itself had serious repercussions, unexpected at that for all the countries in the region. With Soviet military aid, the Arab nations built back their forces and learnt the right lessons. The Yom Kippur War was to be a vindication of that.

In the end, it needs to be remembered that though the Six Day War was an impressive achievement, it is highly unrepresentative of the nature of combat. That remains true for AAA and its performance. Drawing lessons solely on the basis of the conduct during the war is to err into making the wrong assumptions, as Israel would find out, much to its dismay, just six years later. They lost forty-eight aircraft (all but ten to ground fire).[27] Attrition by anti-aircraft artillery was severe. Considering that thirty-eight Israeli aircraft were shot down by ground fire, Israel lost 20 per cent of its air force to anti-aircraft fire in just three days. In addition, twenty-one aircraft were badly damaged and most likely were not available for operations during the rest of the war.[29] If the badly damaged aircraft are included, Israel lost nearly a third of the total aircraft held. Operations with such a magnitude of attrition are unsustainable and it is only pure luck that on the first day the Egyptian AAA had been restrained and told not to fire; the losses would have been far worse.[28] The breakdown of Israeli Air Force losses is as given below:

Air to Air Combat	3
AAA	38
Accidents	3
Fratricide	1 (Shot down near Dimona)
Unknown	3
Total	48

Conduct of further air operations would not have been possible after a couple of days. It was this coincidence that favoured Israel more than anything else. It needs to be considered that, even after the pounding of its air bases, the Egyptian Air Force was still carrying out operations all throughout the war. When it is projected as 193 aircraft destroyed on the first day, it looks bad but, in overall terms, the Egyptian Air Force still had over 250 combat aircraft left, as against 150-odd IAF aircraft. The way we look at losses makes all the difference.

The Arab air forces were not totally grounded and continued their operations during the six days.[30] They lost sixty to seventy-nine aircraft to Israeli aircraft in aerial combat and about fifty to Israeli ground-based air defences.[31]

The only air defence system not to have acquitted itself well was the SA-2 missile system. Egypt had eighteen to twenty-five batteries of SA-2s, but they proved to be ineffective. Not one Israeli aircraft was lost to an SA-2, of the dozen or so fired during the war. The reason for their failure was more to do with technical limitations than anything else. Designed to take on high-flying aircraft like the U-2, these SAMs were at sea against low-flying high-speed jet like the Mystères and Vautours. The story of SAMs would be different next time around.

Buoyed by the outstanding performance of the Israeli air and armoured forces, Israel built up these two even further at the expense of the rest of the armed forces. This was to have wholly unforeseen and very undesirable consequences in the subsequent wars.

Chapter 5

The War of Attrition

Following defeat in the Six Day War, Egypt launched the War of Attrition with the idea of inflicting as many Israeli casualties as possible, thereby testing Israel's ability and determination to hold onto its gains from the war. The post-ceasefire hostilities had been going on ever since June 1967 and there had been no diplomatic effort to resolve the problems at the heart of the Arab-Israeli conflict.

Egypt started building up its armed forces almost immediately after the war. The Soviet Union had supplied more than 130 aircraft by the end of June, ferried by An-12s and re-assembled in Egypt. These were MiG-21FLs and MiG-21 BFMs from the USSR and East Germany, much better aircraft than the Mig-17s and -19s they were replacing. The advantage Egypt had in re-building its air force was that it had lost fewer pilots since most of its aircraft losses had been on the ground. As Brigadier General Qadri al-Hamid, Egyptian Air Force said: 'We had a new air force because we did not lose many of our pilots or ground support personnel.'[1]

The War of Attrition started soon after the ceasefire in June 1967 with the first attacks taking place as early as July 1967. The initial attacks were confined to artillery and shallow raids as Egypt used its guns to attack Israeli positions along the canal, in addition to small raiding parties, to harass the Israelis. In the first incident itself, Israel lost one soldier and had thirteen wounded. Israel retaliated but it was the air force rather than the artillery that was used to respond to the Egyptian attacks. These skirmishes continued and were reportedly a ploy by Egypt, on Soviet insistence, to maintain pressure and create a situation of hostilities so that the sitting UN Security Council meeting would ask Israel to withdraw from the captured territories.

The Egyptian Air Force carried out tens of fighter-bomber sweeps over Sinai and tried to engage the Mirages. Into the bargain, Egypt lost six aircraft while one Mirage III was shot down by an Egyptian SA-2 surface-to-air missile.[2]

The war was to intensify following the Arab League Summit held in September 1967 in Khartoum, Sudan, when the participating Arab states proclaimed the 'Three Nos' of the Khartoum Resolution: no peace with Israel, no recognition of Israel, no negotiations with Israel.[3] Soon enough, Nasser proclaimed: 'what was taken by force, will not be restored except by force.'[4] The stage was being set for the long-drawn war of attrition.

Showing its adherence to the declaration of restoring its status by force, Egypt launched one of the first artillery assaults in September from its fortified position at the Green Island in the north of the Gulf of Suez on Israeli shipping within Israeli waters. Israel retaliated and the artillery fights were being carried out all along the canal, with Ismailia and Suez coming directly under fire. Thousands of Egyptians were forced to leave their homes.

This was followed by the sinking of the Israeli Z-class destroyer INS *Eilat* on 21 October 1967. The destroyer was sunk by Styx missiles fired by Komar-class Egyptian missile boats. This was the first time in history that a major naval ship had been sunk by missile fire from another vessel. Israel retaliated with a massive concentration of artillery fire in the south – targeting the oil refineries and storage facilities in Suez. The refinery and oil depots kept burning for four days, killing eleven people and injuring ninety-two. It was an unexpectedly severe reaction by Israel and one which forced Egypt to stop its artillery attacks for some time.

In November the United Nations passed Resolution 242, seeking an end to hostilities and for Israel to withdraw from the capture territories. A lull prevailed for a year or so, a period used by both Israel and the Arabs to complete the 'defensive rehabilitation' of their forces.

Egypt re-organized its armed forces with infusion of Soviet weapon systems and equipment and, by September 1968, had regained the total strength they had before the Six Day War. With newer weapons systems – MiG-21s replacing the earlier series of aircraft and the newer, better T-54 and T-55 tanks – Egypt had much stronger armed forces. They had approximately 550 T-54 and T-55 tanks, 300 heavy artillery guns, 450 field artillery guns and more than 800 light armoured vehicles.

US Army soldiers with an American trailer-mounted 90mm M118 anti-aircraft gun. The wheels on which the weapon is transported have been removed and are at left. Painted on the side of the artillery piece is the sign: 'The Roaring Bitch'. (*Public domain*)

North Vietnamese SAM crew in front of a SA-2 launcher. (*Public domain*)

Quadmount used for convoy security along Route 9, Vietnam 1968. (*Public domain*)

M42 Duster, MACV compound at Quang Tri City, February 1968 (*CC BY-SA, Sciacchitano*)

42 Duster, used for security along Route 9 in 1968. (*Public domain*)

An F-105D *Thunderchief* after being hit by an SA-2 missile, February 1968. (*Public domain*)

A North Vietnamese S-75 site. (*Public domain*)

Egyptian S-125 anti-aircraft missiles in the Suez Canal vicinity. (*Public domain*)

Anti-aircraft systems that the North used against US aircraft during Operation Linebacker and Linebacker II. (*Public domain*)

An Egyptian missile site, captured by Israelis. (*Public domain*)

A destroyed Egyptian aircraft. (*Government Press Office* (*Israel*), *CC BY-SA 4.0*)

Launch of a Hawk missile. (*Public domain*)

Aerial reconnaissance image of a Middle Eastern S-125/SA-3 Goa site. (*Public domain*)

Waleed Karim with his F-86 Sabre Jet. (*Public domain*)

Indian 40mm L/60 AA Gun deployed somewhere in the Western Sector during the 1965 India-Pakistan War. Dr S. Radhakrishnan, President of India visiting a AA gun detachment. (*Press Information Bureau, India*)

The Egyptian Air Force by now had 110 Mig-21s, eighty MiG-19s, 120 MiG-17s and forty Su-7 in fifteen squadrons, two of them all weather, forty Il-28 light bombers in two squadrons and twenty Tu-16 bombers in two squadrons. In addition, Egypt had four squadrons each of transport aircraft and helicopters. The combined strength of the EAF was 15,000 personnel with almost 750 pilots. In order to avert a repeat of the losses it suffered on the ground in the previous war, Egypt built up the protective systems on the air bases. Hangarettes were built for most of the aircraft as were bomb-proof shelters. Six new air bases were constructed and five highways upgraded and made available for emergency use by the Egyptian Air Force, as were civil airports.

One of the major decisions taken by Nasser to re-organize and develop his armed forces was the creation of a separate Air Defence Command. Signed in by Presidential Decree No. 199 on 1 February 1968, it made the Egyptian Air Defence Forces a separate branch of the armed forces with all the air defence weapons and equipment coming under a unified command.[5] On 23 June 1969 Lieutenant General Mohammed Aly Fahmy was appointed as the first commander of the Air Defence Forces.[6] The Air Defence Forces had about thirty batteries of SA-2 surface-to-air missiles and over 1,000 AA guns. Besides, several squadrons of MiG-21 interceptors were placed under the Air Defence Command, a replication of the Soviet model of air defence forces.[7] These were used to defend the military bases, transportation and logistic centres. This was to have a major bearing on the conduct of future wars, not only the War of Attrition but also the Yom Kippur War years later.

Israel for its part had turned to the USA for help in building up its defence forces as France had imposed an arms embargo following the war. Although the HAWK missile system had already been acquired from the United States in 1964, the United States had earlier refused to supply either the A-6 Intruder or F-4 Phantom. A-4 Skyhawks had been approved for sale to Israel in 1966 but the delivery had been stopped because of the outbreak of war in 1967. The United States, post the Six Day War, cleared the delivery of forty-eight A-4H and TA-4 aircraft, the first of which were received by Israel in 1968 and the first squadron of A-4s was operational by mid-1968. By the end of the year, two squadrons of the newly arrived A-4 Skyhawks, three squadrons with sixty Mirage

IIIs, one of Super Mystères with twenty-five aircraft, one squadron of Mystère IV-As with thirty-five aircraft and fifteen Vautours in a light bomber squadron were operational.

The Israeli Defence Forces had moved ahead its HAWK batteries and AA guns to protect the air bases in Sinai-Bir Gafgafah, Al Arish, Etzion and Jabal Libni, as also its important military installations.

Both sides had used the period well to build up their defence forces and were ready for the next phase which was to commence in September 1968. The two sides had continued with minor skirmishes all through the period with occasional forays by the respective air forces. Both also suffered losses in the air; Egypt lost about ten aircraft, both to IAF jets and AAA. Israel's losses were two jets over Egypt and four over Jordan. The losses over Jordan were more than over Egypt as, in the words of an Israeli air base commander, 'Israeli pilots were taking more risks over Jordan. Egypt's ground defences were known to be stronger and more effective and therefore we took more care from the beginning.'[8]

The uneasy calm that had prevailed along the Suez and over Sinai was shattered by a massive artillery assault using over 1,000 guns, supported by mortars and tanks, along a sixty-five-kilometre front. Egypt claimed to have inflicted heavy losses on Israel and it was hailed as a great victory. Egypt lost twenty-six dead in the Israeli artillery fire. Egypt repeated the fire assault some weeks later. This time, Commando parties attacked Israeli defences on the other side of Suez claiming almost fifty Israeli soldiers killed.[9] This invited a severe reaction from Israel who used a deep strike over 350 kilometres inside Egypt to deliver a simple message that Israel could strike at will, even deep inside Egypt. The IDF, in a raid on Nag Hammadi (Operation SHOCK) in the heart of Egyptian territory, had sabotaged bridges and power stations. The message was received by the Egyptian High Command and yet another period of relative calm returned at the front which was to last till March 1969.

The IDF used this period to begin the construction of a fortified line, the Bar Lev line, named after Haim Bar Lev, the IDF chief of the general staff at the time, all along the Suez canal. Years later, this defensive fortification was to prove to be one of the primary reasons for the initial setbacks suffered by Israel in the Yom Kippur War.

The artillery exchange continued along the canal although the fortifications lessened the effect and there was a resultant reduction in Israeli casualties. To keep up the pressure, Egypt continued with the harassment of firing at all possible opportunities- any movement picked up, Egyptians would fire. Raids by Israel also continued.

On 3 March Nasser announced that Egypt was no longer bound by the ceasefire agreement and renewed his vow of liberating the captured territories. He formally announced the beginning of the 'War of Attrition' on 8 March 1969. The third phase of the plan was now to be executed. Starting as large-scale shelling along the Canal, accompanied by pinpoint sniping and commando assaults, fighting intensified as summer approached.[10]

The activity in the air was rather subdued in the beginning, more of probing missions. In April the Egyptians advanced two SA-2 missile batteries to the Canal, limiting the IAF's freedom of action in the skies. Egypt lost a MiG-21 on one of the missions over Sinai to a HAWK surface-to-air missile on 24 May 1969, the first time an *enemy* aircraft had been shot down by the HAWK system in the Middle East although it had been in service with Israel since 1964. However, the date of the 'kill' is given as 21 March in some accounts.

> In the War of Attrition, HAWK batteries were deployed in Sinai in order to reinforce the existing array. In March 21 1969, a first worldwide kill was signed to the HAWK system. Before noon a new HAWK battery, which was deployed at Baluza, north to the town of Kantara in the Sinai region detected, by controller assistant Yariv Geva, an Egyptian MiG-21 aircraft which took off from Port-Said airport. Geva alerted the sirens and put the battery in a state of alert. The controller, Yair Tamir, tracked the aircraft on the radar, in its flight from north to south along the Suez canal, and when the MiG-21 broke to a course heading towards the HAWK battery, a missile was launched upon it and it was shot down.[11]

With the shelling, raids and snipers becoming regular features, both armies were being sapped although Egypt, with more manpower and superior artillery, was better placed to sustain the attrition war. Israel had suffered major losses during the period May to July as it lost 194 troops killed or wounded. Such losses were not only bad for morale but were unsustainable. Israel turned once again to its air force to demonstrate its superiority and the resolve to fight the static continuing war and make it costly for Egypt. In mid-July Israel's Prime Minister Golda Meir escalated the Israeli air attacks as the IAF initiated a series of air battles against Egypt's MiGs near the Suez, in the sectors codenamed 'Texas' and 'Arizona'. About twenty MiGs were shot down in these dogfights. Israel was slowly getting control back over the skies. Egypt lost nearly a dozen aircraft over Sinai. Israel now started attacking targets in the Nile valley and along the Suez. Egypt contested these raids and suffered losses in doing so. On 2 July the EAF lost four MiGs, shot down by attacking Israeli aircraft.[12]

Despite Israeli retaliation, Egypt continued with the artillery attacks and raids. On 10 July it ambushed an Israeli armoured patrol. It was time for Israel to strike back and strike hard.

On 19/20 July 1969 Israel carried out a raid (Operation BULMUS 6) on Green Island, a small island in the Gulf of Suez in which special operations units of the Israeli Defence Forces (IDF) commandos were used to raid and destroy an Egyptian early-warning radar and ELINT station. The island was well defended by a company of infantry and had fourteen machine-gun positions, two 37mm anti-aircraft guns, and four 85mm anti-aircraft guns. The main target was the early-warning radar and an electronic intelligence (ELINT) station. Although Israeli Air Force A-4 Skyhawks struck the island before the attack commenced to soften the defences, Israel suffered heavy casualties during the raid. Almost half the commandos were killed or wounded although they completely destroyed the Egyptian radar and the ELINT station.[13]

The Egyptian air defences now had a hole in the early warning network. This gap in air defence cover was exploited by Israel to launch Operation BOXER. It was the first major IAF operation since the 1967 Six Day War, signalling a new phase in the War of Attrition.[14] It was a large-scale assault on Egyptian positions on the western bank of the canal, to be launched at the northern tip of the canal, where defences were relatively weak, and then rolling southwards. A strike by a pair of Mirages against an SA-2 battery west of Port Said at 14:00 on 20 July 1969 was the commencement of Operation BOXER 1. Once the missile unit's acquisition radar had been disabled, IAF A-4 Skyhawks struck and destroyed the remaining elements of the battery.

Following this, Israeli Skyhawks, Dassault Super Mystères, Dassault Ouragans and Vautours flew 171 sorties in the next three hours against Egyptian positions all along the sector. The Egyptian Air Force, having lost the radar at Green Island, was caught by surprise and could not challenge the IAF strikes. As the IAF strikes were tapering off by the evening, the EAF launched its own assault on Israeli positions using almost sixty aircraft. Egypt lost two MiG-17s and a MiG-21 in the ensuing air battles while it shot down two IAF Mirages (it claimed nineteen Israeli aircraft).[15] Israel, on its part, claimed five Egyptian aircraft – three in the air and two by air defences; one MiG-17 was reportedly shot down by the HAWK surface-to-air missile battery while an Su-7 fell to AA guns.[16]

The next day, 21 July, Israeli A-4 Skyhawks attacked an AA battery deployed near Qantarah as it continued heavy raids along the Suez. On the 24th, when BOXER 2 started, the day's operations began with the destruction of a radar station at Gebel Ataka by two IAF Mirages. Israel carried out 161 sorties through the day along the central section of the canal, focusing primarily on Egyptian SAM and AA sites. In the retaliatory attacks by Egypt on Israeli positions, the EAF lost two SU-7 and one MiG-21 to the IAF. In addition, an Israeli HAWK battery shot down two MiG-17s while an Su-7 was claimed by AAA.[17]

On 25 July, in an avoidable incident of friendly fire, a Mirage III was damaged by an Israeli aircraft although it luckily made it back to base.[18] Operation BOXER continued for three more days. The three days saw the Mirages battle it out with the Egyptian Mirages but further success eluded both sides. Israel carried out almost 500 sorties during the nine days, seriously degrading the Egyptian air defences and damaging the fortifications and defences along the Suez Canal. The operation was successful only to the extent that it temporarily scaled down the fighting along the canal, but the Egyptians were not deterred for long. The setbacks only made Egypt more resolute and served to escalate its operations all along the front.

In August, Egypt cut back its air activities but, to continue contesting the Israeli Air Force, pushed up additional surface-to-air missile batteries and AA guns. Egypt was now relying more on its artillery to attrite Israeli defences. Israel was continuing primarily to use its air, more as flying artillery,[19] to attack Egyptian positions and artillery emplacements. Well dug in and defended by AA, Egyptian artillery was not an easy target and Israel suffered some considerable losses as it continued attacking them. In a notable incident, on 19 August, Egyptian AA defences claimed to have shot down three IAF aircraft while Israel admitted to having lost one A-4.[20]

By September Israel had carried out 1,000 sorties over enemy territory and claimed to have lost only three aircraft while Egypt lost twenty-one aircraft over Sinai.[21] Continuing its attack on Egyptian air defences, Israel mounted a raid on the Egyptian military base at Ras Abu-Daraj on 9 September. Israel destroyed twelve Egyptian outposts, operated for almost twelve hours deep inside Egypt, and also destroyed the radar station which was the primary target of the raid. It had sunk two torpedo boats at Ras-a Sadat the previous day. It was an audacious raid, thirty miles inside its territory. The raid had demonstrated the reach of Israel and exposed the chinks in the Egyptian defences.

It was not only the ground raids that were causing losses. On 11 September Egypt lost eleven aircraft – seven MiG-21s, three SU-7s and one MiG-17 – to Israeli aircraft and AAA. Only one aircraft was lost by Israel.

The arrival of first shipment F-4E Phantoms in September 1969 gave a qualitative edge to the Israeli Air Force as the twin-engine aircraft equipped with advanced electronic counter-measures (ECM) equipment had the capability to operate with relative impunity and strike deep inside Egypt. As General Hertzog of the Israeli Air Force was to claim, 'The front line with Egypt is not necessarily the Suez canal but the whole of Egypt'.

Soon after the first squadron of F-4s became operational, the IAF launched a 'limited air offensive' in October 1969 against the Egyptian air defence system. Egypt struck back with a massive strike by its fighter-bombers, accompanied by MiG-21s, against targets in Sinai and claimed to have destroyed eight IAF aircraft for the loss of only one aircraft. Israel suffered the first loss of its F-4Es on 18 November 1969 even as it had downed a MiG-21 just a week back to claim its first air-to-air victory.[22]

By November, Israel had carried *out about 500 sorties against the SAMs alone* and claimed to have *crippled Egyptian SAM defence.*[23]

One of the reasons for the IAF's success in crippling the Egyptian air defences was the use of equipment captured during the Six Day War to learn their vulnerabilities and develop counter-measures. This knowledge, coupled with the US experiences in Vietnam, gave the IAF the edge over Egyptian air defences. While this was effective against most of the air defence systems, Israel was finding it difficult to deal with the newer radar systems. The Soviet P-12 radar was one of the newer radars, and immune to counter-measures, as yet. As they served as the primary early-warning radar of the Egyptian air defences providing early detection of incoming aircraft, they were one of the prime targets of IAF.

One of the P-12 radars was damaged during a raid in September 1969 but it came back on-air in a different configuration. The IAF launched reconnaissance missions to locate the radar which was subsequently located at Ras-Arab.

The immediate IAF response was to destroy the new radar station with an aerial strike, but the attack was aborted just minutes before it was to be launched. The new plan called for it to be captured intact. According to another account, the IAF had carried out the strike mission and destroyed a radar at Ras-Arab, but it turned out to be a dummy radar during the post-strike damage assessment. The assessment also showed the actual radar located nearby, unprotected and without any AA defending it. It was then that the plan to capture the radar was prepared. Notwithstanding the actual narrative about locating the radar, Operation ROOSTER 53 was prepared and executed.

The plan of the operation was prepared on 24 December. The intention was to capture the radar and carry it back, using the newly received Sikorsky CH-53 helicopters as they were the only helicopters capable of carrying the entire radar station, estimated at seven tonnes.

The operation was finally launched at 2100 on 26 December 1969. A-4 Skyhawks and F-4 Phantoms attacked the Egyptian positions along the western bank of the Suez Canal and Red Sea to cover the noise of approaching helicopters. The paratroopers, carried by three Super Frelons, were able to surprise the Egyptian contingent at the radar station and quickly took control of the site. The radar was dismantled and two CH-53s were called in to ferry it back. With great difficulty, the helicopters managed to take it back to Israeli-held territory. The radar was handed over to Israeli Intelligence. Its study helped provide Israel with new counter-measures against the Egyptian air defences, removing a threat to Israeli air superiority over the Suez Canal. The radar was later handed over to the USA, as was other equipment captured previously.[24]

With relentless operations against Egyptian air defences, Israel had achieved aerial supremacy over the Suez Canal by the end of 1969 and had completely degraded the Egyptian air defences. The next step was to make the continuation of war so costly for Egypt that it would be forced to accept cessation of hostilities.[25] Moshe Dayan, in a press conference, claimed that 'a significant percentage of Israeli air strikes between September and December attacked the Egyptian Integrated Air Defence Network and caused serious damage to it'. Israel went on to claim that Egypt alone had lost sixty aircraft to Israeli fighters, AAA and HAWK missiles during the period, while Israeli losses were fifteen, two in dogfights and thirteen to AA defences.[26]

By January 1970 Israel had one operational squadron (No. 201) of F-4Es while a second squadron (No. 69) was being formed.

With this end, Israel decided to take the war deeper inside Egyptian territory and launched Operation PRIHA (BLOSSOM) in January 1970. The operations started on 7 January with a strike by two F-4 Phantoms on the SA-2 operators' school near Halwan and another pair attacking Egyptian army command posts near Cairo. The targets during the later IAF strikes included radar stations at Baltim, Jebel Obeid, Abu Suweir, Domyat, Ras Obeid and Wadi Zur and SAM sites in the Delta at Dahshur, El Mansourah, Qassasin and Manzala.[27]

Reacting to these strikes, Egypt bombed targets in the Sinai on 10 January and claimed to have destroyed a HAWK missile site. An Israeli A-4 Skyhawk was shot down a week later – admittedly the sixteenth loss for the IAF during the war. While the strikes continued by both air forces, a new factor seemed to change the equation between the two opposing sides. It was the F-4 Phantom.

The F-4Es with Israel had changed the air defence equation and threatened to render the Egyptian air defences totally ineffective. The reason was simple enough – it lay in the ability of the Phantoms to exploit the weaknesses of the Integrated Air Defence System as it existed in January 1970. The strikes usually involved two or three pairs of F-4Es, one of which flew a decoy mission to distract Egyptian Air Defence Command (ADC) from the actual target. Exploiting the inability of Egypt's Soviet-supplied radars to locate and track targets flying below 1,000 feet, the Israelis operated along routes on which they were unlikely to be detected until about forty to forty-five kilometres from their objective. From that moment on, they could expect that the Egyptians would need between three and four minutes to scramble MiG-21 interceptors from nearby air bases, and then another two to four minutes to catch the Phantoms. In practice, while operating at low altitudes, the F-4E could fly faster than any of the MiG-21 variants then in service with Egypt. This meant that the Israelis could withdraw east of the Suez Canal before the Egyptians were able to intercept them.[28]

The well laid out air defence network appeared to be redundant against the new threat posed by the Phantoms. This was a major factor which made Nasser turn to Moscow, once again, for help. Looking at the grim situation as the Soviet air defence systems were not able to counter the Israeli air threat, the Soviet Union decided to up the ante.

The Soviet chief of air defence forces had visited Egypt in December 1969 and had a first-hand look at the Egyptian air defence network. The same month, based on his feedback, the General Staff of the Soviet armed forces and the General Staff of the air defence forces developed and presented to the leadership the plan for Operation KAVKAZ which called for deployment of a Soviet air defence corps in Egypt. The corps was to have an aviation group, a special AA division and an electronic warfare group. After the request from Nasser, Moscow gave the go-ahead for Operation KAVKAZ. The Soviet troops had started arriving in Egypt by February 1970. The AA element was to be the 18th Special Air Defence Missile Division. The military aid package included 100 MiG-21MFs, improved S-75 and S-75M variants of the SA-2 but, more importantly, Moscow agreed to provide SA-3 SAMs and ZSU-23-4 Shilka self-propelled anti-aircraft guns.[29]

The 18th Special Purpose Air Defence Missile Division comprised three brigades equipped with SA-3s, each with six air defence battalions and one technical battalion. To provide close defence to the SAM sites, a platoon of three ZSU-23-4s and six two-man teams armed with 9K32 (SA-7 Grail) man-portable air defence systems were available in each SAM site. The EW group included a radio electronic intelligence (ELINT) station, a short-wave ECM company and a signals ECM (VHF) company.

Soviet flying units detached to Egypt included the 135th Fighter Aviation Regiment with forty MiG-21Ms and the 35th Independent Reconnaissance Aviation Regiment with thirty MiG-21Ms and MiG-21Rs. These were based at Beni Suef and Kom Awshim air bases (135th IAP) for the air defence of Cairo, and Jiyanklis air base (35th ORAP) for the protection of Alexandria and Mersa Matruh. The third Soviet flying unit, the 90th Independent Reconnaissance Aviation Squadron, was equipped with An-12PP ELINT/SIGINT reconnaissance aircraft, Tu-16R reconnaissance bombers, and Beriev Be-12 anti-submarine amphibians and was based at Cairo West.[30] This squadron was to support Soviet Navy units active in the Mediterranean.

The first Soviet-manned SA-3 sites became operational in mid-February 1970. Each site was protected by a platoon of Shilkas, deployed at a distance of 200 to 300 meters from the radar positions while the AA gunners manning the Strela-2s were positioned two to three kilometres from the centre of the SAM site.[31]

Israel, while it continued its attacks, initially stayed away from areas protected by the new missile systems although the A-4 Skyhawks did carry out raids to try and disrupt the construction at the SAM sites. During these strikes, IAF F-4 Phantoms bombed a scrap metal processing plant at Abu Zambal on 12 February killing sixty-eight civilians and injuring another ninety-eight. The deep strikes came with their own risks of increased collateral damage. While the Israeli government stressed that this was a mistake, such accidents began to be repeated. Just about a month later, forty-six schoolchildren were killed in a raid by two F-4Es at Bahr al-Baqr. The strikes, however, continued.

To extend the missile cover, Egyptian Air Defence Command began constructing new SAM sites around fifty kilometres (thirty-one miles) west of the Suez Canal. As soon as these were ready in April 1970, it moved two SA-2 battalions closer to the waterway during the night of 24/25 April. A counter-attack by Israel the following morning to destroy these sites before they became fully operational failed: the Air Defence Command continued its 'creeping' advance towards the Canal in which additional Egyptian SAM battalions followed by Soviet units were moved closer to Suez. As a reaction to the IAF raid over its SAM sites, Egypt attacked the Israeli MIM-23 HAWK SAM sites although the damage caused could not be ascertained. It was in the course of these redeployments that the Soviets scored their first 'kill' of Operation KAVKAZ.

On 15 May 1970 one of their SA-3 sites shot down a UARAF Il-28U aircraft on a training mission, killing two crew members. The first kill was in fact a case of fratricide. An account in a Soviet Army Veteran's site, however, mentions the date of the incident as 14 March 1970. According to the account, the radar operator confirmed from the nearby base commander before firing at the Egyptian aircraft.

One of the first anti-aircraft missile battalions to arrive in Egypt was deployed near Cairo in temporary positions and stood on alert on the night of 13–14 March when it detected an aircraft. After confirming from the Egyptian duty officers on the airbase who confirmed that no Egyptian aircraft were in air, the SAM commander launched two missiles.

Both the missiles struck the target at an altitude of 200 meters. It was 06:19 a.m. on 14 March 1970. The Soviet SAM had its first kill.

The commander of the division received a report from the command post: 'The target was destroyed, the expense is two.'

Only the aircraft shot down was an Egyptian Il-28BM – a reconnaissance aircraft returning to its base after completing a mission over the Mediterranean. The direct hit of two missiles at low altitude did not leave the crew any chances; the pilots Major Salah Rashid and Lieutenant Dorri Riad Sakr were killed. The plane fell right at the beginning of the runway.[32]

Such lapses continued as a Strela-2M missile operator fired at an Egyptian civilian An-24 aircraft on 18 March.

On 18 March the gunner of the anti-aircraft PZRK Strela-2 from the platoon of the close defence of the S-125 battalion stationed in Alexandria launched a missile on an Egyptian civilian An-24 aircraft flying over the position of the division from the sea at an altitude of about 1,000 metres. The missile hit the right engine, which caught fire. Despite one non-working engine, the crew continued to fly and landed safely.

The reason for this incident was an order issued by the Air Defence Brigade which said: 'planes flying below 6 km and closer than 25 km, to be counted as enemy planes and destroyed.' That the anti-aircraft gunner did.

The divisional orders laying down all 'planes flying below 6 km and closer than 25 km' as enemy aircraft was the reason that the second incident occurred. Similarly, an Su-7B aircraft entered a no-fly zone and was fired upon by a Strela-2M missile unit. The Air Defence Command followed up with rigorous training to avoid recurrence of such incidents.

The initial days were filled with disappointment and missed opportunities for the newly arrived Soviet AD troops as IAF aircraft could not be engaged by them. Lack of early warning, limiting the reaction time available to the AA gunners, was the prime reason for the same. The Soviets were still fine- tuning to deploy their weapon systems, especially the radars, in the best possible manner. The terrain at most of the times prevented a clear line of sight, and giving safe corridors to attacking IAF aircraft was the main hurdle. It was not only the missile systems that had failed to engage the intruding aircraft. Even the AA guns, which should have been able to fire with minimal warning, failed to engage the IAF aircraft.[33]

As the Soviet AD troops started deploying in the hinterland, the Egyptian Air Defence Command began moving thirteen of its SA-2s into what became known as 'the SAM box', about fifty to fifty-five kilometres west of the Great Bitter Lake. These were supported by three Soviet SA-3s units. Early on the IAF carried out what appeared to be only reconnaissance sorties over these sites and, on 6 June 1970, two MiG-21s ambushed a pair of Phantoms which had been detected while approaching low over the Mediterranean and claimed to have shot one down. The new air defence network was making its impact.

With all its units ready, the Air Defence Command launched Operation HOPE, expanding the box and increasing the number of SAM sites within it. This increased the radar surveillance cover also, providing better warning to the AD elements. On 1 July the AD radars picked up two pairs of Israeli fighter-bombers while approaching the canal at about 12,000 metres. The SA-3 missile unit fired a ripple of two volleys of three SA-2s each but could not do any damage. Fired at by the new missile system, the IAF responded strongly. Shortly before sunset, twenty-four fighter-bombers attacked the three easternmost Egyptian surface-to-air missile sites. The Air Defence Command claimed to have shot down five A-4 Skyhawks, including two by the shoulder-fired SA-7s, while losing two SAM sites knocked out and one damaged. The IAF launched a second wave, on the northern and southern flanks of the Egyptian position about half an hour later, but these were dummy sites and the IAF aircraft flew straight into a carefully-prepared ambush. One F-4E was shot down by a Soviet SA-3 at a range of eleven and a half kilometres, the crew managing to eject. The neighbouring SA-3 site hit another F-4 Phantom at a range of eighteen kilometres, but a second missile self-detonated nearly four kilometres short of another target, which managed to escape. The third Israeli wave had its leading Phantom damaged by two Soviet SA-3s and then shot down by a third missile. Three pairs of Skyhawks delivered the final Israeli attack. While they failed to inflict any damage, the Soviets claimed one A-4 shot down.[34]

The crew of eleven Egyptian SA-2 and three Soviet SA-3 sites re-deployed their equipment during the night, so that by the morning all the missiles were in completely different positions to those of the previous day. The Israelis re-appeared at around 1630 hours on 2 July, when a group of twelve Skyhawks and Phantoms attacked an exposed Egyptian SA-2 site. It responded with three missiles but they all missed. The SA-2 missile site was knocked out by the IAF.

The remaining ten SA-2 sites were again moved to new positions, this time to cover the approach from the north, the direction taken by most of the Israeli attacks. The IAF strikes by A-4 Skyhawks on 3 July not only proved ineffective but the Egyptians claimed to have shot down two A-4s and damaged two more. The follow-up strike by F-4E Phantoms also could not do any damage; the SA-2 missile unit claimed to have shot down one Phantom.

The IAF strikes on 4 July could not inflict any damage as most of the attacks were on dummy sites. One F-4 Phantom was reportedly damaged by SA-7s.

On 5 July twenty-four Israeli aircraft attacked the remaining ten Egyptian and three Soviet sites at around 1500 hours. The first formation of fourteen Phantoms approached the SA-3 site but failed to damage any position. One F-4 was claimed to have been hit by the SA-2 as the aircraft was pulling up after its bombing run. A further group of ten Phantoms attacked two Egyptian SA-2 sites an hour later, but could do no damage in the face of heavy AA fire.

Faced by relentless SAM fire, the IAF ended the suppression of enemy air defence (SEAD) missions against the SAM Box on 5 July. The IAF had lost ten aircraft during the period between 30 June and 5 July, with two more damaged, according to Egyptian and Soviet claims, and had been able to damage three SA-2 sites.[35] Those SA-2 units were reportedly repaired and put back in to service.

The IAF, however, admitted to the loss of three aircraft only although it did ask for electronic counter-measures pods for its F-4Es from the United States after this experience.

A break in IAF strikes gave an opportunity to the Egyptian Air Defence Command to once again re-deploy its SA-2 and SA-3 batteries, and prepare more dummy sites. The dummy sites were specially prepared at the older missile sites, the ones whose approximate location was known to the IAF. The close defence resources were also beefed up – no fewer than thirty-four shoulder-fired SA-7 detachments were deployed at each of the new missile sites for their protection. These new sites were primarily on the southern and northern flanks of the SAM Box.

The IAF had meanwhile received the new jamming pods and put these to use on 18 July, the day they resumed their SEAD missions.

The SAM sites picked up a target at about 1000 and opened fire as per their standard operating procedure. The target, however, was an Egyptian Su-7B which was damaged by a SAM-7 missile.

At 1330 the Israelis attacked. At least fourteen F-4Es were picked up by the Soviet radars as they assembled over Sinai and moved towards the Suez, splitting up into four groups of four F-4Es each. Two flights of Mirages gave them cover, one above the Phantoms and one below them, flying on a north-south axis. The strike element included a flight of Skyhawks equipped with ECM pods. The first Phantom four-ship strike group Israeli crossed the canal north of the SAM box before turning left, trying to strike the SAM sites it in co-ordination with the second group, which had come in directly from the east.

The ECM equipment carried by the F-4Es was able to jam the Egyptian SA-2s which then switched over to the alternate operational frequency. The F-4E strikes, however, failed to make any impact as all they could target were dummy sites.

As the Phantoms were attacking the SA-2 sites, the first of SA-3 fired, detonating just fifty metres from the leading aircraft, damaging it and causing it to crash minutes later. The second F-4E group which had come in from the east was also engaged by the SA-3s and one F-4E was badly damaged although the aircraft managed to make an emergency landing at Refidim. One of the F-4Es of the third group, coming in from the north, suffered a direct hit by the SA-3. The fourth F-4E group was lucky as it destroyed an Egyptian SA-2 site and then badly damaged the command post of an SA-3 site.

Israel claimed to have destroyed four SAM sites and damaged three others for the loss of one F-4E and another damaged. Egyptian and Soviet troops claimed to have shot down two F-4Es and damaged one. Admittedly, one Egyptian and one Soviet SAM site were temporarily knocked out. The claims and counter-claims do not agree on the losses, as they rarely do, but what was obvious was that, in spite of the improved electronic warfare equipment and refined tactics, the IAF had failed to make any headway against the Egyptian SAM defences. This was the first time since June 1967 that Israel had lost the air superiority it had enjoyed for so long.[36]

The opportunity to regain control of the skies was presented soon enough by the Soviet MiG-21 pilots eager to engage the Israelis. On 25 July no fewer than ten Soviet-flown MiG-21s scrambled from Beni Suef to intercept the IAF aircraft attacking the Egyptian positions along the Canal. The MiGs caught the IAF by surprise and were able to engage one A-4 Skyhawk with an R-3S (A-2 Atoll) air-to-air missile (AAM).

On 27 July the MiGs were scrambled to intercept an incoming Israeli mission but failed as they arrived late, by which time two Egyptian aircraft had already been destroyed by the IAF. The next encounter, on 30 July, was an unmitigated disaster for the Soviets as they lost five MiG-21s to the Israelis, and failed to cause any damage. This gave the Israelis a false sense of having wrested the control of air back from the Egyptian-Soviet air defence as they soon found out to their peril on 3 August when an Egyptian SA-2 site near Ismailia shot down a Mirage III. As Israel attempted to hit back, with sixteen F-4Es attacking the SAM sites, it lost one F-4E Phantom to the SA-3. The crew, who managed to eject, were captured by the Egyptian army. Another F-4E was shot down by a neighbouring SAM site. Any doubts about the SAM defences that Israel may have had were put to rest.

After this incident, the Air Defence Command was emboldened to move the entire SAM box to within ten kilometres of the Canal, extending the missile cover way beyond the Suez. This move was heavily contested by the Israeli Air Force but they failed to prevent the move forward of the SAMs.

The Israeli air operations had failed to achieve the intended aim. Moreover, the expanding Soviet presence in Egypt and the increased likelihood of a confrontation with Soviet forces prompted the Israeli government to call off further air strikes. The public pressure that Israel was hoping to build against the war in fact made the Egyptians rally behind their government. It had another unintended effect. Nasser turned to the Soviet Union for more military aid and drew the Soviet Union further into the conflict. The air strikes had only increased tensions and led to further escalation in the War of Attrition.

Alarmed by increasing Soviet involvement, Washington pressured Israel into accepting a temporary ceasefire. The emerging situation eventually enabled Egypt to increase the number of SAM sites along the Suez Canal to thirty and then to fifty. The Air Defence Command was in complete control of the skies. This was demonstrated by the Egyptians when an SA-2 shot down an IAF Boeing KC-97G used for electronic reconnaissance, about twenty-seven kilometres east of Ismailia in September 1970, after the War of attrition had come to an end.

The war had ended with both Israel and the Arabs agreeing to the 'Rogers Plan' as proposed by United States. The details were finalized after months of negotiations; the Egyptians had announced their acceptance on 23 July while Israel agreed to do so on 30 July. The ceasefire came into effect on 8 August.

Both sides suffered heavy losses although there are no common grounds to agree on the actual number of casualties. Israel claims to have shot down over 100 Arab and Soviet aircraft in the air for the loss of only four.[37] It also claims to have downed at least twenty-five aircraft with its HAWK missiles and AAA. Israel admitted to losing twenty-two aircraft to air defences. The Egyptian Air Defence Command on the other hand claims to have shot down twenty-one Israeli aircraft in July 1970 alone. During the entire duration of the war, Arabs and various guerrilla groups claimed to have downed 300 Israeli aircraft.[38] Considering the total strength of the IAF, this seems to be an exaggeration. According to US sources, Egypt lost 109 aircraft in the air between June 1967 and July 1970 while it shot down two Mirage IIIs in air combat and its air defences shot down fifteen aircraft – seven by SAMs and eight by AAA.[39]

While the numbers are important to understand the attrition, and success achieved, the real impact of this war was beyond mere casualty count. The War of Attrition was different from all other Middle Eastern conflicts. There was hardly any involvement of the standing armies, except for the ambushes and raids carried out by them. The real war was fought in the air – between the Israeli Air Force and Egyptian Air Defences and, for the first time, ground-based air defence systems prevailed over a modern air force.

Perfecting the lessons learnt during the war, the Soviet Union fielded a much more advanced and effective air defence system during the Yom Kippur War in which the redoubtable SA-6 had been added to the SA-2s and SA-3s. While it is common to discuss the air defence battles fought in the October 1973 war, it was during the War of Attrition that the air defence weapons and tactics were refined. The War of Attrition needs to be studied for this single reason, more than anything else.

Chapter 6

The Bangladesh War 1971

War returned to South Asia just six years after the September War of 1965 but, unlike the two bloody wars in the past, the trigger this time around was not Kashmir but the long drawn oppression and the resultant simmering discontent in the (then) East Pakistan which had come to the boil with the launching of Operation SEARCHLIGHT by the Pakistani Army in March 1971, leading to an armed struggle by Bengali nationalists for self-determination and independence which was supported by India, first covertly and then overtly. While the claims and counter-claims of who initiated the war remain conflicting, the pre-emptive strike by the Pakistan Air Force on Indian air bases on 3 December 1971 is commonly considered to be the formal initiation of the war. This is not to disclaim the various local operations carried out by the Indian Army and *Mukti Bahini* (the Bangladesh guerilla freedom fighters) from June 1971 onwards in the east. While the two opposing armies slugged it out in a series of skirmishes in the east, the air forces had kept away, except for the Boyra incident on 22 November 1971 when four intruding Pakistan Air Force (PAF) F-86s were intercepted by Gnats of No. 22 Squadron IAF, shooting down three of the F-86s. The other air violations by the PAF, including in the west, had not resulted in any interceptions by the Indian Air Force.

Matters came to head when the Pakistan Air Force launched Operation CHENGIZ KHAN on 3 December, hoping to emulate its success achieved in 1965 when it had attacked the Indian air bases on 6 September 1965 and destroyed over thirteen Indian aircraft.[1] The results were, however, quite different this time round. The only damage Pakistan could inflict was one light air observation post (AOP) aircraft at Faridkot and minor damage to the communication equipment of Amritsar Signal Unit for the loss of one F-104 Starfighter.[2] Even as it had caught the Indian Air Force offguard, Pakistan failed to achieve its aim. The only achievement was that it managed to obtain surprise and carry out the raids without being detected and intercepted. With a better radar network and co-ordinated defences, it should not have been so, with the Indian Air Force having invested in bolstering up its radar network, but such are the vagaries of war. All the radars deployed in the west failed to give any warning of the Pakistani air raid.

The Pakistan Air Force had a better radar cover in 1965 but this time round it was not so. Pakistan had two US-built high-powered FPS-20 radars which were linked with the sector operations centres in north and south. Since 1965, it had introduced three medium-powered and five low-looking radars. Altogether these radars provided barely 25 per cent of the high-level cover required over sensitive areas, and a mere 7 per cent of the desired surveillance at low level. The network left some dangerous gaps in the Kashmir region and in the area south of Multan between Sukkur and Hyderabad.[3]

Sakesar with the high-powered FPS-20 radar was the PAF's Sector Operations Centre (North). The other major radar locations were Chuhr Kana, Muridke and Tatepur near Multan which provided medium-level cover with the Condor radars. Low-level cover was provided by four AR-1 radars located at Rafiqui, Cherat, Kallar Kahar and Kirana. Sector Operations Centre (South) was located at Badin with an FPS-20 providing high-level radar surveillance. Keeping in mind the importance of Karachi, the Pakistan Air Force had moved a P-35 radar from the east (ex-Dacca) to Malir. Jacobabad was also to have a P-35 radar which was moved from Malir midway in the war but it was to become operational only when the war ended. The other radars were a vintage Type-21 near Khanpur, a civil aviation ASR-4 radar at Karachi Airport and an AR-1 radar at Pir Patho. A mix of vintage and new radars was what Pakistan had.[4]

Unlike in 1965 when the Indian Air Force had only one high-power P-30(M) radar, at Amritsar, it had built up a rudimentary but functional air defence network by integrating the radar units and visual observation posts and flights. In addition, the IAF re-deployed its radars to have a better low-level cover. A P-30 radar was moved from Adampur to Amritsar to cater for the contingency of the signal unit at Amritsar being damaged. Similarly, a P-30 radar was moved from Jodhpur to Uttarlai while a radar was moved from the east to Ahmedabad to cover the gap between Jamnagar and Jodhpur. A more important change that the IAF did was to initiate the Base Air Defence Centre (BADC) concept wherein the nominated air bases were given autonomous control over the deployed aircraft and AD weapons.[5] This was to mitigate the inadequacy of low-level cover and dedicated communications available to the IAF. The concept proved to be of much advantage during the war although it had its limitations which were exposed by the first strike by the PAF on 3 December. Still, it proved to be a far better radar and early warning network than what Pakistan could muster with its resources.

As with the radar network upgraded after the 1965 war, India built up an effective military machine, efficiently trained. The Indian Air Force possessed over 1,200 aircraft, some of them belonging to the very advanced category and the remainder of substantial capabilities. The inventory comprised 232 MiG-21s, 128 Su-7s, 165 Gnat fighters and fifty-four indigenously produced HF-24 Maruts. These were backed by some 300 relatively old but still operational aircraft, including 199 Hawker Hunters, sixty-one Mystères and eighty-five Canberra light bombers. Even the obsolete Vampires, 224 in all, and the fifty-odd Ouragon fighters could be used in areas uncontested by the Pakistan Air Force, to add to the IAF's overwhelming numerical superiority.

Pakistan had combat aircraft which, performance-wise, could match the IAF to a reasonable degree but, when it came to numbers, the Pakistan Air Force was at a tremendous disadvantage. Compared with 1965, the PAF also lacked, due to unavoidable circumstances, the desired balance between offensive and defensive aircraft. The US embargo had degraded the spares support for the F-86, F-104 and B-57 force and the inescapable dependence on the Chinese F-6, a short-range air defence fighter, had meant that only a single squadron of Mirage IIIs constituted the main offensive element of the PAF.[6]

Following the embargo placed by the US after the 1965 war, Pakistan had to look for arms from other countries. China became a major arms supplier and, by 1971, a large share of the arms and armament with the Pakistani armed forces were of Chinese origin; amongst them were the 37mm and 14.5mm quad AA guns with the Pakistan air defence artillery. The guns were to prove invaluable during the war. Details available indicate that the Pakistan Army AAA had the following resources:

- Three anti-aircraft brigades, responsible for defence of Pakistan Air Force installations and the Naval Dockyard at Karachi.
- Anti-aircraft units organic to field formations.
- Anti-aircraft *Mujahid* companies under command logistic areas.[7]

The highest priority was accorded to the air installations, followed by Naval dockyards and some important bridges. Due to inadequate resources, a large number of assets like the oil installations and railways remained largely unprotected. Anti-aircraft *Mujahid* sub-units were provided to some strategic assets but, as their equipment was defective and the personnel were all ex-servicemen, the degree of air defence provided by them was always suspect.[8]

The situation was different in the east. Both India and Pakistan had, for different reasons, not given the required emphasis to its air defence network in the east. While the Indian Air Force had moved a radar from the east to Ahmedabad, Pakistan had moved a radar from Dhaka to Malir even as it (Pakistan) claimed that it was strengthening its defences and moving more troops to the east. Its strategy, however, remained that 'Defence of the East lies in the West'. With just one squadron of PAF (No. 14 Squadron) in the east, the Indian Air Force could afford to move its assets to the west but, faced with a far superior opponent, the Pakistan Air Force could have retained the radar at Dhaka. Maybe it was admission of an impending defeat that made Pakistan shift its radar out of (then) East Pakistan.

The imbalance in terms of squadrons and air defence regiments was equally stark. The Indian Air Force had ten squadrons in the east, not including a Gnat squadron which had moved to the west on 5 December. Opposing it was a lone F-86 squadron based at Tezgaon. As against a lone air defence regiment of Pakistan, India had deployed nine air defence regiments to provide close air defence to air force bases and installations, and field formations of which four were equipped with 40mm L/70 LAA guns and five regiments continued with Second World War vintage 40mm L/60 LAA guns.[9]

In the west, the balance was not so skewed although the Indian Air Force still outnumbered the Pakistan Air Force two-to-one. The Indian Air Force had twenty-four fighter/fighter-bomber squadrons deployed in the west as against the fourteen of Pakistan. For low-level air defence, India had twenty-six AD regiments. It had also deployed the surface-to-air missile squadrons to cover the Admapur, Halwara, Ambala-Chandigarh and Delhi areas.[10]

Eastern Sector

India had nine air defence regiments in the east, grouped under two independent brigade headquarters. Of these, only four regiments were equipped with radar-controlled 40mm L/70 guns while the remaining five regiments were still equipped with the older L/60 guns. The deployment of the AD regiments had been done by April 1971 and, as the situation progressed, some AD units and sub-units were placed under field formations although the deployment was overwhelmingly on Air Force assets, primarily because of the anticipated pre-emptive air strike by the Pakistan Air Force, as was the case in 1965.

The Indian Air Force was equally prepared to defend its bases and installations. It had five air defence squadrons – two of MiG 21s and three of Gnats. The entire Eastern Command theatre was divided into two air defence sectors. The area west of Siliguri corridor, comprising West Bengal and Bihar, was the responsibility of Advance HQ Eastern Air Command (EAC) while the area east of Siliguri was looked after by No. 3 Air Defence Direction Centre (ADDC). The IAF, learning from the experience of the 1965 war, had built up a well co-ordinated radar network and had three surface-to-air missile squadrons deployed to cover their more important bases.[11] The Pakistan Air Force was going to find the going tough this time around.

Pakistan had a functional air defence network in name only, relying on a single AR-1 radar located at Mirpur, about ten miles north-west of Dacca. As the prevailing situation was not favourable for the deployment of mobile observation units or posts (MOU), the radar with its line of sight range of about forty kilometres, which gave a reaction time of barely three minutes once intruders were detected, was the only asset providing some semblance of early warning. Pakistan had had another radar at Dacca, a P-35, but it had been withdrawn in October 1971 and re-deployed at Malir in West Pakistan.[12] Tezgaon had been left to fend for itself with just about enough resources to put up a decent fight.

The first air engagement of the war occurred on 22 November when four F-86 Sabres of the Pakistan Air Force intruded into Indian territory at Boyra and were engaged by Gnats of No. 22 Squadron, IAF.[13] The regimental records show that a troop of 48th AD Regiment was deployed in the area which engaged the Sabres although the official history of the war does not record this. Although the ack-ack guns only proved to be of little deterrence and not much else, a junior commissioned officer of the regiment was awarded a Mention in Despatches for his action during the incident. The presence of anti-aircraft artillery in the area is also borne out by an account of the battle by a Pakistan Air Force pilot who is reported to have strafed the ack-ack guns. 'At that time, the leader, Wing Commander Choudhry, was attacking a AAA battery that was noticed to be firing at them.'[14]

The three F-86s were shot down by the Gnats.

The Pakistan Air Force did not undertake any action against the Indian Air Force or the ground troops thereafter until the outbreak of full hostilities. Due to the presence of just one squadron of Sabres, down to sixteen F-86s, Pakistan did not carry out a pre-emptive strike in the east on 3 December, unlike in the west where the Pakistan Air Force struck Indian air bases and radar installations at dusk.

When the news of Pakistani raids along the Western Sector came in, Eastern Air Command did not have any aircraft to retaliate immediately, during the night of 3/4 December. Instead, it asked for resources from Central Air Command (CAC) which detailed eight Canberras of No. 16 Squadron based at Gorakhpur for the mission. Four Canberras took off for Tezgaoan and Kurmiltola, each armed with 1,000lb bombs. The aircraft faced no opposition except for the anti-aircraft guns and even though they spent about an hour over the targets, they failed to cause any damage.[15] Luckily for them, the Canberras did not suffer any loss or damage from the ground fire.

The Pakistan anti-aircraft unit at Tezgaon was 6th Light Air Defence Regiment, which had acquitted itself well during the September War, also in the same sector. It was earlier equipped with Bofors 40mm L/60 guns but the accounts available indicate it now had 37mm AA guns and 20mm quad light AA guns. Based on Indian Air Force accounts, the regiment was deployed not only at Tezgaoan but also at Kurmitola, Chittagaon and

Jessore. As Pakistan had raised some ad hoc anti-aircraft batteries, for its assets had not provided regular AAA resources, it is likely that some of the anti-aircraft units deployed outside Dacca may well have been such irregular batteries. They performed reasonably well and scored quite a few hits on Indian aircraft during the course of the war.

Coming back to the air operations, in the early morning of 4 December, Pakistan launched two combat air patrols (CAPs), anticipating Indian air raids at dawn itself, but it seemed that the Indian Air Force had other plans as the CAPs did not find any Indian aircraft and came back without any incident. Just as the second CAP landed back at Tezgaon, the radar at Mirpur picked up Indian aircraft coming in towards Tezgaon.[16] This was the first offensive mission by the Indian Air Force in the east.

Hawker Hunters of Nos 17 and 37 Squadrons had taken off at 0630 and were escorted by MiG-21s. As they vectored towards their target, they were picked up by the Pakistani radar and a CAP was launched to intercept them but it failed to deter the intruding aircraft. The raid at Tezgaon, however, did not do much damage either to the aircraft parked on the ground or to the runway.

The Indian Air Force launched 112 counter-air missions on the Pakistani air bases of Tezgaon and Kurmitola during the day in which the Pakistan Air Force lost three F-86 Sabres in aerial battles over Dhaka and three civilian aircraft were destroyed on the ground, but the Indian Air Force was not able to deliver a decisive blow to the Pakistan Air Force and, at the end of the day, Pakistan still had the majority of its aircraft safe, and ready for another round.[17]

Even this limited success had come at a heavy cost as the Indian Air Force lost seven aircraft of its own, all but two to anti-aircraft fire. The losses included two Hunter aircraft of No. 7 Squadron shot down by anti-aircraft fire at Lal Munir Hat. The Pakistani anti-aircraft artillery had been very active throughout and took a heavy toll of the intruding Indian aircraft. Not only did the anti-aircraft shoot down three aircraft over Tezgaon, they hit and damaged at least four more aircraft – two Sukhoi Su-7s and two MiG-21s. Luckily, these aircraft managed to get back, otherwise Indian losses would have been higher. Another disappointment was that some of the F-86s claimed by the IAF to have been destroyed on the ground at Tezgaon turned out to be dummies.[18] A further disappointment for the Indian Air Force was its failed attempt to try and locate an AR-1 radar suspected to be located near Kurmitola. The only consolation was that it did not suffer any loss during this mission

During these raids by the IAF, the real attrition was caused by Pakistan anti-aircraft fire. No raid by the IAF went uncontested as the anti-aircraft put up a heavy barrage, unexpectedly so. As one IAF pilot said,

> All those losses that we suffered were not from any enemy aircraft, but just ground fire. We never expected such heavy ground fire.... It was like a barrage of ammunition dotting the sky and everyone who flew through that would have been lucky to get through.... We decided we will not hit Dacca at low level, because we were going against heavy flak.[19]

It was not that the Pakistan anti-aircraft artillery did not have their own losses. The second Indian wave, comprising Sukhois, over Tezgaon had been greeted by the anti-aircraft guns, damaging two of them. The Sukhois had, however, managed to reach their base. It was in the third wave, of two Hunters from No. 37 Squadron, that the Pakistan anti-aircraft artillery got its first kill. The second Hunter, piloted by Flying Officer V.K. Arora, was also hit by anti-aircraft fire but luckily his aircraft was not seriously damaged. In fact, Arora decided to hit back at the anti-aircraft artillery and, as the first Hunter crashed near the anti-aircraft gun position, Arora dived directly on to the gun's position, destroying it with his front guns. This was the first loss of the Pakistani anti-aircraft artillery.[20] He strafed another gun position but could not cause any further damage.

On balance, the Pakistani flak had held the upper hand during the day. As Jagan and Chopra write in their book *Eagles over Bangladesh*, 'PAF sat tight and let its AA guns do the hard work when the IAF came calling in numbers'. The hard work of the anti-aircraft guns had surely paid off on day one.

It was not only at Tezgaon that AAA tasted success. The light AA guns deployed at Lal Munir Hat destroyed two Hunters on 4 December as they attacked the railway station.[21] The IAF lost two aircraft from its fifty-five close air support missions on Day One, a rather heavy attrition rate of over 3.6 per cent. Overall, the loss of seven aircraft, with two more damaged badly, and two flame-out incidents, painted a not too rosy picture for the IAF. Coupled with its failure to locate the AR-1 radar, the Indian Air Force would have wished for a better way to end the day.

On 5 December, the Indian Air Force tried to bait the Pakistani Sabres to come out and fight but the Pakistan Air Force, most likely warned by the AR-1 radar of the superior numbers of the Indian Air Force, stayed away. The only option then for India to put down the Pakistanis was to try and take out the runways – but again the conventional use of rockets had not given the desired results. The Indian Air Force decided to change tack and try out the Soviet FAB-500 M-62 bombs against the runways. The first trial was to have been against the AR-1 radar and Kurmitola airfield but, as the AR-1 radar remained elusive and out of the reach of IAF, the M-62 could not be tried out. Incidentally, the radar remained elusive throughout and out of the reach of the Indian Air Force for the duration of the war. However, Kurmitola airfield was another story. The Indian Air Force was able to damage it enough to make it unusable. Luckily, there were no losses to anti-aircraft fire at Kurmitola during the day. Even during close air support missions, there were no losses, although one Sukhoi SU-7 of No. 221 Squadron was hit by small arms fire near Jessore.

As the threat from the Pakistan Air Force was now minimal, Nos 7 and 30 Squadrons, IAF, were given orders to move to the Western Sector. In addition, three SAM squadrons were also released for the west as was an AD battery of 40mm L/70 guns which was airlifted to Agra. Until then, Agra had only a battery of vintage L/60 guns and was badly in need of more air defence troops, especially after the special attention given to it by the Pakistan Air Force during the night 3/4 December.[22]

IAF MiG-21s used the Soviet-built M-62 bombs against Tezgaon on 5 December. The heavy AA presence meant that the MiGs could not use the regular tactics of releasing the bombs at low level at about 900 metres above ground level (AGL) and pulling up from 600 metres. The MiGs perforce had to change tactics and release the bombs at about 1,400 to 1,500 metres and pull up from 1,000 metres, keeping well outside the effective ceiling of the anti-aircraft guns. Not only the height of bomb release had to be changed, the MiGs came in at a steep dive angle of

35 degrees – another first. The changed tactics paid off, however, and the MiGs were able to place the bombs right where they wanted, on the runway, putting it out of use.[23]

The Pakistani anti-aircraft gunners had also changed their tactics and had now placed the guns at both sides of either end of the runway. These were four-barrelled 14.5mm quads with a higher rate of fire than the 37mm guns. As the MiGs had streaked in, the anti-aircraft guns opened up but, as the IAF aircraft were well above the effective ceiling, the anti-aircraft fire proved ineffective. The MiGs were followed by Hunters of No. 14 Squadron which came in, escorted by Gnats providing top cover, with Napalm to try to neutralize the guns. Luckily for the Pakistani gunners, most of the Napalm failed to ignite. All throughout this, the anti-aircraft fire remained as fierce as before, making one of the Hunter pilots 'duck in his cockpit' as the AA shells burst all around him.[24]

The other raid by the Indian Air Force, on Kurmitola, was uneventful in comparison as no major opposition was faced by the Indian aircraft.

The only loss of the day, the first MiG-21 lost in the east, was during the close air support. The Indian Air Force provided forty CAS missions to the Indian Army's IV Corps during the day. The first fourteen sorties had gone in without any loss, the only damage being the small-arms hits on the MiGs, but the mission flown by No. 4 Squadron was not to have the same fate. At Brahmanbaria, as two MiGs went in against a Pakistani position, one of the MiGs was hit by small-arms fire. The damage was serious enough and even as the pilot, Squadron Leader D.P. Rao, tried to head back to the base at Guwahati, the engine flamed out, forcing him to eject.[25]

This incident, and the fact that a large number of aircraft were being hit by small-arms fire, forced the IAF to advise the pilots not to to fly at excessively low level and avoid taking risks.[26]

For the first time the Pakistan Air Force ventured out of Dacca airspace on 6 December to provide close support to the Pakistan Army, albeit just about twenty miles away, although the Sabres were reportedly seen over Comilla also. The F-86 Sabres were reportedly recovered back from an airstrip at Barisal, about eighty kilometres from Dacca. While the confirmation of use of the airstrip at Barisal was not available, it did add a target for the Indian Air Force to neutralize and to be tasked for counter-air missions. Although the reports (of use of Barisal) later proved to be false, the Indian Air Force did carry out counter-air missions against Barisal the next day.

Tezgaon was again raided, this time by a solitary MiG armed with M-62 bombs on the early morning of 7 December and was followed by Hunters later in the day. As the runway was damaged beyond repair, the Pakistani F-86 Sabres were effectively grounded and the opposition was limited to anti- aircraft fire but it was serious enough – damaging one of the Hunters of No. 14 Squadron. The damaged Hunter tried to reach its base but the engine flamed out, forcing Gupta, the pilot, to eject.[26] This was not the end of action at Tezgaon. The Hunters were followed by MiGs of No. 28 Squadron. This time around, the anti-aircraft fire again found its mark, hitting one of the aircraft but the damage was not serious enough and the crippled MiG was escorted back safely to base. The runway at Tezgaon was not so lucky – it was so badly damaged that it could not be repaired to be in action by morning.

By 8 December Tezgaon was damaged beyond repair and could not be used further by the Pakistan Air Force, effectively grounding it for the rest of the war. Even so, the Indian Air Force did not stop the counter-air missions against it and, in a new experiment, used Caribous, the lumbering transport aircraft, to bomb the runway. The Indian Air Force could afford to do so as not only the Pakistan Air Force but the anti-aircraft artillery was losing its sting. The ammunition supply for the Pakistani anti-aircraft guns was getting so low by 8 December that orders were issued to minimize expenditure and conserve ammunition. The AA gunners were asked to use not more than three rounds per attack and the quad guns were to use only two barrels at a time with ammunition restricted to twelve rounds per barrel.[28]

With the Pakistan Air Force effectively neutralized, all Indian air defence regiments in the east, except those deployed at some radar stations, were released for the Western Sector by 8 December.

The absence of the Pakistan Air Force in the skies freed up more Indian Air Force resources for close support to the army. This had an unintended effect also as the Indian pilots were rather reckless while carrying out the support missions. They flew low and made repeated passes over targets, presenting an easy target to ground fire. The number of aircraft coming back with bullet holes was testimony to that. While most were lucky enough to come back, there were occasions as on 10 December when the ground fire was so intense that it resulted in the loss of an aircraft. While providing close support at Hilli, a Hunter of No. 7 Squadron was hit by small-arms fire and resulted in the aircraft going down. This loss was, however, attributed as 'technical loss' by the IAF after an inquiry.[29]

In another incident, a MiG-21 of No. 28 Squadron was lost to anti-aircraft fire over Tezgaon on the 12th. Even with restricted ammunition, Pakistani anti-aircraft artillery was no pushover and it continued to take a toll until as late as 15 December when a Canberra was shot down over Tezgaon, bringing the total of aircraft lost in combat related incidents to thirteen, ten of them to anti-aircraft/ground fire.[30]

The IAF had flown over 2,000 sorties in the Eastern sector and, in terms of numbers, the attrition rate of 0.63 per cent may seem to be manageable but, if only the counter-air operations are considered, the attrition rate goes up to 1.79 per cent, with seven losses in 390 sorties. This was very high considering that the Pakistan Air Force had only one squadron and that, too, with only sixteen aircraft – three of its nineteen F-86 Sabres had been destroyed on 22 November, well before the war. To be fair to the Indian Air Force, the high attrition during counter-air operations was more due to anti-aircraft fire than the solitary PAF squadron. Also, losses to anti-aircraft continued throughout the fourteen-day war as the ground-based air defences could not be suppressed. According to Pakistani Army claims, batteries of 6th Light Anti-Aircraft Regiment itself, deployed in various sectors, shot down ten Indian aircraft between 4 and 16 December.[31]

For close support to the Indian Army, the Indian Air Force flew a total of 1,384 sorties in which it suffered six losses, an attrition rate of about 0.43 per cent. As 6th LAA Regiment of Pakistan was deployed primarily at the PAF air bases of Tezgaon and Kurmitola, most of these losses came from small-arms fire, as was the case of the Mi-4 helicopter hit during the heli-borne operations at Sylhet and the loss of the MiG over Hilli.

As there were no counter-air or counter surface force operations by the PAF, Indian Air Defence regiments did not have any kills to their credit during the entire fourteen-day war.

With the bomb line moving fast and the ground battle progressing faster than anticipated, incidents of fratricide and collateral damage could not be avoided. The destruction of the MVs *Padma* and *Palash* of Task Force Alpha of the Naval Wing of *Mukti Bahini* on 9 December by Gnats of the IAF and the bombing of an orphanage at Karwan Bazaar on 9 December by Caribous of No. 33 Squadron were the more serious of such incidents. There were some close shaves, also, which thankfully did not result in any losses.

With the surrender of the Pakistani Army on 17 December, the war came to an end in the Eastern Sector and a new nation, Bangladesh, had come into being.

Western Sector

The Pakistan Air Force launched Operation CHENGIZ KHAN on 3 December, the decision for which was reportedly taken on 30 November 1971. The objectives of the strike were:

- To surprise the IAF by attacking its forward airfields when it was least expected.
- To neutralize these in order to obtain at least temporary battlefield air superiority in the West.
- To counter-balance the Indian numerical advantage by hitting the forward operating bases of the Indian Air Force as a measure reducing the weight of expected counter-attacks on PAF's own bases.

The first strikes were launched at 1740 hours on 3 December as the Pakistan Air Force struck Pathankot and Amritsar. The Indians were caught off-guard with the air raid sirens giving the first warning as the Pakistani aircraft swooped down on the two air bases. The attacking aircraft were engaged by the anti-aircraft guns only and suffered no loss. However, the Pakistani strikes failed to have any impact, except for some damage to the runway at Pathankot which was soon repaired.[32]

Pakistan launched the second wave with two of its F-104 Starfighters against the P-30 (M) radar at Amritsar and claimed to have put it out of action for nearly an hour. The official records, however, mention only a limited damage to its communication equipment. The Pakistan Air Force suffered its first loss in the Western sector, an F-104 Starfighter which was shot down by AAA over Amritsar.[33] The damage caused to the radar was soon repaired and it was operational in the night itself.

> Amritsar radar was also attacked, with both pilots claiming to have hit the antenna; some damage to the communication equipment is acknowledged by the IAF. The lead F-104 (tail no 56–804) was equipped with a locally developed radar homing device, which was the only one of its type in the PAF. Trials had shown it to be a promising gadget and, as expected, had been instrumental in locating the well-camouflaged Amritsar radar. Damage to the radar was, however, short-lived as it became fully operational sometime during the night, which warranted a repeat mission the next morning.

Amritsar airfield and the radar were both defended by 27th Air Defence Regiment. This time around, Amritsar airfield was better protected with almost two batteries of radar-controlled 40mm L/70 guns. The F-104 was, however, not shot down by 27th AD Regiment but by a gun detachment of 26th Air Defence Regiment which had a troop (six guns) deployed at Amritsar airfield to beef up the defences. The first kill, and the first gallantry award, of the war was won by anti-aircraft artillery at Amritsar. Lance Naik Shreepati Singh of 26th Air Defence Regiment, who was the radar operator of the detachment that shot down the F-104 Starfighter, had the honour of being the first AA gunner to win a gallantry award during the war.

The next wave of the Pakistani strikes with fifteen B-57 Canberras, four T-33s, and one C-130 was directed against Ambala, Agra and Halwara at around 1800 hours and continued in single- or two-ship formations through the evening until at least 2230 hours. The B-57s flew seven single-ship sorties. These strikes were more effective as they caused significant damage, especially at Uttarlai and Halwara. Four Pakistani aircraft were reportedly shot down during the raids although official records mention only one F-104 and a B-57 to have been destroyed by anti-aircraft fire.[34] More importantly, no Indian aircraft were damaged or destroyed during these raids which continued through the night.

One reason why the Pakistani pre-emptive strikes failed to achieve their objective is that the Pakistan Air Force did not press home the attacks and just went through the motions, executing the attacks at high speed, thereby compromising accuracy. This was ostensibly to keep the aircraft safe from Indian anti-aircraft fire and minimize attrition. Another reason, as mentioned by some analysts, was that the strikes were more to instigate and provoke the Indian Air Force to retaliate and thereafter take on the Indians over Pakistani territory from a position of advantage. As hostilities had already started in the east with the Indian Army making regular forays into Pakistani territory, there is some merit in this assumption and it is borne out by Air Commodore Mansoor Shah of the PAF in his book *The Gold Bird*.

> An interesting rationale for the initial strikes has been elaborated in his book, *The Gold Bird* by Air Cdre Mansoor Shah, who was the Assistant Chief of Air Staff (Operations) during the war. Shah claims that these strikes were meant to provoke IAF into retaliating against PAF bases, which were the only well-defended target sets in the country. He goes on to state that it was important to keep the IAF's attention focused on the bases or else, it might have switched to countrywide interdiction of lines of communications, where the PAF was defenceless.[35]

The failure of the Pakistan Air Force owes much to the fact that the air defences at almost all the Indian bases and installations were far better and more robust than in the previous war. The number of air defence regiments in Western Command of the Indian Army was thirteen at the beginning of the war, compared to eleven in 1965, not counting three air defence regiments which moved in from the Eastern Sector during the course of the war. Of these, all but four were deployed on strategic and air force bases and installations. The increased number of regiments with radar-controlled guns, nine to be precise, was another factor that contributed to providing more lethal air defence.

The Pakistani raids were not without their own faux pas. One of the B-57s which raided Agra narrowly escaped being shot down by its own anti-aircraft artillery as it returned.

The raid on Agra airfield was significant as it was the deepest target attacked by any PAF aircraft. Two Mianwali-based B-57s staged through Rafiqui and managed to reach Agra 375-nm away, without being intercepted en route. The effort was only a partial success as the first B-57 failed to produce any results due to dud bombs. The second B-57 flown by Flt Lt Mazhar Bukhari with Flt Lt Nasim Khan as navigator, was able to carry out the attack successfully (2105 hrs), though it barely survived a mistaken AAA barrage on recovery at Rafiqui.[36]

To add to their woes, Pakistani air raids largely missed their targets.

Of the 130 sorties flown by B-57, T-33 and C-130, forty per cent were reported by the aircrew – in all candour – to be unsuccessful, either due to armament malfunctions or because the targets could not be located and bombs were dropped in general target vicinity on 'dead reckoning'.

The Indian Air Force retaliated immediately with Canberras of Nos 5, 16, 35 and 106 Squadrons carrying out twenty-three strikes against the Western Pakistani airfields of Murid, Mianwali, Sargodha, Chander, Risalewala, Rafiqui and Masroor, inflicting heavy damage to Sargodha and Masroor. The IAF strikes were carried out without any loss.[37]

The Indian Air Force launched counter-air operations on 4 December with S-22s, HF-24s, MiG-21s and Hunters against Pakistani airfields and radar stations. These strikes were quite successful with the Indian Air Force destroying thirteen Pakistani aircraft on the ground, comprising seven F-86s, two MiG-19s, one Mirage-III, two B-57s and one C-130. The IAF, however, paid a heavy price for this, losing seven aircraft; three Hunters and one Su-22 were shot down by Pakistani aircraft while three aircraft were shot down by Pakistani anti-aircraft fire.[38]

Pakistani accounts of the day's raids, on the other hand, paint a grim picture of Indian exploits, claiming that the Pakistan Air Force shot down ten Indian aircraft during the day and damaged four more. Pakistani anti-aircraft, according to their claims, shot down four Indian aircraft as against three admitted by the IAF.[39] These were not the only losses of the day. Pakistan lost two more aircraft, one B-57 and an F-104 shot down over Amritsar, while India lost an Su-22 in an accident during take off, killing the pilot.

On 4 December Pakistan carried out the first close support missions against the Indian army in the Chamb and Jammu sectors. No major losses were reported, even as anti-aircraft artillery tried to engage the Pakistani aircraft and hit several of them. Flight Lieutenant Israr Ahmed was one of the Pakistani pilots providing close support to the Pakistani army in the sector whose aircraft was hit by anti-aircraft fire. His citation for Sitara-e-Jurarat reads:

> On 4th December, 1971, Flight Lieutenant Israr Ahmad was detailed to fly a mission over the Chamb-Akhnur sector. While over the battle area, his aircraft was hit by enemy ground fire and the pilot was seriously injured. In spite of his injuries, the pilot climbed to height, flew the aircraft and landed at a base during an air raid warning.[40]

The radar station at Barnala and airfields at Amritsar, Pathankot and Srinagar were also attacked by Pakistani aircraft which managed to put the radar off the air for nearly twelve hours.

The Indian Air Force focused on counter-air operations during the day but it did provide close support also to the army, totalling 109 sorties during the day all along the Western Sector. Two Su-22s were hit by ground fire near Dera Baba Nanak as they were attacking Pakistani armour in the area. Both aircraft were badly damaged, forcing the pilots to eject. These were the first losses of Indian aircraft to anti-aircraft fire during close support missions.[41]

Further south, the Indian Air Force provided close support and attacked Pakistani positions at Islamgarh and Gazi Camp. One HF-24 Marut was lost to ground fire during the day while the Indian Air Force suffered its first Canberra casualty on the night of 4/5 December, when two Canberras failed to return from Masrur and Mianwali. A Canberra was shot down by a Pakistani Mirage III over Mianwali while the second was shot down by Pakistani anti-aircraft fire although Pakistani accounts mention the loss of a Canberra to have occurred over Sargodha.

On the night of 4/5 December, during an attack by a Canberra, Sargodha runway was cratered and, remained unusable for several hours. A second bomb dropped in the same run landed at an engineering facility, killing two officers who were at work. One of the vintage 3.7" guns of 52 Medium Air Defence Regiment was able to exact instant retribution, so it seemed, when a well-aimed shot hit the intruder. The Canberra struggled to stay aloft for a few minutes, but finally went down near Bhalwal, killing its crew of two.[42]

The Indian Air Force also carried out tactical reconnaissance missions in the Naya Chor-Umarkot-Dhanarao area while the Pakistani Air Force attacked Srinagar airfield on 5 December, damaging its runway. An Indian Alouette helicopter was also shot down during the raid. The Pakistani Mirage IIIs which raided Pathankot, however, could not cause any damage. Having learnt its lessons from the faux pas during the 1965 war, Pathankot was well prepared. Elsewhere, PAF F-104s raided Amritsar, of which one was shot down by the anti-aircraft guns and the pilot was captured as he ejected over Indian territory.[43] Pakistani attempts to put down the Amritsar radar had again failed.

> The Amritsar radar busting project came to a halt at mid-day on 5 December, when the specially-equipped F-104 flown by Sqn Ldr Amjad Hussain was shot down by AAA, while carrying out a strafing pass over the radar. Amjad ejected and was hauled up as a POW. The 12-odd sorties flown for 'suppression of enemy air defences' did not yield the desired results. The F-104s were, therefore, promptly moved to Masroor in the south, where the F-86s were eagerly waiting to be relieved from their largely blind night patrols.

Pakistani B-57s carried out a total of nine raids during the day on Indian installations and bases at Amritsar, Pathankot, Adampur, Nal and Bhuj but could not cause any serious damage. The only damage was at Okha where the Pakistan Air Force hit the main oil depot, setting it on fire. During these raids, three B-57s were shot down by anti-aircraft fire at Amritsar, Jamnagar and Bhuj. An account of the B-57 raids during the night 5/6 December mentions

Three B-57s, along with their crew, were lost to AAA during raids on the night of 5/6 December. In the north, Flt Lt Javed Iqbal (P) and Flt G M Malik (N) met a tragic end after being shot down at Amritsar. Though they had managed to eject, both were badly beaten up by the mob that had swarmed at the place of landing and were fatally injured as a consequence. In the south, Sqn Ldr Ishfaq Qureshi (P) and Flt Lt Zulfiqar Ahmad (N) went down at Bhuj and Sqn Ldr Khusro Shadani (P) and Sqn Ldr Peter Christy (N) went down at Jamnagar. Apparently, the benefit of attacking an airfield in moonlit conditions – a 17-day old waning moon, about 85% of its full illumination – worked both ways and, would have helped the AAA gunners in sighting and tracking the attacking bombers.[44]

The Indian Air Force, for its part, focused on the Pakistani airfields in the north which could be used for close support missions against the Indian army resulting in Pakistan withdrawing many of its aircraft to bases in the depth. This did have a marked impact on the quantum of close support available to the Pakistani army from 6 December onwards. Of the seven Canberras sent to attack Sargodha, the IAF lost one, shot down by anti-aircraft guns defending the air base.[45]

As part of the counter-air operations, Indian Hunters and Su-22s attacked the high-power FPS-20 radar at Sakesar and damaged one of its antennae, putting it off the air for two days. The anti-aircraft guns deployed to defend the radar extracted some consolation as they shot down one of the Su-22s. Three more Hunters were lost in aerial combat. Although the radar was put off, Indian Air Force had paid a rather high price. IAF accounts of the raid on the Sakesar radar mention it thus:

> On 5th December, he was leading a formation of two aircraft on the strike mission to Sakesar Radar Station which was very heavily defended. The aircraft flown by his Number two became unserviceable at take off. Undeterred by this, he proceeded alone on this mission. After reaching the target, he attacked the Radar Station in the face of heavy ground fire and succeeded in damaging and putting the radar station off the air.[46]

The damage to the radar is also acknowledged by Pakistan:

> The attack by the Hunter pilots was not in vain, as they managed to pull off two strafing runs each. The FPS-20 surveillance radar and the FPS-6 height finder antennae were badly damaged, while considerable electronic equipment and cables were destroyed. The radar remained out of operation for three days, before spares were rushed in and repairs carried out.
>
> Later that afternoon, a lone intrepid Hunter was able to sneak in for yet another successful attack on Sakesar radar, adding to the damage and destruction caused by the previous Hunter pair.[47]

In the raids by the Indian Canberras over Murid, Shorkot, Mianwali and Masrur, one PAF B-57 was claimed to have been destroyed on the ground as was the bulk petroleum installation (BPI) at Masrur. The B-57 destroyed in the raid was the last of the RB-57Bs, bringing to an end the association of these surveillance aircraft with the Pakistan Air Force.

For the IAF 5 December was an eventful day as it stemmed the Pakistani armour advance at Longewala, destroying forty tanks over that day and the next. The four Hunters of No. 122 Squadron operating from Jaisalmer, were all that stood between the Pakistan Army and Jaisalmer and Ramgarh. A Pakistani infantry brigade, supported by an armoured regiment, had attacked the Indian position at Longewala on the night of 4/5 December and, as the army was not in a position to provide any immediate support, it was the Indian Air Force that rose to the occasion and achieved a remarkable feat in destroying the Pakistani thrust.

The close support operations to the north were not so fortunate as three Indian aircraft were lost to anti-aircraft fire and one to air action in close support missions in XI Corps' sector. In addition, several aircraft were damaged by Pakistani anti-aircraft artillery although they managed to return to base. One such pilot was Flight Lieutenant Vijay Kumar Wahi, who was carrying out an interdiction mission against Bhawalnagar railway station.

> While attacking the train the port wing of his aircraft was damaged by anti-aircraft fire. Undeterred and unmindful of his safety, he

pressed home his attack and destroyed a large number of tanks. After pulling out of the attack he found the port wing of his aircraft on fire. With great presence of mind and skillful flying, he brought the crippled aircraft back to base safely.[48]

Pakistan did not carry out any counter-air missions during the day on 6 December and attacked Indian air bases only at dusk and in the night. They could cause only marginal damage to the runways at Srinagar and Amritsar. Attempts to damage the radar at Amritsar made no headway. The Indian Air Force, as the day before, concentrated on air bases which were used to provide close support to the Pakistani army although the extent of damage caused could not be ascertained.

Meanwhile, Longewala remained a high priority for the Indian Air Force and the Pakistani army brigade and armoured regiment continued to be targeted by the Hunters. In I and XI Corps' sectors, India lost three Su-22s and a Mystère suffered engine flame-out. Indian anti-aircraft artillery with the field formations opened their account, shooting down three F-86s in 26th Infantry Division's sector.[49]

The Indian Air Force further reduced the counter-air missions the next day, attacking only the Pakistani air bases at Risalwala and Murid. The reduced efforts against the air bases was to free more aircraft to step up the close support missions for the army. The Pakistani counter-air missions were also low key although they managed to hit and set on fire the oil tanks at Barmer railway station. No damage was caused to either of the air forces on these missions although the close support missions were not without losses. India lost an Su-22 to air action during the close support missions while Indian anti-aircraft guns shot down three Pakistani aircraft. One of these was at Shakargarh and the pilot was taken prisoner of war:

> The PAF was asked for only 6 sorties of interdiction in support of this formation (Major General Abid Zahid's 15 Division) but lost an F-6 to enemy flak on 7 December; the pilot, Flight Lieutenant Wajid Ali was taken PoW.[50]

The Pakistan Air Force suffered its single biggest loss on the ground when Indian Hunters destroyed five F-86s at Murid on 8 December.[51] In a rare acknowledgement of its losses, this incident was confirmed by the PAF and is mentioned as under:

> On the ground the PAF's biggest single loss occurred at Murid on 8 December when a Hunter attacked a lone F-86 which was thoughtlessly parked, after being refuelled and re-armed, next to a cluster of 4 covered pens; within these pens stood 4 F-86s fully armed with bombs for the next mission. The base paid the price for this inexcusable lapse by losing all 5 aircraft when the exploding bombs of the exposed Sabre triggered detonations in the other four.

In other raids during the day, India attacked Chaklala and Risalwala when one Su-22 was lost. The Indian Air Force also attacked the oil storage tanks at Attock and Karachi, and the storage area at Drigh Road airfield. Writing about the raid on Attock, Tufail mentions that the IAF was able to get away without any losses due to absence of a radar cover:

> The AAA defences were taken by surprise, but by the time the guns opened up, the damage had been done. The Hunters survived the AAA barrage and, with no interceptors on patrol, they made good their escape.[52]

Indian attempts to locate the elusive radar at Lahore failed yet again. The Indian Air Force had long suspected that a high-power radar was located there which was used to track all Indian air activity, and had been trying to pinpoint it ever since the war started, but had failed to do so. The Pakistan Air Force on its part attacked Amritsar and Avantipur radars but could not cause any damage. Pakistan suffered further losses of three MiG-19s, one C-130 and a light aircraft during the day.

The battle of Chamb was still raging and the Indian Air Force carried out twenty-eight sorties in support of the army which accounted for a number of Pakistani tanks and guns, at the cost of a MiG-21 shot down by Pakistani anti-aircraft fire. In other missions, India lost a Mystère and a Hunter to anti-aircraft fire at Arruka and Hasilpur[53] while Indian anti-aircraft artillery shot down an F-86 in Chamb on 8 December.

On 8 December, Flt Lt Fazal Elahi of No. 26 Squadron was fatally hit by ground fire while performing a close support mission in Chamb area. Apparently, the AAA shell hit the bomb fuse, causing the F-86F to blow up in mid-air.[54]

The intense resistance offered by the Indian anti-aircraft artillery to the Pakistan Air Force in the Chamb sector was, in a rare gesture, also duly acknowledged by the Pakistan Air Force:[55] 'PAF fighters providing cover to own troops in this area met with fierce opposition from Indian AAA.'

On 9 December the Indian Air Force was asked to provide all possible support to the army, especially in the Chamb area. While this was being carried out, the Indian Air Force attacked Chander and Risalwala air bases to try and keep the Pakistan Air Force away, losing one Su-7 over Chander.

Nawabshah, Hyderabad and Jacobabad were the other airfields attacked by the Indian Air Force. the Pakistani anti-aircraft artillery deployed at Hyderabad shot down an HF-24 Marut during the raid.[56]

For its part the Pakistan Air Force attacked Srinagar and Pathankot but failed to cause any serious damage. A new development during the day was the use of F-104s for a raid on the Indian Navy base at Okha in Gujarat, one of which was shot down by the anti-aircraft guns deployed there. This was the first time the Starfighter was observed in this sector and they may have been moved south to strengthen the Pakistan air defence around Karachi which had been a regular target for the Indian Air Force.[57]

An unverified claim is of the Indian Air Force having launched four SA-2 missiles at Halwara airfield against the attacking Pakistani aircraft during the night of 10/11 December. Although this raid is not mentioned in the *History of India Pakistan War 1971*, it is mentioned in various Pakistani accounts. Details available indicate that the raid was carried out by B-57s, of which one aircraft was targeted by the SAM battery at Halwara. The missiles failed to hit and the B-57 continued with its mission. Both the pilot and the navigator were awarded with gallantry awards for 'courage, determination and devotion to duty'.

Squadron Leader Abdul Basit was detailed on an air mission against the I.A.F. Base at Halwara on the night of 10/11th December, 1971.

He flew the mission as planned. While a few minutes short of the target four surface-to-air missiles were fired at his B-57 aircraft. He displayed great courage, skill and devotion to duty, evaded these missiles, continued on his mission and successfully attacked the target even though there was all the likelihood of the enemy firing more SAMs. For his courage, determination and devotion to duty Squadron Leader Abdul Basit has been awarded Sitara-i-Juraat.[58]

The Pakistan Air Force scored its first kill on the ground when it destroyed an HF-24 at Uttarlai airfield during an attack on the base on 11 December. Amritsar, Jammu and Srinagar were also targeted by Pakistan and it lost an F-86 to anti-aircraft fire at Amritsar. Close support missions were launched all along the western sector by the IAF during which one Su-22 was lost to the Pakistan Air Force near Shorkot.

While not mentioned in Indian accounts, Pakistan acknowledged the loss of an F-86 to Indian anti-aircraft defences in the Chamb sector on 11 December:

Enemy ack ack continued to take its toll and on 11 December Flight Lieutenant Shahid Raza's F-86 was shot down and he was lost.[59]

After having earlier targeted the radar at Sakesar, the Indian Air Force turned its attention towards the high-power FPS-20 radar at Badin but the damage caused by the first raid by the MiG-21s could not be ascertained. Badin was again targeted by four MiG-21s, in co-ordination with three Hunters attacking Talhar airfield. Not only did the Indian Air Force lose two Hunters over Talhar, shot down by F-86s, but a MiG was shot down by anti-aircraft fire at Badin. The defences at Badin were as intense as before – they had shot down a Canberra in the previous war.

Srinagar was the main target of the PAF on 14 December as it was attacked by six F-86 Sabres. The day saw an unequal fight as Flying officer Nirmaljit Singh Sekhon of No. 18 Squadron took on single-handedly the intruders in a Gnat and shoot down an F-86. He hit another Sabre before he was himself shot down. He was awarded the country's highest gallantry award for his valour above and beyond the call of duty.

As the Pakistan Air Force activity had petered off by now, India carried out counter-air operations against only one Pakistani airfield during the day (15 December).

The Indian Air Force had also been carrying out interdiction missions, without facing much opposition. In the absence of adequate radar cover the Indian Air Force could approach the targets in the hinterland, undetected, at low level as was the case in the attack on Mangla dam.[60] The anti-aircraft defences, even if deployed at these targets, hardly got any early warning and largely proved ineffective.

> The dam was defended by AAA, but the attackers were able to catch them unawares by ingressing low. Lack of early warning also precluded the possibility of any interception.

As the war wound down, Indian anti-aircraft artillery shot down a PAF MiG-19 at Shakargarh on the last day of the war:

> On 17 December, the last day of the war, Flt Lt Shahid Raza of No. 25 Squadron volunteered for a mission from which he was fated not to return. During ground attack, his F-6 was hit by enemy AAA near Dharman, close to Shakargarh. He was heard to be ejecting but sadly, nothing more was ever learnt about him. He was awarded a Tamgha-i-Jur'at posthumously.[61]

The air operations came to an end in the Western Sector at 2000 hours on 17 December with the acceptance by Pakistan of the ceasefire offer.

It was a short but intense war. The PAF was defensive throughout, as if waiting for the enemy to come and attack them. The pre-emptive strikes on 3 December were launched with inadequate numbers which could not have caused any serious damage. The beefed-up Indian defences not only prevented any real damage to Indian bases and installations but also shot down five aircraft over the 288 counter-air sorties carried out by the Pakistan Air Force.

For the Indian Air Force, the hostile air defence environment over Pakistani air bases was a major deterrent in execution of its counter-air missions. As the *History of India Pakistan War 1971* notes:

Changing its strategy in the face of these heavy losses, the IAF gave up its all-out attack on the PAF bases, and the tempo of counter air operations was reduced from 6 December.

The counter-air operations further reduced after 8 December as 'again it (IAF) had to avoid heavy losses'. The only saving grace was that the numerically smaller Pakistan Air Force was equally affected by the heavy attrition and kept away from the skies for the most part, leaving the IAF largely free to operate.

The Pakistan Air Force was more cautious in 1971 as it well understood the fact that the numbers were stacked against it and India had considerably built up its armed forces since the last war. Pakistan did not venture over Indian bases as in the past. The beefed-up defences at Pathankot, with almost an AD regiment deployed to defend, were a major change since 1965 when only a battery and a troop were deployed at the airfield. Amritsar airfield was another example.

Early warning remained a problem area as the proximity to the international border, as in the case of Pathankot and Amritsar, and the terrain, e.g. at Srinagar, precluded any meaningful warning to be available to Indian defences and it is creditable that the anti-aircraft defences rose to the challenge and performed so well. It is all the more remarkable as the control and reporting system was rudimentary at best. The anti-aircraft troops were dependent on the nearest air base or the nearest air force radar for early warning. At times, the anti-aircraft guns and detachments were so widely dispersed that they had to function autonomously under pre-assigned control orders.

Pakistan had a smaller geographical spread to contend with but had more incidents of fratricide, the most prominent one being the shooting down of Squadron Leader Cecil Chaudhary:

> Only five days earlier (on 6 December) Cecil himself had been shot down in error by Pak Army ack ack, but was safely recovered to fly another day.[62]

Earlier, on 4 December, Pakistani anti-aircraft artillery had engaged a PAF aircraft at Risalewala. Kaiser Tufail writes about the incident in his blog *Air Defence in the Northern Sector*:

As the attackers approached the airfield, Flt Lt Javed Latif easily positioned behind one of them while Riffat cleared tails. Firing all three of his cannon, Latif waited for some fireworks. Noticing that the aircraft was still flying unharmed, he fired another long burst till all his ammunition was exhausted. Just as he was expecting his quarry to blow up, he felt a huge thud. Thinking that he had been hit by the other Su-7, he broke right and then reversed left but found no one in the rear quarters. Checking for damage, he found that the left missile was not there and the launcher was shattered. The AAA shells bursting in puffs all around the airfield confirmed his suspicion that he had taken a 'friendly' hit, but luckily the aircraft was fully under control. Pressing on, he started to look for the escaping Su-7s and, within moments, was able to pick one of them trailing a streak of whitish smoke. Convinced that it was the same one he had hit earlier, and assuming it to be crippled, Latif decided to go for the other Su-7. He spotted it straight ahead, flying over the tree tops at a distance of two miles. Engaging afterburners, he closed in for a Sidewinder shot but could not get a lock-on tone. To his dismay, he realised that the missile tone was routed through the circuitry of the left missile which had been shot off. Getting below the Su-7, he fired without a tone nonetheless, half expecting it to connect, if at all it fired. Moments later, he heard Riffat's excited voice on the radio, 'Good shooting, leader, you got him!' Not sure if he had really hit him as he had not seen any explosion, Latif was soon relieved to see the Su-7 roll over inverted and hit the ground.[63]

It is not that the Indian Air Force did not have such incidents. Sinking the MVs *Padma* and *Palash* in the Eastern Sector, and the shooting down by friendly fire of Flight Lieutenant Ashok Balwant Dhavle on 11 December in a case of mistaken identity were two such occurrences. Incidentally, Dhavle is one of the 'Missing Fifty-One', the missing Indian Armed Forces personnel believed to be still languishing in Pakistani prisons and never acknowledged by the Pakistan government.[64]

About the total losses suffered by the two sides, there are conflicting figures, claims and counter-claims yet to be authenticated officially by either side. According to *India Pakistan War 1971*, the IAF suffered a total of fifty-two losses, of which thirty-four were to anti-aircraft/ground fire. However, A.K. Tiwari in *IAF in Wars* states that the total losses suffered by the IAF were seventy-five, of which thirty-four were to ground fire, including anti-aircraft guns. While the figures for the overall losses are disputed, the loss of thirty-four Indian aircraft to anti-aircraft/ground fire can be considered to be reasonably accurate. Although no official figures have ever been released by the Pakistan Air Force, it claims that a total of 104 Indian aircraft were destroyed during the war, including thirty-nine by anti-aircraft/ground fire.

However, the impact of anti-aircraft artillery should not be seen only in terms of number of aircraft shot down. It was instrumental in degrading the efficacy of air strikes as its presence itself made the opposing air forces change tactics and adopt more defensive techniques.

This was the real success of AAA during the war. Forcing the opposing air force to change tactics, blunting the offensive edge by its relentless barrage and, even when short of ammunition, making every round count and causing irreplaceable attrition. The missions flown by the air forces, in trying to suppress the air defence, however small it may have been in this war, could have been used for more offensive tasks and this virtual attrition of air force did add up to a considerable effort. And in direct confrontation between the anti-aircraft gunner manning his vintage guns and the blue-blooded air force pilot, the humble gunner came up on top in his own quiet, but deadly, manner.

Chapter 7

Conclusion

More aircraft were lost to AAA than any other weapon system during the Second World War. It was not much of a contest really, with only AAA and aircraft vying for the honours as surface-to-air missiles had not been operational during the war. *Wasserfal*, *Enzian* and other German 'Wonder Weapons' were produced in such limited numbers that they could not have made any impact even if they had been used by Germany during the war. Of the two weapon systems available for air defence, i.e. guns and aircraft, it was primarily the AA guns that caused most of the attrition. The AA guns, ranging from 20mm multi-barrelled cannon to the much heavier 130mm AA guns, performed well during the war, notching up an impressive number of kills.

It was the same AA guns that faced the more advanced jet aircraft when war broke out in Korea. The main AA gun with North Korea was the Soviet 37mm that could fire approximately 160 rounds per minute and had an effective range of some 4,500 feet. A few 85mm guns that could fire to nearly 25,000 feet were also available. The bulk of AAA though was 20mm or smaller calibre guns which had much less range. The limitation in capability of these guns was made up for by numbers, although it was not the numbers of the types of AA guns that were important but the manner in which they were employed.

The surface-to-air missiles had not become operational as yet. The world's first surface-to-missile, the US Nike Ajax would not enter service until one year after the end of the Korean War. The shoulder-fired Redeye missile had still not been conceptualized – it was in 1948 that the US Army sought air-defence weapons for the infantry as the guns were considered to be ineffective against jet aircraft, but the results of the study to develop a suitable weapons system would be finalized only in 1954. It was back to the guns to shoulder all the responsibility of ground-based air defence systems.

The main AA guns used in the wars during the period were Soviet AA guns of Second World War vintage, as also their Chinese versions. The 37mm AA gun M1939 (61-K) was the mainstay of North Korean air defences. Developed in the late 1930s, it had proved its mettle during the Great Patriotic War, shooting down 14,657 Axis aeroplanes, using 905 rounds on average to shoot down one aircraft. Although replaced by the ZSU-57-2 self-propelled AA guns in the Soviet Union, the M1939 saw service in both Korea and Vietnam, as did the 100mm KS-19 AA gun. The 85mm M1939(52-K) AA guns which were with the Soviet AA divisions in Korea could also be used as anti-tank guns, like the German 88mm. However, they were fewer in numbers and had been replaced largely by the 100 and 130mm guns in the Soviet Army. Numerically the ZPU-1/ -2 and -4 AA guns were the more commonly used AA guns with North Korea.

These vintage guns faced the most formidable air force of the day and were responsible for over 88 per cent of all USAF losses but their real impact was not in the number of aircraft shot down but the effect they had on the conduct of air operations. The AA guns made it difficult for the coalition aircraft to press home with their offensive missions and reduced the efficacy of their weapon delivery,

Massed AAA made close air support and delivery of weapons hazardous. The presence of AAA meant a change in speed and altitude of weapon delivery – reducing their accuracy. Taking the example of napalm, this should normally be delivered at a flat pass at an altitude of about 100 feet and at relatively slow speed to obtain good results. When AAA was present, passes had to be made at speeds up to 450mph with immediate pull-ups to above 2,000 feet to escape the small-arms range. Such changed tactics obviously reduced the accuracy of the napalm drops.

To counter the increasing interference by the Communist AAA, the coalition forces tried out a number of active measures. From directly attacking the AA sites by air and from field artillery, the USAF changed its tactics to make flak suppression more effective but failed in their mission to suppress the AA, although the newer methods did reduce losses to ground fire.[1]

The electronic counter-measures were also adapted by the USAF to degrade the North Korean radars. The radars with North Korea were a mixed lot, ranging from German *Freya* systems captured by the Russians, Soviet systems like the truck-mounted early warning (EW) RUS-2 radar and its fixed-base version, the P2M, the EW and GCI radars; Kniferest and Token and a Soviet copy of the American SCR-584 fire-control radar. Numbering about 100 in all, they were 'of good quality and intelligently used', according to a US Navy report.[2]

Electronic reconnaissance and signal intelligence flights by Boeing RB-50G Superfortresses from SAC's 55th Strategic Reconnaissance Wing over Korea started from August 1951 to garner details of the North Korean radars. Chaff was used by the USAF to confuse the radar operators, but the US was hesitant in using more direct methods like jamming as it was felt that such measures might reveal US capabilities and they could be used against the US in case of a direct war between the USA and the Soviet Union. Faced with hostile AAA, the USAF did resort to spot jamming as the threat of AAA could not be simply wished away.

The USAF also tried other measures, including painting the underside of its bombers black, direct attacks on radar-controlled searchlights and use of nightfighters. This was necessitated as the Communists had started using the *helle Nachtjagd* (illuminated night-fighting) technique which was first used by the Germans in the Second World War. In this, the radars were used to detect the incoming bombers and then direct the searchlights on to them; the MiGs would then attack the illuminated bombers.

Such was the AA threat that USAF planners tried every possible means to reduce losses – moonlit nights were avoided, missions planned on nights when cloud cover would block searchlight beams, and bombers made to fly at altitudes where contrail formation would be minimum. All to reduce the chances of being detected by air defences.

Shoran (Short Range Navigation) was a technique adapted by the USAF to have better results during its bombing missions and was effective in the initial stages but the North Korean air defences were quick to map the routes that the USAF was forced to take, and deployed the AA guns along the likely routes – inflicting higher casualties on the intruding aircraft. It was in fact the same for all interdiction missions. Initial success followed by disappointing results.

The most widely publicized of the special-purpose campaigns was Operation STRANGLE. Like its predecessor, the operation looked fairly successful at first but soon enough the Communists developed counter-measures. While in the extreme north it was the MiGs that forced the USAF to abandon its attacks on the railroads, it was the AAA that was used with telling effect in the south. Automatic AA weapons were emplaced along stretches of track and the fire from those weapons was so intense that it forced the attacking aircraft to abandon their highly effective glide attacks and carry out the less accurate, but also less vulnerable, dive-bomb attacks. Forced to carry rockets and proximity-fuzed bombs for flak suppression, the effective bomb loads were reduced.

The reduced accuracy and decreased bombloads of the fighter-bomber attacks, coupled with the huge amount of effort the Communists were expending on fixing the broken rails, resulted in such a decline in the effectiveness of Operation STRANGLE that the US was forced to acknowledge that the Communists 'have broken our railroad blockade of Pyongyang and ... won ... the use of all key rail arteries'.

The next interdiction campaign, Operation SATURATE also met the same fate. It looked good at first and then became less effective as the enemy developed counter-measures which were rather direct this time around. The Communists placed AA guns along nearly all their railway lines, effectively contesting the USAF over all the targets. Before it could achieve any worthwhile results, the operation ended in a failure.

In all the interdiction campaigns, one of the primary reasons why they failed to achieve their objectives was the *ability of Communists to devise effective countermeasures for various types of attack.*[3]

In a way, that summed up the entire Korean War: a string of air campaigns which ultimately met with great resistance and counter-measures that prevented them achieving the desired results.

The war in Vietnam proved to be no different. The presence of a large number of surface to air missiles, notably the SA-2 Guidelines added to the overall effectiveness of North Vietnam's air defences. The three components, viz. the MiGs, AAA and SAMs acted in perfect harmony, making it difficult for the US air forces. With the overlapping air defences, no space was safe enough for US aircraft.

To evade the small-arms fire US pilots flew at higher altitudes, but this exposed them to the integrated air defence. The radars detected the planes at the higher altitudes, deprived their missions of the element of surprise, and vectored MiG fighters to intercept them. The higher altitudes also brought the planes into the effective range of AAA of various calibres, from the 12.7mm guns to radar-guided 100mm guns effective to altitudes of 40,000 feet. Because AA guns were the most effective weapons in bringing down US aircraft, their presence forced US aircraft to fly above AAA range, but this brought them into the range of SAMs. To counter the SAMs, US aircraft with devices mounted on their wings for electronic counter-measures (ECM) against the radar flew in formation with other planes, which enhanced the ECMs but reduced the planes' manoeuvrability and made them more vulnerable to attacks by MiGs. When a SAM was actually coming at them, pilots performed a tight turning dive to outmanoeuvre the missile, but this tactic had the undesirable effect of bringing them down again into the range of AAA.

The estimates of the number of US aircraft, both fixed-wing and rotary, shot down during the war vary according to the source and may never be truly known. But downing the aircraft was never the only way the AA affected air operations in Vietnam. The changes in air tactics, development of defensive measures, advancement in electronic warfare capabilities, use of unmanned craft, precision-guided munitions, were all in more than one way an outcome of the hostile air defences faced by the US.

The Viet Cong deployed their AA guns in unconventional manner, in formations of triangles, diamonds, and pentagons. They routinely used 'dummy sites' and often moved the guns to new sites, all to confuse the pilots and to concentrate the fire on selected aircraft. It was not uncommon for them to place the guns on high ground, covering the most likely landing zones. A remarkable feature was the very high standard of fire discipline. They fired for effect, making it difficult for the USAF to operate, especially at low level. The following example would suffice to illustrate this:

> They made each bullet count. On December 22, 1972 a Vietnamese anti-aircraft unit using a single-barrel 14.7mm gun shot down an F-111 supersonic fighter-bomber. What was remarkable was the anti-aircraft gun had only 19 shells left when they spotted the American aircraft.[4]

One of the important factors that contributed to strengthening of AA defences was the large presence of Chinese AA troops. Between August 1965 and March 1969, a total of sixty-three regiments, organized into sixteen AA divisions, served in Vietnam. On 9 August 1965, they shot down a US F-4 using 37mm and 85mm AA guns, the first US aircraft to be shot down by Chinese AA troops, and went on to claim 1,707 US aircraft shot down and a further 1,608 damaged.[5]

The presence of an integrated air defence network, incorporating North Vietnamese troops, Chinese AA divisions and Soviet advisors, made it all very difficult for the US to use their air forces without dedicating large resources for protection and escort duties. This was chipping away at the number of aircraft that could be used for offensive missions, and came to be called 'Virtual Attrition'. It came to be recognized as a recurring feature during the war when many US aircraft had to be diverted to ECM duties, flak suppression, anti-SAM operations and to escort the bombers, denuding the overall offensive effort available. Further, carrying self-protection jammers and EW suites reduced the bomb-carrying capability.

It was not that the aircraft that went through with their missions performed optimally. Some just did not attack certain areas, while others simply jettisoned their loads and aborted their missions although the most common measure adopted was to fly higher and try to get out of the range of ground fire. This itself reduced the effectiveness of the bombing attacks.

Faced with increasingly effective AA, the US resorted to using weapons that did not require a low-level delivery. From using the Mk82 500-pound general-purpose bomb to the Mk83 and Mk84, 1,000- and 2,000-pound bombs against hardened targets, such as bridges or other concrete structures, it was not long before special weapons like the AGM-62 Walleye or AGM-12 Bullpup were being used to avoid losses.

The single most contributory factor which affected the air operations was the SA-2 missile system. It did not shoot down the maximum number of US aircraft but its mere presence affected the air tactics as no other weapon system did. AA guns could be avoided by simply flying at an altitude which was beyond their range but, with an effective ceiling of 20,000 metres, the SA-2 could not be avoided and the aircraft had to fly through its envelope. The proliferation in SAM sites was not checked at the initial stages and this lapse proved costly for the USAF.

The North Vietnamese adopted their own deployment patterns, different from the 'classic' clover-leaf pattern followed by the Soviets and built up a large number of dummy sites, as they did for AA guns. Moving around the SAM launchers was a common feature which made it difficult for the USAF to spot the SAM sites. Once located, US aircraft tried to take them out but, more often than not, failed to do so. The efficiency of the SAMs came down in the later years but they were still formidable as the following figures of missiles fired, and US aircraft shot down during LINEBACKER II reveal. A total of 266 missiles were fired between 18 and 29 December, shooting down fourteen B-52s and seriously damaging another four. The average number of missiles required to shoot down one B-52 was nineteen. If the claims are considered, a total of thirty-six US aircraft were shot down for 266 missiles, bringing down the missile expenditure to 7.3 missiles per aircraft.

As mentioned elsewhere, these figures are contested by both the US and North Vietnam (and Soviet Union). Soviets claimed a much better performance by the SA-2. Soviet claims are that North Vietnam was provided with ninety-eight missile systems and 7,500 missiles and finished the war with forty-five sites and 2,300 missiles. Another source state the total of SAM missile systems provided was ninety-five along with 7,658 missiles, of which 6,806 were expended (including defective missiles and lost in battle), shooting down a total of 1,046 US aircraft. There are, however, no substantiated records of the actual number of US aircraft shot down, or the number of missiles fired.

The surface-to-air missiles played a similar role in the Middle East although the Israeli Air Force was better prepared to face the threat and did not suffer major losses to the SA-2, the only SAM in service with the Arab Air Forces during the Six Day War. A factor that contributed to the SA-2's relative failure was the manner in which it was used by the Arabs. Fixed sites with hardly any tactical variation in its use made it more of a sitting duck than a formidable air defence system. This was corrected to some extent by Egypt during the War of Attrition but, even so, the major losses were to AAA.

India had acquired the SA-2 before the India-Pakistan War of 1965 but there are no records of it having downed any Pakistani aircraft. The missile was used against the Pakistan Air Force B-57 at Halwara air base on the night of 10/11 December 1971 but all four missiles failed to hit the target. This is the only documented use of a surface-to-air missile during the India Pakistan Wars of 1965 and 1971.

These wars were low key affairs and the air power was not used to its optimum. The counter-air operations were restricted by both air forces in 1965 due to heavy losses to AAA and, even in 1971, the Pakistan Air Force seemed to only go through the motions of attacking Indian bases. Suppression of air defence missions were limited to attempts to knock off selected radars – the radar at Amritsar was the main target for the Pakistan Air Force in both the wars, while India tried taking out the Pakistani radar at Badin. Otherwise there were no SEAD missions per se.

There are some common threads in all the wars. Air power was resisted more by the opposing AAA than the rival air force. More losses occurred due to ground fire than any other cause. Fratricide was an unfortunate fact which could not be eliminated. Not only were own aircraft targeted by friendly ground fire but even by friendly air force(s). The air defences influenced the air operations, forcing them to adopt newer techniques and technologies. The numbers were important, but more important was this indirect influence which shaped the conduct of air forces.

Number of aircraft lost to AA? Well, with no clear answers to how many aircraft were shot down or damaged, it would be safe to just say *more than any other cause*. On that account, there is no dispute.

Attrition trends in the Jet Age

One of the commonly referred to methods to judge efficacy of the air defences is the attrition caused on the air force(s). There are no commonly accepted norms of what is an acceptable attrition rate, or what constitutes an unsustainable attrition although 2 to 3 per cent is generally said to be within acceptable limits although even seemingly low attrition rates can result in failure, and defeat, over time.[1] One example is the defeat of the Luftwaffe in the Battle of Britain during the autumn of 1940 as a result of a per-sortie attrition rate of less than 5 per cent. Nazi Germany had to give up its ambitious plans of subjugating the UK by its air campaign. On the other hand, during the Six Day War of 1967, the Israeli Air Force lost nineteen aircraft on the first day itself, a loss of more than 10 per cent of its total combat aircraft inventory, and yet went on to not only sustain its air campaign but emerged victorious at the end of the short and

During the Second World War, the British air defences averaged an 8 per cent attrition rate while the attrition by German air defences was about 4 to 8 per cent, and 4 per cent for Japanese Air Defences.[2] These were much higher than the commonly acceptable figure of 2 to 3 per cent, but they did not halt the air campaigns and both the Allies and the Axis powers continued with their air campaigns. It, however, needs to be considered that, if the overall Allied air operations during the war are taken into account, the attrition rate falls to just about 0.97 per cent. This is considering that the Allies suffered a combat loss of 40,000 from 41,200,000 sorties.[3] The same figure can also be viewed differently – that the Allies suffered a loss of eighteen to nineteen aircraft every day, on all days, for the entire duration of the war. This may appear to be a very high figure, yet in terms of attrition rate seems manageable.

Attrition in prolonged wars

In this context, if the figures of 1,230 US aircraft lost in 720,980 sorties during the Korean War are taken, it reflects an attrition rate of 0.17 per cent. The low attrition rate is due to the large number of support missions which resulted in a lower attrition rate. The maximum losses were during close air support (CAS) and interdiction which were only 34 per cent of the total. If only the combat sorties are considered, the attrition rate works out to be 0.2 per cent or 2 per 1,000 sorties.[4]

Whichever figure is taken, what needs to be considered is that the Korean War was an asymmetric war with North Korea facing a far more formidable opponent in the air unlike the Second World War when two (*almost*) equal opponents faced each other in the air, and both sides suffered heavy losses in air-to-air combat. In Korea, the lesser number of US losses to air combat resulted in a lesser number of overall losses, and a lower attrition rate. A comparison with the attrition rate of the Second World War would thus be incorrect.

The same trend continued during the Vietnam War. The US Air Force flew a total of 5.25 million sorties over South Vietnam, North Vietnam, northern and southern Laos, and Cambodia, losing 2,251 fixed-wing aircraft, 1,737 because of hostile action and 514 for operational reasons.

This works out to an attrition rate of only 0.4 losses per 1,000 sorties which compares favourably with a 2.0 rate in Korea and the 9.7 figure during the Second World War. In sheer numbers, however, the US lost almost 10,000 fixed-wing and rotary-wing aircraft during the war. A low attrition rate does not hide this simple fact.

Similar to the experience in Korea, the US air forces suffered much higher attrition during their air campaigns against well-defended targets. To put this in perspective, the USAF suffered 21.4 per cent attrition while attacking industrial targets in the period from August 1964 to December 1967 and a 19 per cent loss on power stations and iron and steel plants, all targets which were well defended.

Taking the numbers of losses for specific aircraft, again a different perspective can be observed. The US lost 334 F-105s and 671 F-4s during the war, i.e. 12 per cent of its entire fleet. Similarly, 40 per cent of all the F-105 Thunderchiefs ever produced, i.e. 334 aircraft of the total 833, were lost during the war. Looking at the losses during Operation LINEBACKER II, the USAF lost thirty-one B-52s (fifteen according to its own records) from 741 sorties. The loss rate of 4.2 per cent (2.02 per cent if US figures are taken) is way beyond the overall attrition rate.

This only highlights the fact that the prolonged asymmetric wars in Korea and Vietnam, with a very large number of support sorties and an unevenly distributed AA network, resulted in a low attrition rate which is not necessarily a true reflection of losses suffered during a conflict.

Attrition in short wars

One of the first major, but short, wars in the jet age was the India-Pakistan War of 1965. The twenty-two-day war saw Indian and Pakistani air forces slug it out for the first time to end in a stalemate with no clear winner although the numbers and attrition rates reflect a win for the Indian Air Force. The Pakistani Air Force carried out a total of 2,364 sorties, suffering a loss of forty-three aircraft, i.e. an attrition rate of 1.82 per cent while the Indian Air Force had an attrition rate of 1.50 per cent with fifty-nine losses from over 3,937 sorties although some accounts suggest that the Indian Air Force had seventy-one losses, which means an attrition rate of 1.80 per cent, i.e. the same as the Pakistan Air Force.

Looking at some specific details, during the limited air superiority battle the IAF suffered an attrition rate of 20 per cent whereas the PAF suffered 12.5 per cent attrition. In the face of the heavy attrition both sides stopped using fighters by daylight, for counter-air battle.

In an example of an air force continuing in spite of suffering heavy losses, the Israeli Air Force continued with its counter-air operations even after having lost nineteen aircraft on Day One (5 June) of the Six Day War of 1967. These were lost from 490 sorties flown against Egypt and meant an attrition rate of just below 4 per cent. Overall, Israel undertook 1,000 sorties on Day One and suffered twenty losses – bringing down the attrition rate to 2 per cent.

Seen in numbers alone, the loss of twenty aircraft meant an attrition rate of 7 per cent on Day One alone and a loss of 9 per cent by Day Two when the losses went up to twenty-six.

Israel had achieved total air superiority by Day Two, i.e. 6 June, and thereafter carried out air operations in support of its army. During the remaining four days it lost a further twenty-two aircraft. A simple fact to remember is that losses to ground-based air defence cannot be *controlled* and will continue even if an air force is not opposed by the *enemy's* air force in the skies. Complete air superiority does not mean that there will be no further losses.

Overall, during the war Israel flew a total of 3,279 sorties and had an attrition rate of only 1.5 per cent.

During the India Pakistan War of 1971 the Indian Air Force flew a total of 7,300 sorties and suffered a loss of seventy-five aircraft while the Pakistan Air Force had forty-two losses from 3,027 sorties. The attrition rates for the Indian and Pakistani Air Forces were 1.02 and 1.4 per cent respectively.

The low attrition rate for the Indian Air Force is not reflective of the comparably high attrition suffered during the counter-air operations, similar to its experience in the previous war of 1965. The Indian Air Force carried out 400 counter-air operations and lost twenty-three aircraft, i.e. it had an attrition rate of 5.75 per cent, not as high as in 1965, when it had 20 per cent losses but still way above the average attrition rate. However, the Indian Air Force did not stop the counter-air operations with this attrition rate.

For close air support to the Indian Army, the Indian Air Force flew a total of 1,859 sorties and lost twenty-eight aircraft. The attrition rate was 1.5 per cent. The lowest attrition rate was in air defence missions when it lost only two aircraft from over 2,000 sorties.

Attrition by Cause

Asymmetric wars are characterized by minimal, if any, opposition by rival air forces and the AAA was the main contributory factor towards attrition. This is borne out during both the Korean and Vietnam Wars when the losses to AAA were over 95 per cent of the total suffered by the US/Coalition air forces in Korea and 83 per cent in Vietnam. The higher losses in Vietnam to enemy air forces were due mainly to better aircraft, like the MiG-21s available with the Communist air forces.

The high attrition from AAA can also be seen in the short intense wars. During the India Pakistan War of 1965, the Indian Air Force lost fifteen aircraft in the air to the Pakistan Air Force and ten to AAA while the Pakistan Air Force lost eighteen aircraft to the Indian Air Force and twenty-five to Indian AAA. During the 1971 War, the Indian Air Force lost double the aircraft to AAA than it lost to the Pakistan Air Force. For the Pakistan Air Force, there were more losses to the Indian Air Force (ten) than to AAA (seven).

Lower losses to AAA in such situations are due to fewer close support and offensive missions flown by an air force as it becomes defensive, trying to preserve its strength, as was done by the Pakistan Air Force in the 1971 war.

Note: Figures for 1965 War are of the Pakistan Air Force and of the Indian Air Force for the 1971 War.
During the Six Day War, it was the Arab AAA that claimed almost all the Israeli aircraft lost during the war as it shot down thirty-eight of them. Only three Israeli aircraft were lost in air-to-air combat during the six days.

An analysis of the attrition trends reveal that losses to AAA will continue even if an air force has gained complete control of the skies.

The only way to prevent, or control, losses to AAA is to curtail offensive missions and be on the defensive.

SAM Effectiveness

As the first surface-to-air missile had entered service after the Korean War, it was the AAA only which served as the ground-based air defence weapon system during that war. By the time the Gulf of Tonkin incident took place and the USA commenced its retaliatory air campaigns, surface-to-air missiles were operational with both the USA and the USSR. The United States' Nike Ajax was the world's first operational surface-to-air missile, entering service in 1954, which was followed by the Soviet S-25 Berkut in 1955. The first missile to be used against an enemy aircraft was, however, the Soviet S-75 Dvina (SA-2) which was used by China to shoot down a Taiwanese RB-57D Canberra high-altitude reconnaissance aircraft near Beijing on 7 October 1959, although news of this was deliberately kept under wraps to prevent the US from gaining any information about the capabilities of the new missile system.

The S-75 missile system and its capabilities were first revealed to the public when the newer version with longer range and higher-altitude capability, the V-750VN (13D) missile, was used to shoot down the U-2 of Francis Gary Powers overflying the Soviet Union on 1 May 1960. The S-75 system was also deployed in Cuba during the Cuban missile crisis, when it shot down another U-2 on 27 October 1962.

In 1965 North Vietnam was supplied with the S-75 missile system by the Soviet Union and it saw extensive use during the war. The missile was also supplied to Egypt and Syria and was used during the Six Day War and also in the War of Attrition.

Designed to take on high-flying aircraft, up to an altitude of 25,000 metres, the missile had a limitation in that it could not engage targets below 3,000 feet, thus restricting its efficacy against low-flying aircraft. This seriously affected its overall performance and the S-75 has often been criticized for having a very low kill ratio. The commonly referred to figures state that it took almost fifty Guideline missiles to shoot down an aircraft. The manner in which the missile system was deployed affected its use – from one SAM battery in 1965, North Vietnam deployed twenty-five batteries the next year and about thirty-five to forty by 1968. The SAM firings also increased proportionally, from about thirty launches per month in the initial stages to about 270 per month between July 1966 and October 1967.[1] The firings peaked during LINEBACKER II although the average firing rate was 220 missiles per month. According to Werrell, 5,366 to 6,037 missiles were fired between October 1967 and March 1968, claiming 115–128 US aircraft.

The SAM effectiveness at these figures comes to a very low kill ratio of just about 2 per cent, with an average of forty-seven missiles required to shoot down one aircraft. This was much lower than the initial kill probability of 5.7 per cent achieved by the S-75 in 1965 when a total of 194 missiles was used to shoot down eleven aircraft.[2] Momyer states that 150 aircraft were shot down by North Vietnam, firing 9,034 SAMs to have an overall kill ratio of 1.66 per cent or sixty missiles were used to shoot down one aircraft.

However, another US study on Vietnam air losses between 1961 and 1973, by Chris Hobson,[3] mentions the total losses to be 205 of which 195 were by SA-2 and ten by SA-7. Assuming the same number of missiles fired, the kill ratio achieved is 2 per cent which is more, but only marginally so, than the figures given in the earlier study.

As SA-2 was the front-line Soviet missile system, its performance was monitored keenly by the Soviets. The after action report, *Combat Actions of the Air Defense Forces and Air Forces of the Vietnamese People's Army in December 1972*, by Colonel General Anatoliy Ivanovich Khyupenen, who directed the Soviet air defence advisory effort in 1972, discusses the missile performance in detail.[4] The performance of the SA-2 was of interest to the Soviets as the B-52 was the primary US bomber that would be used against the Soviet Union in the event of a nuclear war. The aforementioned study is considered to be a detailed and balanced one, giving a fairly accurate account of the SA-2's performance.

The main areas of contention are the number of missiles fired by the North Vietnam Air Defences and the number of B-52s shot down. Taking details of the last campaign, i.e. LINEBAKER II, the number of missiles launched, as reported by the USAF, was 800 to 1,000 while the North Vietnamese and Soviets claim to have expended 266 missiles. The difference in numbers comes from the way the number of launches

Date and Time	Strike region	Total aircraft	Strike aircraft	Number combat ready AD Bns in strike region	Number of Bns participating in fight	Number of missiles at start of raid	Number of engagements	Missiles expended	Number of downed aircraft	Effectiveness of engagement	Average missile expenditure
12/18/1972 1935–2030	Hanoi	61	21	9	6	119	11 & 2	20 & 4	2 & 2	0.18 & .1	10.2
12/18/1972 2335–0030	Hanoi	70	24	9	2	99	4	9	No data	0	Nul
12/19/1972 0440–0546	Hanoi	66	24	9	9	90	19	35	1	0.05	35
12/19/1972 2000–2035	Hanoi	53	15	10	3	67	4	7	1	0.25	7
12/19/1972 2315–0036	Hanoi	106	42	10	3	60	4	6	0	0	Nul
12/20/1972 0430–0535	Hanoi	41	9	10	3	80	4	7	1	0.25	7
12/20/1972 1925–2050	Hanoi	82	36	9	4	73	4 & 2	10 & 3	3 & 1	.75 & .5	3.3 & 3
12/21/1972 0446–0554	Hanoi	69	21	9	6	83	13 & 1	20 & 1	4 & 0	.31 & 0	5 & 0
12/22/1972 0325–0418	Hanoi	69	21	9	6	88	10	17	3	0.3	5.7
12/23/1972 0445–0536	Hai Phong	52	18	5	5	59	11	20	2	0.18	10

12/26/1972 2215–2320	Hanoi	86	36	13	13	125	24	45	6	0.25	7.5
12/26/1972 2215–2320	Hai Phong	49	15	5	3	62	3 & 3	6 & 6	1 & 2	.33 & .67	6 & 3
12/27/1972 2230–2339	Hanoi	145	51	12	11	101	17 & 3	30 & 6	4 & 0	.25 & 0	7.5 & nul
12/28/1972 2140–2235	Hanoi	130	48	11	4	79	4 & 1	6 & 2	2 & 0	.5 & 0	3 & nul
12/29/1972 2300–2340	Hanoi	94	9	8	3	71	3	6	1	0.33	6
Total		1173	390				135 & 12	244 & 22	31 & 5	.23 & .43	7.9 & 4.4

Table 1: Missile ADA combat repelling mass raids by Strategic Aviation.
Note: Strike aircraft in column 4 are only those B-52s that entered the missile engagement zone.
Note: Columns 8–11 show first the engagements with B-52s and second with tactical aviation.

are detected and reported. They are counted and reported by anyone who sees them. Taking all reports into account, it is difficult to calculate how many were actually fired. Even electronics intelligence (ELINT) can only detect launch signals, but not actual launches, as many launch sequences may be initiated but not completed. There is also a tendency for air forces to exaggerate the number of missiles fired at an aircraft and avoided by them.

Considering that the missile supply by the Soviets was dependent on the expenditure, it can be assumed that they would have a better count of the same. The missile expenditure and number of B-52s shot down, as indicated in the Soviet report is shown on the previous page.

Quoting from the report:

> The number of missiles affected firing effectiveness. Most firings (99 of 135) were carried out with two missiles, downing 23 B-52 aircraft (firing effectiveness 0.23); 31 firings used one missile, downing 4 aircraft (effectiveness – 0.13); five firings were carried out with three missiles, downing 4 aircraft (effectiveness – 0.8).

The overall missile expenditure to shoot down one B-52 was 7.5 missiles, a far better performance than that claimed by the USAF – *'fifty SA-2 were required to shoot down one aircraft'*. It also merits consideration that the SA-2 was first fielded in 1957 and was a fairly obsolete and cumbersome system by 1972 standards. To judge its performance in a role for which it was never designed may not be correct, even though the way it changed the rules of air operations is no mean achievement.

Appendix I

The Soviet View of the North Vietnamese Ground Air Defense

At the start of the LINEBACKER-2 air operation, the air defence missile forces of the Vietnamese People's Army had thirty-six air defence missile battalions armed with the Soviet-manufactured SA-75 M 'Dvina' [SA-2 Guideline] missile system. They were supported by nine technical battalions. The SA-75M missile system was a three-component variant employing the V-750M missile with a P-12 [Spoonrest] target-acquisition radar and a target-engagement station.

These battalions were organized into nine air defence missile regiments and these were further organized into four air defence divisions. The divisions were assigned to three air defence groups (Hanoi, Haiphong and the 4th Combat Zone).

The bulk of this force was concentrated on the approaches to the capital of the DRVN, Hanoi. In this region were the Hoi Bai, Kep and Gia Lam airbases; the Dong-An and Yuen-Vien railyards; the port and industrial region of Hai Phong; as well as the crossing sites, roads, road intersections and force concentrations in the provinces of the 4th Combat Zone – Thanh-Hoa and Nghe-An Provinces.

While warding off the massive strikes by US strategic, tactical and carrier aviation, the missile air defence forces of the Vietnamese People's Army conducted over 180 engagements, two-thirds of which were against B-52s. In all, they destroyed fifty-four aircraft (thirty-one B-52s, thirteen F4s and ten A-6s or A-7s) with the expenditure of 244 missiles against the B-52s, that is to say that an average of 7.9 missiles were expended for every B-52 aircraft shot down. If the tactical and carrier-based aircraft are singled out, then 3.3 rockets were expended for every aircraft shot down. (See Tables 1 & 2). Without going into technical details, during the course of this combat, they overcame various types of interference and obstacles employed by the US aircraft to interrupt missile engagement, while warding off the strikes of strategic, tactical and carrier aviation in December 1972.

Let us look at two typical fights over Hanoi on the early morning of 19 December and the night of 26 December 1972.

In the first example, there were nineteen engagements which shot down one aircraft out of sixty-six strategic bombers [table shows twenty-four strategic bombers out of sixty-six total aircraft]. In the second example, the air defence missile forces conducted twenty-four engagements which expended forty-five missiles and shot down six B-52s out of a force of more than eighty aircraft, including thirty-six strategic bombers (see Table 1). The average effectiveness of the engagement was 0.25 and the average expenditure of missiles to down an aircraft shrank to 7.5. The success was due to the growth of co-ordination among the personnel teams of the command posts at all levels and their increase in combat experience.

In the second example, the combat teams of the regimental and battalion command posts were more confident and determined than earlier, they were tactically skilled in selecting targets for engagement, they were more capable of fully utilizing the missile navigation system to destroy the target despite an electronic interference backdrop, and skilfully employed the missile navigation system through chaff and jamming. The missile launches were at an optimum distance. Thus, thirty-six of forty-five rockets were fired at a range of twenty-five to thirty-five kilometres. In five engagements, in which targets were destroyed, the launch distance was twenty-eight to thirty-two kilometres. However, besides this, there was a series of mistakes. Two detachments of B-52s were mistakenly identified as groups of F-4s and were not engaged. Several battalions conducted only a single engagement when the air situation and the number of ready missiles [elevated on launchers] would have allowed them to conduct no less than three engagements. As before, they violated the rule as to the number of missiles that should be fired at a target in an engagement [three]. For example, four of twenty-four engagements involved only one missile launch and two of these were 'tail chasers' pursuing a target that had already passed over the firing point. In only one engagement were the prescribed three missiles launched and in the rest of the engagements, only two missiles were launched.

One of the techniques of missile combat during this period was to engage using the concentrated fire of several missile battalions on a single target or group of targets. This technique proved most effective. During twenty-three raids, this massed engagement technique killed thirteen B-52s while using a total of ninety-eight missiles. At the same time, massed engagements which concentrated the fires of over three battalions was ineffective due to problems with command and control of multiple battalions.

During the first two days, the missile forces participated in the effort to ward off five mass raids by strategic aviation. In these fights, the effectiveness of the engagements was somewhat lower and achieved an overall 0.9. Over nineteen missiles were expended to knock down each of the four aircraft.

The effectiveness of the engagements increased through the acquisition of combat experience and the growth of the capabilities of the personnel of the air defense missile forces of the Vietnamese People's Army. Thus, on the following days, the combat readiness grew and the average effectiveness of the engagements rose to 0.27 while the average expenditure of missiles to down a single aircraft decreased to 6.6.

Analysis of the general character and effectiveness of the engagements against strategic aviation shows that the effectiveness that they achieved confirmed the high combat attributes of the Soviet SA-75M air defence missile.

The air defence missile forces repelled the air attacks under conditions of various forms of interference which were applied in the course of the US aviation raids. There was jamming, chaff and impulse-response jamming.

Further, the combat positions of the air defence missile battalions were repeatedly subjected to blast and fragmentation bombs and Shrike anti-radar missiles. However, only nine strikes (eight blast and fragmentation bombs and one Shrike) were successful for the enemy: they put six battalions out of action temporarily. These strikes destroyed the early-warning antenna station, five DES-75 diesel-powered electric generators, nine missile launchers, fifteen missiles, one ATS-59 tractor and damaged cables in three battalions. One air defence missile battalion was put out of action by the Shrike missile that knocked the missile-guidance system off-line. This unit had switched on their high-voltage radar for eighty seconds (if the high-voltage radar is turned on for fifteen to twenty seconds or less, the anti-radar missile does not lock onto the target). It is possible that the jamming supporting the B-52 strike groups interfered with the tactical air force's ability to launch anti-radar missiles.

The missile crews were inadequately trained to fight when jammed and under aerial attack. Fearing Shrike anti-radar missile strikes, the battalion launch crews tried to fire at the B-52s without turning on the high-voltage radars at all during the firing cycle, which prevented them from detecting targets under jamming and switching to manual guidance.

[Author's note: this commentary on the lack of US anti-radar missile effectiveness contrasts with Khyupenen's own words in another piece he wrote about the activities of the 'Radar Troops' during LINEBACKER II: 'It should be noted, however, that there were no serious instances of material damage despite the large number of anti-radar projectiles that were launched against the radar companies' positions.' Author Drenkowski interviewed a returning PoW who had been driven past a large 'park' of wrecked radar vans in a region near Hanoi. He was able to count over 400 damaged vans in the single park. Many had pieces of Shrike or Standard ARM AGM78 missiles plainly visible in the wrecked equipment. Many or most could have been damaged during the preceding aerial combat of Operation LINEBACKER (May-October 1972) as well as during Operation LINEBACKER II. However, it is apparent from his information that the anti-radar missiles and attacks may have been far more effective than Khyupenen was willing to admit in his reports.]

The most successful missile firings against B-52s combined the active and passive guidance operating mode. Switching on the radar for five to seven seconds prior to a missile launch made it possible to clarify the aerial and jamming conditions and, of particular importance, to evaluate the presence of chaff in the area where the missile was expected to intercept its target. Then, the missiles were launched with the radar switched off to provide protection against anti-radar missiles. The operator then turned on the radar for the missile guidance terminal phase (fifteen to eighteen seconds before intercept), in case a target blip could be detected. Three

B-52s were brought down with the conventional method where the radar acquired the target and stayed on for the entire engagement. Three B-52s were destroyed out of seven attempts using the active and passive guidance operating mode.

Proper selection of missile launch distance had a major impact on the effectiveness of the firings at B-52 aircraft in jamming conditions (Map 3). The most effective firings were those with a launch distance of thirty-thirty-five kilometres.

When the strategic bombers deployed chaff during the raid, 64 of 244 missiles reached their targets, thirty-seven self-destructed at terminal guidance, and the rest exploded in the target area but did not destroy the target aircraft. Chaff deployed by the B-52s caused some missiles to detonate. This was possible with tail-chasing as well as head-on firings since the lead aircraft dumps chaff into the lower hemisphere. Not a single B-52 was destroyed in six tail-chasing firings, although all the missiles detonated in the area of the target.

The number of missiles affected firing effectiveness. Most firings (99 of 135) were carried out with two missiles, downing twenty-three B-52 aircraft (firing effectiveness 0.23); thirty-one firings used one missile, downing four aircraft (effectiveness – 0.13); five firings were carried out with three missiles, downing four aircraft (effectiveness – 0.8). This confirms that the most effective firings were those with three missiles. Notwithstanding air attack and jamming, the DRVN's air defence missile forces were able to inflict considerable damage on US strategic aircraft. A combination of missile and anti-aircraft artillery fire was particularly effective.

Anti-aircraft artillery was used primarily against US tactical and carrier-borne aircraft with missile forces participating only when they were not engaging B-52s.

Most of the firings (more than 76 per cent) at tactical and deck-based aircraft were carried out in jamming conditions of one kind or another with 0.47 effectiveness. The reason for this relatively high effectiveness is that the firings were carried out selectively and in favourable conditions, i.e. with weak or moderate jamming and no target manoeuvre. Seventy-five per cent of the firings were at non-manoeuvring targets. About 37 per cent were carried out with one missile, and more than 58 per cent

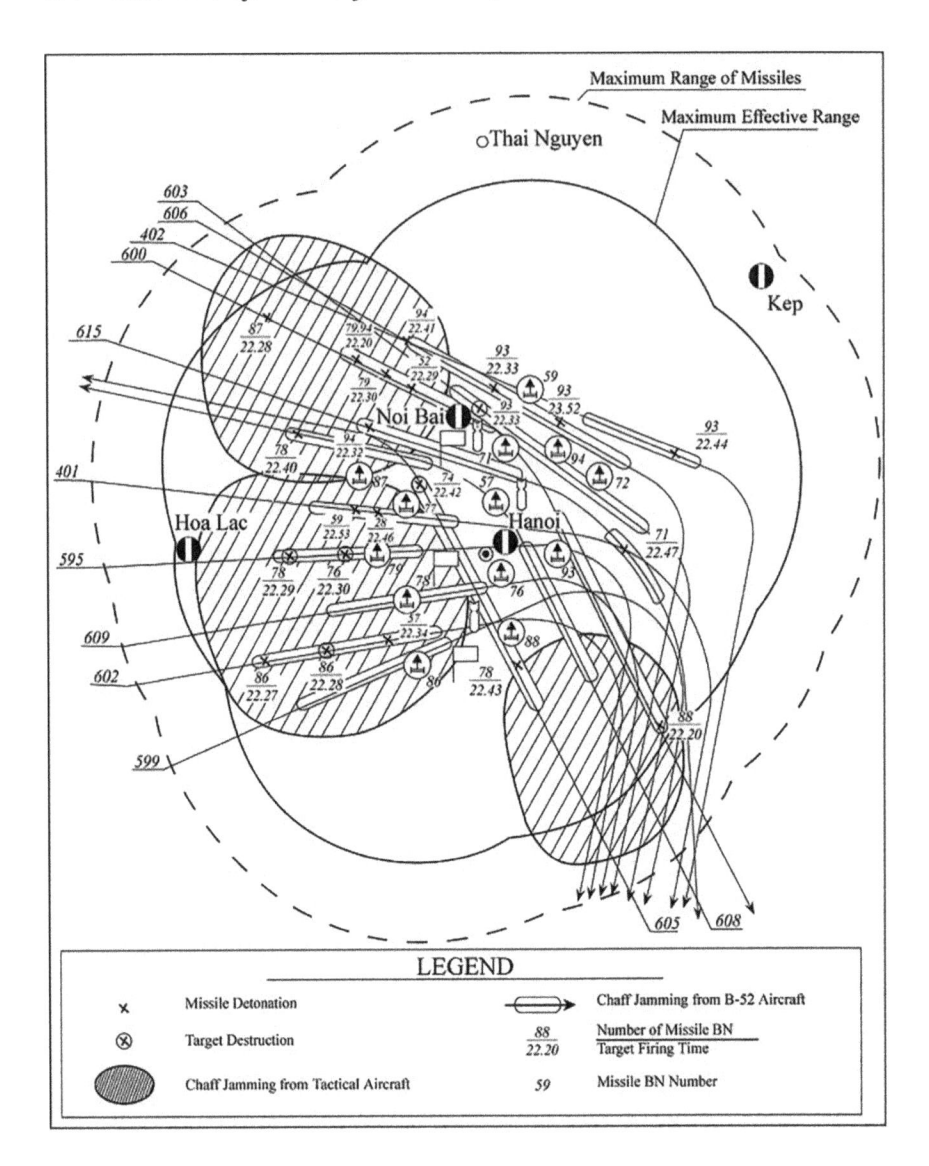

174   Anti-Aircraft Artillery in Combat, 1950–1972

[Figure: Map showing missile engagement zones around Hanoi, Noi Bai, Hoa Lac, Kep, and Thai Nguyen, with maximum range of missiles and maximum effective range indicated.]

LEGEND

Symbol	Meaning	Symbol	Meaning
×	Missile Detonation	⇐⇒	Chaff Jamming from B-52 Aircraft
⊗	Target Destruction	88 / 22.20	Number of Missile BN / Target Firing Time
(shaded)	Chaff Jamming from Tactical Aircraft	59	Missile BN Number

with two. Of forty-six firings at tactical and carrier-borne aircraft, eighteen (or 39 per cent) were at targets flying at low altitude (up to 1,000 metres), where aircraft have limited maneuverability. There were eleven tail-chasing firings and eight aircraft were destroyed (firing effectiveness 0.72). [See Table 2 on page 176].

The reasons why tail-chasing firings were highly effective are as follows. The aircraft generally discontinued anti-missile manoeuvres

The Soviet View of the North Vietnamese Ground Air Defense   175

after passing the battalion's position. Jamming became much less intense and anti-radar missiles were limited by the large flight-heading angle.

Firings were more difficult when aircraft flew at altitudes above 1,000 metres. Here the aircraft were making anti-missile course and altitude manoeuvres. Jamming was effective at these altitudes and Shrike anti-radar missiles were most likely to be used.

The EB-66 jammer aircraft jammed the frequency band of the P-12 [Spoonrest] radar. Usually, one or two of the four radar frequency channels were less jammed. This made it possible to select a frequency channel with minimal noise and track targets for one to two minutes, after which the enemy would again jam the selected frequency channel. US Navy vessels in the Gulf of Tonkin also conducted jamming.

Tactical aircraft (F-4 and F-105) jammed only in the frequency band of the SA-75M target-tracking channels. Jamming was rarely used on the missile channels and did not disrupt missile guidance because they had a high level of anti-jamming protection.

Farther away from the missile battalion launch positions (fifty to sixty kilometres), the tactical aircraft usually flew in wings in a wedge, echelon or paired stack formation. Their jammers were switched on at a distance of seventy to ninety kilometres. Since every aircraft in the group was jamming, they could not be acquired by radar.

F-105 aircraft that were detecting and attacking anti-aircraft defences did so without jamming in order to locate electronic equipment and strike it with anti-radar missiles. These aircraft usually switched on their jammers after detecting a missile launch.

F-111A low-altitude flights were made with jammers switched off, allowing for a stealth approach to the strike object. Jammers were only switched on when a missile launch was detected. The aircraft would simultaneously perform an anti-missile horizontal turn. A blip from an F-111A could still be picked up at eight to ten kilometres against background noise, making it possible to track the target manually using angular data and distance.

Carrier-borne aircraft used special jammers and impulse response jamming by strike aircraft and cover and support group aircraft. This caused thirty to forty blips from real and false targets to appear simultaneously on the operators' screens even at five kilometres range.

Date and Time	Strike region	Total aircraft	Strike aircraft	Number combat ready AD Bns in strike region	Number of Bns participating in fight	Number of missiles at start of raid	Number of engagements	Missiles expended	Number of downed aircraft	Effectiveness of engagement	Average missile expenditure
12/19/1972 0410–0510	Hai Phong	30	20	7	4	89	4	5	2	0.5	2.5
12/19/1972 1130–1240	Hanoi	30	12	10	6	71	6	10	2	0.33	5
12/20/1972 0030–0115	Hai Phong	35	25	7	1	78	1	1	1	1	1
12/20/1972 0400–0600	Hai Phong	15 to 20	10 to 15	7	2	78	2	3	2	1	1.5
12/20/1972 0700–0800	Hai Phong	15 to 20	10 to 15	7	7	82	10	17	6	0.6	2.8
12/22/1972 0526–0600	Hai Phong	16	10	5	4	55	4	7	2	0.5	3.5
12/23/1972 1345–1430	Hanoi	54	16	12	3	95	3	6	2	0.67	3
12/27/1972 1330–1430	Hanoi Hai Phong	100	40	17	1	134	1	2	0	0	Nul
12/27/1972 1555–1635	Hanoi	32	12	12	3	101	3	4	1	0.33	4
Total		327–337	155–165				34	55	18	0.53	3

Table 2: Missile ADA combat in repulsing mass raids by Tactical and Carrier Aviation.

Jamming from B-52s was detectable at a distance of 180 to 200 kilometres. Jamming from the B-52s was more stable in terms of width, clarity and intensity than noise bands from tactical aircraft, and they left a deeper residue (tailing). Jamming was most effective at a distance of twenty-four to twenty-five kilometres and a flight altitude of 10,000 to 12,000 metres.

Source: A. I. Khyupenen, Strategicheskkaya aviatsiya SShA v operatsii 'Laynbeker-2' [*US Strategic Aviation in Operation 'Linebacker-2'*, Voenno-istoricheskii zhurnal [*Military-Historical Journal*], February 2005.

Appendix II

Vietnam War

North Vietnamese AAA Number of Guns in Each Route Pack
October 1967–March 1968

Route Pack	1	2	3	4	5	6A	6B	Total
24 Oct. 1967	1,411	533	550	784	693	2,238	910	7,119
29 Nov. 1967	1,270	514	525	707	686	2,084	784	6,570
20 Dec. 1967	1,190	526	539	673	698	2,104	815	6,545
10 Jan. 1968	1,177	529	561	540	695	2,140	815	6,457
10 Feb. 1968	1,137	340	418	615	695	2,124	962	6,291
20 Mar. 1968	1,065	360	440	609	672	1,712	937	5,795

Although the SAM and MiG threats got more attention, *about 68 per cent of the aircraft losses were to anti-aircraft fire.* As of 20 March 1968, North Vietnam had anti-aircraft artillery at 1,158 sites. A total of 5,795 guns was deployed, of which 4,802 were 37mm to 57mm and 993 were 85mm to 100mm.

Source: Gen. William W. Momyer, USAF (Retd), *Air Power in Three Wars (USAF)*.

North Vietnamese SAM Effectiveness

	Missiles Fired	Aircraft Lost	Effectiveness
1965	194	11	5.7%
1966	1,096	31	2.8%
1967	3,202	56	1.75%
1968	322	3	0.9%
1972	4,244	49	1.15%

Note: North Vietnam deployed the Soviet-built SA-2 Guideline surface-to-air missile in 1965. Its effectiveness diminished as US airmen developed defensive tactics, added electronic counter-measures and sent 'Wild Weasel' aircraft to destroy, deter and intimidate the SAM batteries. A few SA-3s, effective at lower altitudes, were introduced later in the war, as were shoulder-fired SA-7s, which were deadly against slow-flying aircraft in South Vietnam.

Source: Gen. William W. Momyer, USAF (Retd), *Air Power in Three Wars (USAF)*.

USAF Bomb Damage Assessment Claims in North Vietnam

	Mar 1965–Oct 1968		Apr 1972–Jan 1973	
	Destroyed	Damaged	Destroyed	Damaged
AAA Sites	1,682	1,196	217	89
SAM Sites	80	93	40	5
Radar Sites	109	152	55	19

Note: *Bomb damage assessment is both difficult and imprecise. These figures are better taken as a distribution of bombing effort rather than as an exact tally of the damage inflicted.* If the CIA report (mentioned in the text) is referred to, no SAM sites were destroyed, nor were any radars destroyed. The claims of destruction caused to AD sites is speculative at best.

Source: John T. Correll, 'The Vietnam War Almanac', *Air Force Magazine*, September 2004.

Summary of US Fixed-Wing Aircraft Lost to SAMs 1965–1973

Year	SAM Type		Total
	SA-2	SA-7	
1965	13	–	13
1966	35	–	35
1967	62	–	62
1968	12	–	12
1970	1	–	1
1971	7	–	7
1972	63	9	72
1973	2	1	3
Total	195	10	205

Source: USAF in Vietnam, The Air Force Association, https://higherlogicdownload.s3.amazonaws.com/AFA/6379b747-7730-4f82-9b45-a1c80d6c8fdb/UploadedImages/MitchellPublications/TheAirForceandtheVietnamWar.pdf

Losses by Type

F-4 Phantom	52		F-8 Corsair	11
F-105 Thunderchief	31		A-4E Skyhawk	32
A-6A Intruder	10		RA-5C Vigilante	3
RF-101 Voodoo	5		F-104 Starfighter	3
A-1H Skyraider	5		RB-66C Destroyer	2
EF-10B Skynight	1		A-7	14
EB-66	2		O-1 Bird Dog	3
O-2 Skymaster	3		TA-4F Skyhawk	1
RA-5C Vigilante	1		AC-130 Spectre	2
OV-10A Bronco	6		B-52D/G	17

US Aircraft Losses Aug 1964–1967

Target	Sorties Number	Sorties Percentage	Combat Losses Number	Combat Losses Percent	Rate
Industry	1,030	1.0	22	8.7	21.4
Power Stations	630	0.6	12	4.7	19.0
Iron and Steel Plants	280	0.3	8	3.2	19.0
POL	120	0.1	2	0.8	16.7
Land Transport System	75,410	70.5	102	40.5	1.4
Highways	62,000	58.0	40	15.9	0.6
Railways	13,4100	12.5	62	24.6	4.6
All others	30,500	28.5	128	50.8	4.2
Total	106,940		252		2.4

Comparison of Losses during ROLLING THUNDER 1967 and LINEBACKER

Cause	Service	1967 Subtotal	1967 Percentage of Total	Linebacker Subtotal	Linebacker Percentage of Total
AAA	USN	65	20.25	15	15.79
AAA	USAF	101	31.46	11	11.58
AAA	USMC	9	2.80	3	3.16
CFIT	USN	4	1.25	3	3.16
CFIT	USAF	4	1.25	0	0.00
CFIT	USMC	0	0.00	0	0.00
Hostile Fire	USN	1	0.31	0	0.00
Hostile Fire	USAF	1	0.31	0	0.00
Hostile Fire	USMC	0	0.00	0	0.00
Malfunction	USN	5	1.56	0	0.00
Malfunction	USAF	2	0.62	1	1.05
Malfunction	USMC	0	0.00	0	0.00
Mid Air	USN	0	0.00	0	0.00
Mid Air	USAF	4	1.25	0	0.00
Mid Air	USMC	0	0.00	0	0.00
MiG	USN	3	0.93	1	1.05
MiG	USAF	21	6.54	24	25.26
MiG	USMC	0	0.00	0	0.00

		1967		Linebacker	
Cause	Service	Subtotal	Percentage of Total	Subtotal	Percentage of Total
Pilot Error	USN	1	0.31	0	0.00
	USAF	0	0.00	0	0.00
	USMC	0	0.00	0	0.00
SA-2	USN	34	10.59	16	16.84
	USAF	30	9.35	11	11.58
	USMC	2	0.62	1	1.05
Small Arms	USN	14	4.36	1	1.05
	USAF	13	4.05	3	3.16
	USMC	1	0.31	0	0.00
Unknown	USN	2	0.62	3	3.16
	USAF	4	1.25	1	1.05
	USMC	0	0.00	1	1.05
Total		321	100.00	95	100.00

Source: Alfred Price, *The History of US Electronic Warfare, Vol. III* (Arlington, VA: The Association of Old Crows, 2000).

Appendix III

The Bangladesh War 1971

Indian Air Losses of the 1971 War
Total Losses

TYPE	EAST	WEST	TOTAL
MiG-21	2	6 (2)	8
Sukhoi Su-7	1	18 (1)	19
Hunter	12 (3)	11 (2)	23
Canberra	1	4 (1)	5
Gnat	–	3 (2)	3
Mystère IVa	–	5 (2)	5
HF-24	–	4	4
Vampire	–	1	1
Dakota	1 (1)	–	1
Others (Army/Navy)	–	2	2
Helicopters	2 (2)	2 (1)	4
Total	19 (6)	56 (11)	75 (17)

Losses by Cause

Type of Loss	East	West	Total	% age
AAA/Ground Fire	10	26	36	48 %
Air-to-Air Combat	3	15	18	30 %
Destroyed on Ground	–	2	2	2 %
Undetermined	–	2	2	1 %
Accidents	6	11	17	22 %
Total	19	56	75	

The Bangladesh War 1971

Pakistani Air Losses of the 1971 War

Cause	East	West	Total
Air Combat	5	5	10
AAA/Ground Fire	–	7	7
Destroyed on ground -	–	8	8
Accidents -	–	4	4
Destroyed by PAF	13	–	13
Total	18	24	42

Losses by Type

Aircraft Type	East	West	Total
F-86 Sabre	16	12	28
F-104 Starfighter	0	3	3
MiG-19 (F-6)	0	4	4
T-33	2	0	2
B-57 Canberra	0	5	5
Others	5	4	9
Total	23	28	51

Bibliography

Books

Aloni, Shlomo, *Arab-Israeli Air Wars*, Osprey Publishing, 2001.
——, *Israeli Mirage and Nesher Aces*, Osprey Publishing, 2004.
——, *Israeli Phantom II Aces*, Osprey Publishing, 2004.
Amarinder Singh, TS Gill, *The Monsoon War: Young Officers Reminisce: 1965 India-Pakistan War,* Lustre Press, Roli Books, New Delhi, 2015.
Appleman, Roy E., *South to the Naktong, North to the Yalu: United States Army in the Korean War*, Department of the Army, Washington, D.C., 1998.
Bajwa, Farooq, *From Kutch to Tashknet*, Pentagon Books, New Delhi 2012.
Berger, Carl, ed. *The United States Air Force in Southeast Asia, 1961–1973*, Office of Air Force History, Wshington D.C., 1977.
Boniface, Roger, *MIGs Over North Vietnam: The Vietnam People's Air Force in Combat, 1965–75*, Crecy Publishing, Manchester, 2017.
Boose, Donald W., *The Ashgate Research Companion to the Korean War*, Ashgate Publishing Limited, Surrey, 2014.
Bowman, Martin W., *Cold War Jet Combat: Air to Air Jet Combat 1950–1972* Pen and Sword Books, Barnsley, 2016.
Bonds, R. and D. Miller, *Illustrated Directory of Special Forces*, Zenith Imprint, 2002.
Boyne, Walter J., *Beyond the Wild Blue: A History of the U.S. Air Force, 1947–2007* (2nd edition), Thomas Dunne Books, New York, 2007.
Bukharin, Oleg, Frank Von Hippel, *Russian Strategic Nuclear Forces*, MIT Press, 2004.
Chakravorty, BC, *History of The Indo-Pak War 1965*, History Division, Ministry of Defence, Government of India, New Delhi, 1992.
Cheng Guan Ang, *The Vietnam War from the Other Side*, Routledge, Abingdon (U.K.), 2002.
Clodfelter, Mark, *The Limits of Airpower: The American Bombing of North Vietnam*, University of Nebraska Press, Lincoln, 2006.
Clodfelter, Michael, V*ietnam in Military Statistics: A History of the Indochina Wars, 1792–1991*, McFarland & Company, Inc., Jefferson, NC & London, 1995.
Corum, Colonel Delbert; Burbage, Major Paul, eds, *The Tale of Two Bridges and The Battle for the Skies over North Vietnam, 1964–1972*, Air University Press, Maxwell Air Force Base, Alabama, 1976.

Croizat, VJ, *Lessons of the War in Indochina*, Vol. 2, RAND Report RM-5271-PR, RAND, Santa Monica, California, 1967.

Davidson, Philip B. Lieutenant General USA, Ret., *Vietnam at War, The History 1946–1975*, Presidio Press, Novato, 1988.

Dayan, Moshe, *Diary of the Sinai Campaign*, Schocken Books, New York, 1965.

Department of State, *Aggression from the North: The Record of North Vietnam's Campaign to Conquer South Vietnam*, U.S. Government Printing Office, Washington, DC, 1965.

Dor, A., *The Mirage IIIC Shahak* – IAF Aircraft Series No. 3, Milan, Italy, AD Graphics, 1999.

Drew, Dennis, *Rolling Thunder 1965: Anatomy of a Failure*, Air University Press, Maxwell Air Force Base, Alabama, 1986.

Dunstan, Simon, and Peter Dennis, *The Six Day War, 1967: Sinai*, Osprey, Oxford, U.K., 2009.

Dupuy, Trevor, *Elusive Victory: The Arab-Israeli Wars, 1947–1974*, Harper and Row, New York, 1978.

Elliot, David W.P., *The Vietnamese War: Revolution and Social Change in the Mekong Delta 1930–1975*, M.E. Sharp Inc, New York, 2007.

Fall, Bernard, *Hell in a Very Small Place: The Siege of Dien Bien Phu*, J. P. Lippincott, Philadelphia, Pennsylvania, 1966.

Flintham, Victor, *Air Wars and Aircraft: A Detailed Record of Air Combat, 1945 to the Present*, Facts on File Yearbook, Inc., New York, 1990.

Frankum, Robert Bruce, *Like Rolling Thunder: The Air War in Vietnam, 1964–1975*, Rowland & Littlefield, 2005.

Futrell, Robert F., *The United States Air Force in Korea 1950–1953*, United States Govt Printing Office, Washington D.C., 1997.

——, *The United States Air Force in Southeast Asia: The Advisory Years to 1965*, Office of Air Force History, Washington, D.C, 1981.

Greenwood, John, Von Hardesty and Robin Higham, *Russian Aviation and Air Power in the Twentieth Century*, Routledge, 2014.

Hai, Kutub, *The Patton Wreckers*, Times Group Books, New Delhi, 2015.

Hammel, Eric, *Six Days in June*, Clarks Scribner and Sons, New York, 1972.

Head, William P., *War Above the Clouds: B-52 Operations During the Second Indochina War and the Effects of the Air War on Theory and Doctrine*, Air University Press, Maxwell Air Force Base, Alabama, 2002.

Herzog, Chaim, *The Arab-Israeli Wars: War and Peace in the Middle East*, Random House, New York, 1982.

Hobson, Chris, *Vietnam Air Losses, United States Air Force, Navy and Marine Corps Fixed-Wing Aircraft Losses in Southeast Asia 1961–1973*, Midland Publishing, Great Britain, 2001.

Hogg, Ian V., *Anti-Aircraft Artillery*, The Crowood Press, Ramsbury, Marlborough, 2002.

Katz, Sam, *Israeli Elite Units since 1948*, Osprey Publishing, Oxford, 1988.

Jackson, Robert, *Air War Korea 1950–1953*, Motorbooks International, Osceola, Wisconsin, 1998.

Knaack, Marcelle S., *Encyclopedia of U.S Air Force Aircrfat and Missiel Systems, Vol I*, Office of Air Force History, Washington DC, 1978.

Jacob Van Staavern, *Gradual Failure: The Air War over North Vietnam: 1965–1966*, Air Force History and Museums Program, United States Air Force, Washington, D.C., 2002.

Jacob Neufeld and George M. Watson, Jr.(Ed.), *Coalition Air Warfare in the Korean War 1950–1953*, Proceedings Air Force Historical Foundation Symposium Andrews AFB, Maryland, May 7–8, 2002, U.S. Air Force History and Museums Program Washington, D.C., 2005.

Jagan Mohan PVS and Chopra, Samir, *India Pakistan Air War 1965*, Manohar Books, New Delhi, 2005.

Jagan Mohan PVS and Samir Chopra, *Eagles over Bangladesh, The Indian Air Force in the 1971 Liberation War*, Harper Collins, New Delhi, 2013.

Katz, Sam, *Israeli Elite Units since 1948*, Osprey Publishing, Oxford, 1988.

Lal, P.C., *My Years with IAF*, Lancer Publishers, New Delhi, 1986.

Lambeth, Benjamin S., *The Transformation of American Air Power*, Cornell University Press, Ithaca, 2000.

Marolda, Edward J., *By Sea, Air, and Land: An Illustrated History of the U.S. Navy and the War in Southeast Asia*, Naval Historical Center, Washington DC, 1994.

Marshall L. Michel, *Clashes: Air Combat Over North Vietnam 1965–1972*, Naval Institute Press, Annapolis, 1997.

Merky, Peter, and Polmar, Norman, *The Naval Air War in Vietnam*. The Nautical & Aviation Publishing Company of America, Mount Pleasant, South Carolina, 1986.

McCarthy, Don, *The Sword of David: The Israeli Air Force at War*, Pen and Sword, Barnsley, 2013.

McCarthy, James R.; Allison, George B., *Linebacker II: A View from the Rock*, Air University Press, Maxwell Air Force Base, Alabama, 1979.

Morocco, John, *Rain of Fire: Air War, 1969–1973*, Boston Publishing Company, Boston, 1985.

Mossman Billy, *Ebb and Flow November 1950–July 1951*, Centre of Military History, United States Army, Washington D.C., 1990.

Mossman B.C., *The Effectiveness of Air Interdiction during the Korean War*, Office of the Chief of Military History, Department of The Army, Washington DC, 1966.

Moyar, Mark, *Triumph Forsaken: The Vietnam War 1954–1965*, Cambridge University Press, New York, 2006.

Nicolle, David; Cooper, Tom, *Arab MiG-19 and MiG-21 Units in Combat*. Osprey Publishing, Oxford, 2004.

Nordeen, Lon O., *Air Warfare in Missile Age*, Smithsonian, Washington D.C., 1985.

Nordeen, Lon O.; Nicolle, David, *Phoenix Over the Nile – A History of Egyptian Air Power 1922–1994*, Smithsonian, Washington D.C., 1996.

Norton, Bill, *Air War on the Edge – A History of the Israel Air Force and its Aircraft since 1947*, Midland Publishing, 2004.

O'Ballance, Edgar, *Electronic War in the Middle East*, Hamden, Conn: Anchor Books, 1974.

Oren, Michael, *Six Days of War*, Presidio Press, New York, 2003.

Palit, D.K., *History of Regiment of Artillery Indian Army*, Leo Cooper, London, 1972.

Pradhan, R.D., *1965 War, The Inside Story: Defence Minister Y.B. Chavan's Diary of India-Pakistan War* Atlantic Publishers and Distributors Pvt Ltd, New Delhi, 2007.

Prasad, S.N., *India Pakistan War of 1971: A History*, Natraj Publishers, Dehra Dun, 2014.

Rabin, Yitzhak, *The Rabin Memoirs*. Little, Brown and Company, Boston, 1979.

Riza, Shaukat, *Izzat-O-Iqbal, History of Pakistan Artillery 1947–1971*, Published by School of Artillery, Naushera, Pakistan, 1980.

Routledge, Brigadier N.W., *History of Royal Regiment of Artillery: Anti Aircraft Artillery 1914–1955*, Brassey's, London, 1994.

Schlight, Colonel John, *A War Too Long: The USAF in Southeast Asia, 1961–1975*, Air Force History and Museums Program, Washington, DC, 1996.

Schlight, Colonel John, *The War in South Vietnam: The Years of the Offensive, 1965–1968*, Air Force History and Museums Program, Washington, DC, 1999.

Seidov, Igor, and Stuart Britton, *Red Devils over the Yalu: A Chronicle of Soviet Aerial Operations in the Korean War*, Helion and Company, Warwick, UK, 2014.

Shalom, Danny, *Phantoms over Cairo – Israeli Air Force in the War of Attrition (1967–1970)* (in Hebrew), Bavir Aviation & Space Publications, Rishon Le-Zion, Israel, 2007,

——, and Kera'am Be-yom Bahir, *Like a Bolt from the Blue*, Bavir, Rishon Le-Zion, Israel 2002,

Shulimson, Dr Jack and Johnson, Maj. Charles M., *U.S. Marines In Vietnam: The Landing And The Buildup, 1965*, Normanby Press, 2016.

Shulimson, Dr Jack, *U.S. Marines In Vietnam: An Expanding War, 1966*, Normanby Press, 2016.

Singh, Mandeep, *Baptism Under Fire: AAA in India Pakistan War 1965*, Vij Publications, New Delhi, 2017.

Spector, Ronald H., *Advice and Support, 1941–1960, The United States Army in Vietnam*, United States Army Center of Military History, Washington, DC, 1983.

Stewart, Colonel James T., *Airpower – The Decisive Force in Korea*, D. Van Nostrand Company Inc., Princeton, NJ, 1957.

Thompson, Wayne, *To Hanoi and Back: The U.S. Air Force and North Vietnam, 1966–1973*, Smithsonian Institution Press, Washington DC, 2002.

——, and Bernard C. Nalty, *Within Limits The U.S. Air Force and the Korean War*, Air Force History and Museums Program, Washington D.C., 1996.

Tilford, Earl H., *Setup: What the Air Force Did in Vietnam and Why*, Air University Press, Maxwell Air Force Base, Alabama, 1991.

Toperczer, István, *MiG-21 Units of the Vietnam War*, Osprey, Oxford, 2001.

——, *MiG-17 AND MiG-19 Units of the Vietnam War*, Osprey, Oxford, 2001.

Truong, Truong V, *Vietnam War: The New Legion*. Trafford, Victoria BC, 2010.

Tucker, Spencer C. (Editor) and Paul G. Pierpaoli, Jr., (Documents Editor), *The Encyclopedia of the Korean War, A Political, Social, and Military History*, 2nd Edition, Greenwood Publishers.

Tufail, Kaiser, *In the Ring and On Its Feet*, Ferozesons (Pvt) Ltd, Lahore, 2018.

Van Staaveren, Jacob, *Gradual Failure: The Air War Over North Vietnam, 1965–1966*, Air Force History and Museums Program, Washington D.C., 2002.

Van Thai, Hoang; Van Quang, Tran, eds., *Victory in Vietnam: The Official History of the People's Army of Vietnam, 1954–1975*, translated by Merle L. Pribbenow (English ed.), University Press of Kansas, Lawrence, Kansas, 2002.

Varhola, Michael, *Fire and Ice: The Korean War 1950–53*, De Capo Press, Boston, 2000.

Wang, Renshen, et al., *The Air Force: Memoirs and Reminiscences*, People's Liberation Army Press, Beijing, 1992.

Williams, Gary H., *Operation Linebacker II: An Analysis in Operational Design*, Naval War College, Newport, June 1997.

Werrel, Kenneth P., *Archie to SAM: A Short History Operational of Ground Based Air Defence*, Second Edition, Air University Press, Maxwell Air Force base, Alabama, 2005.

Xiaobing Li, *A History of the Modern Chinese Army*, The University Press of Kentucky, Lexington, Kentucky, 2007.

Xiaoming, Zhang *Red Wings Over the Yalu: China, the Soviet Union, and the Air War in Korea*.

Zaloga, Steven J., *Red SAM: The SA-2 Guideline Anti-Aircraft Missile*. Osprey Publishing, Oxford, 2007.

Articles and Papers

'Air War Korea, 1950–53', Air Force Magazine, October 2000 http://www.airforcemag.com/MagazineArchive/Documents/2000/October2000/1000korea.pdf.

Bar-Siman-Tov, Yaacov, 'The Myth of Strategic Bombing: Israeli Deep-Penetration Air Raids in the War of Attrition, 1969–70', *Journal of Contemporary Studies, Vol 19*, SAGE, London, 1984.

Boyne, Walter J., 'Linebacker II', *Air Force Magazine*, Vol. 80, Number 11, May 1997.
——, 'MiG Sweep' *Air Force Magazine*, November 1998.
Brower, Kenneth S., 'The Israel Defense Forces, 1948–2017', *Mideast Security and Policy Studies* No. 150, The Begin-Sadat Centre for Startegic Studies, Bar-Ilan University, May 2018.
Cooper, Tom, 'Operation Kavkaz', *Aeroplane Monthly*, January 2016.
Correll, John T., 'The Emergence of Smart Weapons', *Air Force magazine*, March 2010.
Cox, Fredrick, 'The Russian Presence in Egypt', *Naval War College Review* Vol 2, 1970.
Drenkowski, Dana, and Grau, Lester W., 'Patterns and Predictability: The Soviet Evaluation of Operation Linebacker II', *The Journal of Slavic Military Studies*, Issue No. 20:4, 2007, pp. 559–607.
Drew, Dennis M., 'Rolling Thunder 1965: Anatomy of a Failure', *CADRE Paper*, Report No. AU-ARI-CP-86-3, Air University Press, October 1986.
Fall, Bernard B., 'Dien bien phu: Battle to Remember, *The New York Times*, 3 May 1964, http://www.nytimes.com/1964/05/03/dienbienphu-battle-to-remember.html.
Fullbrook, Captain Jim E., 'LAMSON 719. Part II: The battle', *U.S. Army Aviation Digest* No 32, July 1986.
Grant, Rebecca, 'The Crucible of Vietnam', *AIR FORCE Magazine*, February 2013.
Hershberg James G., and Zubok, Vladislav, 'Russian Documents on the Korean War, 1950–53', *Cold War International History Project Bulletin* Issue 14/15, Winter 2003–Spring 2004.
Jian, Chen, 'China's Involvement in the Vietnam War, 1964–69', *The China Quarterly*, No. 142, Jun., 1995.
Khalidi, Ahmed S., The War of Attrition, *Journal of Palestine Studies* Vol. 3, No. 1 (Autumn, 1973).
Kolcum, Edward H., 'Soviets' Shifting Middle East Balance', *Aviation Week and Space Technology*, 11 May 1970.
Mailes, Yancy 'B-52 played major role in Operations Freedom Train and Linebacker I', *Air Forces Global Strike Command Air Forces Startegic – Air*, 4 December 2012.
Peltz, Stephen, 'Israeli Air Power,' *Flying Review International*, December 1967.
Pfeiffer, Abigail, 'Airpower in Vietnam: A Strategic Bombing Analysis', 15 September, 2011 http://www.abigailpfeiffer.com/2011/09/airpower-in-vietnam-a-strategic-bombing-analysis/
Podeh, Elie, 'The Lie That Won't Die: Collusion, 1967', *Middle East Quarterly*, Winter, 2004.
Rothman, Lily, 'How the Korean War Started', *TIME*, Jun 25, 2015 http://time.com/3915803/korean-war-1950-history/

Schiff, Ze'ev, The Isareli Air Force', *Air Force Magazine*, 1976.

Simha, Rakesh Krishna, 'Vietnam War: The critical role of Russian weapons', *Russia Beyond the Headlines*, 30 April 2015 http://in.rbth.com/blogs/2015/04/30/vietnam_war_the_critical_role_of_russian_weapons_42917

Singh, Rohit, 'Battle of Dien Bien Phu', *Scholar Warrior*, Centre for Land Warfare Studies, New Delhi, Spring 2013.

Smirnov, A., 'Memoirs of a covert Soviet soldier in the Korean War', *Russia Beyond the Headlines*, July 26, 2013 https://www.rbth.com/society/2013/07/26/memoirs_of_a_covert_soviet_pilot_in_ the_korean_war_28427.html

Soltys, Andrew T., 'Enemy Antiaircraft Defenses in North Korea', *Air University Quarterly Review* 7, No. 1, Spring 1954.

Warnock, Timothy, 'Air War Korea, 1950–53', *Air Force Magazine*, October 2000 http://www.airforcemag.com/MagazineArchive/Pages/2000/October2000/1000korea.aspx

Younes, Ali, 'Pakistani Pilots in Arab Israel War', *Opinion*, 10 August, 2012 https://www.webcitation.org/6GYjCNSx0?url=http://www.opinion-maker.org/2012/08/pakistani-pilots-in-arab-israel-war/

Zhai, Qiang, 'Transplanting the Chinese Model: Chinese Military Advisers and the First Vietnam War, 1950–1954,' *The Journal of Military History*, Vol. 57, No. 4, October 1993.

Zhang Xiaoming, 'China, the Soviet Union, and the Korean War: From an Abortive Air War Plan to a Wartime Relationship', *The Journal of Conflict Studies* Vol. XXII No. 1 Spring 2002.

Zhou, Bangning, 'Explaining China's Intervention in the Korean War in 1950', *Interstate- Journal of International Affairs, No 1, Vol 2014/2015*, 2015 http://www.inquiriesjournal.com/articles/1069/explaining-chinas-intervention-in-the-korean-war-in-1950

Notes

Chapter 1: Korea 1950–53

1. Tucker, Spencer C. (Editor) and Paul G. Pierpaoli, Jr, (Documents Editor), *The Encyclopedia of the Korean War, A Political, Social, and Military History*, pp. 113–14.
2. Stewart, Colonel James T., *Airpower – The Decisive Force in Korea*, p. iii.
3. Jackson, Robert. *Air War Korea 1950–1953*, p. 148.
4. Appleman, Roy E., *South to the Naktong, North to the Yalu: United States Army in the Korean War*, Center of Military History, United States Army, 1961, p. 44.
5. Futrell, Robert F, *The United States Air Force In Korea 1950–1953*, p. 86.
6. Ibid., p. 27.
7. Ibid., p. 86.
8. Ibid.
9. Ibid., p.169.
10. Ibid., p.171.
11. Ibid., p. 217.
12. Warnock, A. Timothy, 'Air War Korea, 1950–53', *Air Force Magazine*, October 2000 http://www.airforcemag.com/MagazineArchive/Pages/2000/October 2000/1000korea.aspx
13. Futrell, op. cit., p. 226.
14. Warnock, op. cit.
15. Sandler, Stanley *The Korean War: An Encyclopedia*, pp. 240–1.
16. Futrell, op. cit., p. 288.
17. The Koreans had approached the Soviet Union for AA resources after China expressed its inability to meet Korean demands, as decribed in 'Russian Documents on the Korean War, 1950–53', Introduction by James G. Hershberg and translations by Vladislav Zubok, *Cold War International History Project Bulletin, Issue 14/15* accessed at https://www.wilsoncenter.org/sites/default/files/CWIHPBulletin14-15_p4_0.pdf: *During a meeting with Stalin, Kim Il Sung remarked, 'As a result of the constant intensification of the enemy's bombing we need to build up our anti-aircraft artillery. Recently we asked for 5 regiments of anti-aircraft artillery, but we really need 10 regiments. We asked 5 from you, comrade Stalin, and 5 – from the Chinese comrades. Mao Zedong said that currently it is impossible for China to meet Korea's request. Therefore we are asking you to give us 10 regiments of anti-aircraft artillery.'*

18. Futrell, op. cit., p. 334.
19. Ibid.
20. Werrel Kenneth P., *Archie to SAM: A Short History Operational of Ground Based Air Defence*, p. 75.
21. Futrell, op. cit., p. 338.
22. Werrel, op. cit., p. 6. See also Soltys, Andrew T., 'Enemy Antiaircraft Defenses in North Korea,' *Air University Quarterly Review 7*, No. 1 Spring 1954, pp. 77–80.
23. In 1940 Berlin had 1,080 heavy AA guns and 288 light AA guns deployed for its defence, a number which increased later during the war.
24. Futrell, op. cit., p. 86.
25. For the supply routes' protection, the Communists were using a mix of active and passive measures to keep the supplies going and as Soviet Air Force regiments could have operated only from well-defended airfields, outside the Korean landmass, the airfields would always have been a higher priority. According to Zhou's telegram to Peng on 22 March 1951, the Soviet Union agreed to send eight anti-aircraft artillery regiments to defend the four airfields that were being built for the Soviet Air Force. *Zhou En-Lai Junshi Wenxuan* 1, p. 177. See also, Zhou to Stalin, 23 March 1951 telegram, APRF, p. 143. Zhang Xiaoming, 'China, the Soviet Union, and the Korean War: From an Abortive Air War Plan to a Wartime Relationship' *Journal of Conflict Studies*, Vol. XXII, No. 1, Spring 2002, accessed at https://journals.lib.unb.ca/index.php/jcs/article/view/368/582#49
26. Futrell, op. cit., p. 425.
27. Ibid., p. 446.
28. Ibid.
29. Seidov, Igor, *Red Devils over Yalu: A Chronicle of Soviet Aerial Operations in the Korean War 1950–53*, pp. 558.
30. William, William J., ed., *A Revolutionary War: Korea and the Transformation of the Postwar World*, p. 154; Sarin and Dvoretsky, *Alien Wars: The Soviet Union's Aggression Against the World, 1919 to 1989*, p. 74. See also, Zhang Xiaoming, op. cit.
31. Xiaming Zhang *Red Wings over Yalu: China, the Soviet Union and the Air War in Korea*, p. 127.
32. 'Communist Intentions in Korea,' HR70-14, 14 November 1951, *Current Intelligence Review* https://archive.org/stream/14November1951Current IntelligenceReview/14November1951CurrentIntelligenceReview_djvu.txt
33. Stalin was not willing to provide air cover for the Chinese troops in Korea, as he did not want to be actively involved in the war so as to prevent a direct military confrontation between the United States and the Soviet Union. (Li, Millet, and Yu, *Mao's Generals Remember Korea*, p. 4). See also, Becker, Stefanie, '*Cold War in Asia: China's Involvement in the Korean and Vietnam*

War' accessedathttps://kuscholarworks.ku.edu/bitstream/handle/1808/19013/Becker_ku_0099M_14077_DATA_1.pdf
34. Smirnov, A., *Memoirs of a covert Soviet soldier in the Korean War Artofwar. Ru* 26 July 2013 https://www.rbth.com/society/2013/07/26/memoirs_of_a_covert_soviet_pilot_in_ the_korean_war_28427.html
35. Xiaobing Li, *China's Battle for Korea: The 1951 Spring Offensive*, pp. 63–4.
36. Werrel, op. cit., p. 75.
37. Fifth Air Force Historical Division, *History of the Fifth Air Force*, 1 January 1952–30 June 1952, Appendix 65, US Air Force Historical Research Agency, Maxwell Air Force Base, Alabama, United States, p. 151.
38. Farquhar, John Thomas, *A Need to Know: The Role of Air Force Reconnaissance in Air War Planning*, http://www.dtic.mil/dtic/tr/fulltext/u2/a249785.pdf
39. Thompson and Nalty, op. cit., p. 42.
40. Zhang Xiaoming China, op. cit.
41. Mosman, BC, 'The Effectiveness of Air interdiction During the Korean War', OCMH Study 2–3.7 AD H, Office of the Chief of Military Historian, Department of the Army, Washington DC, March 1966 accessed at https://www.nj.gov/ military/korea/effectiveness.pdf. See also, Muir, Malcolm, *A failed blockade: Air and seapower in Korea 1950–53*, pp. 144–55 accessed at http://www.tha.id.au/adc/Readings/Ops2/150430_1_Ops_R_AFailed Blockade_Muir(Omnipage).pdf
42. Futrell, op. cit., p. 50–5.
43. Sandler, op. cit., pp 113–14.
44. 'Anti-aircraft in Korea (1950–1953): Korean Air Defence', Global Security. Accessed at http://www.globalsecurity.org/military/library/policy/army/accp/ad0699/lesson1.htm#le11
45. 'The Retreat From Chosin Reservoir, Korea, 1950', *Weapons and Warfare*, 16 June 2016 accessed at https://weaponsandwarfare.com/2016/06/16/the-retreat-from-chosin-reservoir-korea-1950/ See also Seelinger, Matthew J., 'Nightmare at the Chosin Reservoir,*Army History*,Army Historical Foundation,Arlington,Virginia, 20 January 2015 accessed at https://armyhistory.org/ nightmare-at-the-chosin-reservoir
46. Futrell, op. cit., p. 431.
47. Ibid.
48. Ibid.
49. Ibid.
50. The TOKEN radar operated in the S-band frequency around 3,000 megacycles. First detected in Moscow in 1951, the new GCI radar could direct several 'fighters simultaneously at ranges up to 70 miles away'. Fifth Air Force Historical Division, *History of the Fifth Air Force*, 1 January 1952–30 June 1952, Appendix 65, US Air Force Historical Research Agency, Maxwell Air Force Base, Alabama, United States.

51. Letter by Brigadier General, USAF, Commanding (FEAF Bomber Command) to Major General John B. Montgomery, Director of Operations, Strategic Air Command, 30 January 1963, in *History of Air Force*, January-July, Vol. 2: Support Document, File number:: K-713.01-38, vol. 2, Jan-27 Jul 1953, US Air Force Historical research Agency, Maxwell Air Force Base, Alabama, United States.
52. Futrell, op. cit., p. vii.
53. Ibid., p. 459.
54. Warnock, 'Air War Korea, 1950–53', *Air Force Magazine*, October 2000, p. 47.
55. Futrell, op. cit., p. 520.
56. Werrel, op. cit., p. 12.
57. Knaack, Marcelle S., Encyclopedia of U.S Air Force Aircrfat and Missiel Systems, Vol I, Office of Air Force History, Washington DC, 1978, p. 9.
58. Wheeler, Keith, *Bombers over Japan*, p. 84; and Joe Baugher, *B-29 in Korean War* accessed at http://www.joebaugher.com/usaf_bombers/b29_12.html
59. Muir, op. cit., pp. 144–55.

Chapter 2: Vietnam
1. Davidson, *Vietnam at War: The History 1946–1975*, pp. 39–40.
2. Ibid., pp. 41–8.
3. Seals, 'Chinese Support for North Vietnam during the Vietnam War: The Decisive Edge '*Vietnam News*, 2008, accessed at https://namvietnews.wordpress.com/chinese-support-for-north-vietnam-during-the-vietnam-war-the-decisive-edge/
4. Victor Flintham, *Air Wars and Aircraft: A Detailed Record of Air Combat, 1945 to the Present*, p. 256.
5. Werrel, *Archie to SAM: A Short History Operational of Ground Based Air Defence*, p.113.
6. Rohit Singh, 'Battle of Dien Bien Phu', *Scholar Warrior*, CLAWS Journal, Spring 2003, New Delhi, p. 147–56. See also, Pham Huy, 'Antiaircraft artillery moved to Dien Bien Phu battle', *Vietnam News*, March 20, 2014 accessed at https://www.vietnambreakingnews.com/2014/03/antiaircraft-artillery-moved-to-dien-bien-phu-battle/
7. Rohit Singh op cit., pp 147–56. See also Fall, 'Dien Bien Phu: Battle to Remember', *New York Times*, 3 May 1964.
8. Werrel, op. cit, p. 113.
9. Fall, 'Dien Bien Phu: Battle to Remember', *New York Times*, 3 May 1964.
10. Ibid.
11. The Viet Minh used American 105mm guns captured in the Korean War so the errant French ammunition drops were important supply channels for the Communists. See Bernard Fall, *Hell in a Very Small Place: The Siege of*

Dien Bien Phu, pp. 31–4, 49, 133, 144, 454–5; William Leary, 'CAT at Dien Bien Phu,' *Aerospace Historian*, September 1984, pp. 178–80, 183; Futrell, *The United States Air Force in Southeast Asia: The Advisory Years to 1965*, Office of Air Force History, Washington DC, 1981, pp. 19–20, 116; and V. J. Croizat, *Lessons of the War in Indochina*, Vol. 2, RAND Report RM-5271-PR, RAND, Santa monica, California, 1967, pp. 292, 302.

12. Truong V., *Vietnam War: The New Legion*, Vol I, p. 419.
13. Truong, op. cit., p. 361.
14. Ibid.
15. Central Intelligence Agency Information Report, '*Situation Appraisal as of 30 November 1963*', (National Security File, Vietnam Country File, Vietnam Memos), Johnson Library, Washington, December 2, 1963. https://history.state.gov/historicaldocuments/frus1961-63v04/d335
16. Qiang Zhai, 'Transplanting the Chinese Model: Chinese Military Advisers and the First Vietnam War, 1950–1954,' *The Journal of Military History*, Vol. 57, No. 4, October 1993, p. 715. See also Bob Seals, 'Chinese Support for North Vietnam during the Vietnam War: The Decisive Edge', *Vietnam News*.
17. Carl O. Schuster, 'The Rise of North Vietnam's Air Defenses', *Historynet*, June 2016, http://www.historynet.com/13703647.htm
18. Clodfelter, *Vietnam in Military Statistics: A History of the Indochina Wars, 1792–1991*, p. 56.
18. Robert Bruce Frankum, *Like Rolling Thunder: The Air War in Vietnam, 1964–1975*, 2005, p. 15.
19. Clodfelter, op. cit., p. 56.
20. Right after the Gulf of Tonkin Incident, it was noted by American intelligence that China had moved 36 MiG fighters to the newly built airfield at Phuc-Yen in North Vietnam, and had substantially strengthened its air strength in southern China. See Raplh B. Smith, *An International History of the Vietnam War*, Vol. 2, p. 300; and Allan Suess Whiting, *The Chinese Calculus of Deterrence: India and Indo-China*, University of Michigan Press, 1975 p. 176. See also, Chen Jian, 'China's Involvement in the Vietnam War, 1964–69' *The China Quarterly*, No. 142, pp. 356–87.
21. Xiaobing Li, *A History of the Modern Chinese Army*, p. 217. Aslo, Liu Yuti and Jiao Hongguang, 'Operations against invading American planes in the Chinese-Vietnamese border area in Guangxi,' in *The Air Force.: Memoirs and Reminiscences*, pp. 559–60. Liu was then the Seventh Army's deputy commander and Jiao was deputy political commissar.
22. Special Report, *Status of Soviet and Chinese Military Aid to North Vietnam*, CIA Report, 3 September 1965, and Intelligence Memorandum, *Chinese Communist Forces in North Vietnam*, CIA Report, 29 September 1966, Freedom of Information Act, accessed on line, http://www.foia.cia.gov on 30 June 2008.

23. Chen Jian, op. cit., pp. 356–87 and Xiaobing Li, *A History of the Modern Chinese Army*, 2007, p. 217.
24. This summary of the operations of Chinese anti-aircraft artillery forces in Vietnam is based on the following sources: Chen Jian, 'China's Involvement in the Vietnam War', *The China Quarterly*, No. 142, June 1995, pp. 356–87; Qu Aiguo, 'Chinese supporters in the operations to assist Vietnam and resist America', p. 43.
25. Xiaoming Zhang, 757. Also Seals, op. cit.
26. Schuster, op. cit.
27. Col Dennis M. Drew, *Rolling Thunder 1965: Anatomy of a Failure*, p. 59.
28. Benjamin S. Lambeth, *The Transformation of American Air Power*, p. 16. See also Abigail Pfeiffer, *Airpower in Vietnam: A Strategic Bombing Analysis*, September 2011, accessed at http://www.abigailpfeiffer.com/2011/09/airpower-in-vietnam-a-strategic-bombing-analysis/ on 19 July 2019
29. Lambeth, op. cit., pp. 16–17. Also, Mark Clodfelter, 'The Limits of Airpower or the Limits of Strategy The Air Wars in Vietnam and Their Legacies', *Joint Forces Quarterly*, Issue 78, 3rd Quarter, 2015, pp. 111–24.
30. Van Staaveren, Jacob, *Gradual Failure: The Air War Over North Vietnam, 1965–1966*, Air Force History and Museums Program, Washington DC, 2002, pp. 84–5.
31. Ibid.
32. Tilford, Earl H., *Setup: What the Air Force Did in Vietnam and Why*, p. 109.
33. Werell, op. cit., pp 117–18 and Cheng Guan Ang, *The Vietnam War from the Other Side*, pp. 96–7.
34. Ibid.
35. Barton Meyers, 'Vietnamese Defense against Aerial Attack', Paper Presented at the 1996 Vietnam Symposium Center for the Study of the Vietnam Conflict, Lubbock, Texas, 19 April 1996, Brooklyn College of the City University of New York accessed at https://www.vietnam.ttu.edu/events/1996_Symposium/96papers/meyers.php
36. Rakesh Krishna Simha, 'Vietnam War: The critical role of Russian weapons', *Russia Beyond the Headlines*, 30 April 2015, http://in.rbth.com/blogs/2015/04/30/vietnam_war_the_critical_role_of_russian_weapons_42917
37. Staaveren, op. cit., p 315.
38. Walter J. Boyne, *Beyond the Wild Blue: A History of the U.S. Air Force, 1947–2007*, p. 152.
39. Staaveren, op. cit., p. 315–17.
40. Patrick Barker, *The Sa-2 And Wild Weasel: The Nature Of Technological Change In Military Systems*, accessed at https://apps.dtic.mil/dtic/tr/fulltext/u2/a281789.pdf
41. Davies, Peter, *F-105 Wild Weasel vs SA-2 'Guideline' SAM, Vietnam 1965–73*, pp. 40, 53, 72, 90 and 'How our S-75 in Vietnam beat the Americans',

Politforums.Net, 27 July, 2015 accessed at https://www.politforums.net/eng/historypages/1438016941.html
42. Ibid.
43. David Freed, 'The Missile Men of North Vietnam: A look at the air war waged from the ground', *Air Space Magazine*, https://www.airspacemag.com/military-aviation/missile-men-north-vietnam-180953375/#JHM5keqoeZPUV0dQ.99
44. Staaveren, op. cit. pp. 164–6 and Werell, op. cit., p. 121.
45. Ibid.
46. Peter Fey, '*The Effects of Leadership on Carrier Air Wing Sixteen's Loss Rates during Operation Rolling Thunder*,' 1965–1968, US Army Command and General Staff College, Fort Leavenworth, Kansas, 2006, p. 54 and VA-163, Command History 1966, Naval Historical Center, Aviation History Branch, Washington DC, p. 25.
47. Edward F. Puchalla, 'Communist Defence against Aerila Surveillance in Southeast Asia', *Central Intelligence Agency*, accessed at https://www.cia.gov/library/center-for-the-study-of-intelligence/csi-publications/books-and-monographs/Anthology-CIA-and-the-Wars-in-Southeast-Asia/pdfs/puchalla-communist-defense-against-aerial-surveillance.pdf
48. Steven J. Zaloga, *Red SAM: The SA-2 Guideline Anti-Aircraft Missile*, p. 17 and Staaveren, op. cit., p. 317.
49. Peter Fey, '*The Effects of Leadership on Carrier Air Wing Sixteen's Loss Rates during Operation Rolling Thunder*,' 1965–1968, U.S. Army Command and General Staff College, Fort Leavenworth, Kansas, 2006 accessed at https://apps.dtic.mil/dtic/tr/fulltext/u2/a451820.pdf
50. John T. Correll, 'Take It Down! The Wild Weasels in Vietnam', *Air Force Magazine*, July 2010 accessed at http://www.airforcemag.com/MagazineArchive/Documents/2010/July2010/0710weasel.pdf and 'The Pioneers: Wild Weasel and the F-100F' accessed at https://www.nationalmuseum.af.mil/Visit/Museum-Exhibits/Fact-Sheets/Display/Article/197491/the-pioneers-wild-weasel-and-the-f-100f/

Carlo Kopp, 'F-4G: Anatomy of a Wild Weasel', *Air Power Australia*, July 1986 accessed at http://www.ausairpower.net/TE-Weasel.html
51. 'A Comparative Analysis of USAF Fixed Wing Aircrfat Losses in Southeast Asia Combat', Project 4363, *Aerospace Vehicle Combat Survivability*, US Air Force Flight Dynamics Laboratory, Wright-Patterson AFB, Ohio accessed at https://apps.dtic.mil/dtic/tr/fulltext/u2/c016682.pdf; John T. Correll, 'Rolling Thunder', *US Air Force Magazine*, March 2005 accessed at http://www.airforcemag.com/MagazineArchive/Pages/2005/March2005/0305thunder.aspx and Earl J. Tilford, '*What the Air Force Did in Vietnam and Why*'.
52. Norman Malayney, 'Gull One Down', *American Aviation Historical Society Journal*, Vol. 52 No. 3, Fall 2007, http://www.cvva.ca/GullOneDown.pdf

53. Patrick Barker, *The SA-2 and Wild Weasel: The Nature of Technological Change in Military Systems*, accessed at https://preserve.lehigh.edu/etd/277
54. Staaveren, op. cit., pp 266–86, 272, 317.
55. Davies, *F-105 Wild Weasel Against the SA-2 Guideline SAM*, Vietnam 1965–73, and Boyne, Walter J., 'MiG Sweep' *Air Force Magazine* November 1998, pp. 46–51.
56. Thompson, *To Hanoi and Back The United States Air Force and North Vietnam 1966–1973*, Air Force History and Museums Program United States Air Force Washington, DC, 2000, and Vaan Staaveren, op cit. pp. 50–2.
57. Ibid.
58. Davies, *US Navy F-4 Phantom II Units of the Vietnam War 1964–68*, pp. 61–2, Peter Fey, op. cit., pp. 59–60 and Staaveren, op cit., pp 27–272 and 320.
59. Drew, Dennis M., *Rolling Thunder 1965: Anatomy of a Failure*, CADRE Paper, Report No. AU-ARI-CP-86-3, Air University Press, October 1986.
60. John T. Correll, 'Emergence of Smart Weapons', *AIR FORCE Magazine*, March 2010, pp 60–4 and Hewitt, *Planting the Seeds of SEAD: The Wild Weasel in Vietnam*.
61. Chen Jian, 'China's Involvement in the Vietnam War, 1964–69', *The China Quarterly*, No. 142, June 1995, pp. 356–87.
62. Fey, op cit., p. 62.
63. Clodfelter, *The Limits of Airpower: The American Bombing of North Vietnam*, p. 20.
64. Ibid.
65. Schlight, Colonel John, *A War Too Long: The USAF in Southeast Asia, 1961–1975*, Air Force History and Museums Program, Washington D.C., 1996, p. 53.
66. The cost in terms of aircraft was high. By 24 December Hanoi's air defense system had downed 171 aircraft (80 Air Force, 83 Navy, 8 VNAF) and damaged 450 (189 Air Force, 250 Navy, 11 VNAF). Losses were largely due to the north's large inventory of anti-aircraft guns: by December 24, 1965, they numbered approximately 2,236, more than twice the number in February of that year, plus several thousand automatic weapons. Although few aircraft were lost to enemy aircraft and SA–2 missiles, they had a significant harassing effect on combat and reconnaissance missions. (Staaveren, op. cit., p. 317).
67. Lambeth, op. cit., p. 17.
68. Mailes, Yancy, 'B-52 played major role in Operations Freedom Train and Linebacker I', *Air Forces Global Strike Command Air Forces Startegic – Air*, 4 December 2012, accessed at https://www.afgsc.af.mil/News/Article-Display/Article/454706/b-52-played-major-role-in-operations-freedom-train-and-linebacker-i/

69. David Fulghum & Terrance Maitland, et al., *South Vietnam on Trial*, p. 142; James G. Burton, *The Pentagon Wars: Reformers Challenge the Old Guard*, p. 10. Also, John T Correll, 'The Emergence of Smart Weapons', *Air Force Magazine*, March 2010 accessed at http://www.airforcemag.com/MagazineArchive/Documents/2010/March2010/0310bombs.pdf.
70. Van Thai, Hoang; Van Quang, Tran, eds., *Victory in Vietnam: The Official History of the People's Army of Vietnam, 1954–1975*, translated by Merle L. Pribbenow (English ed.), p. 293.
71. Michael Casey, Clark Dougan, Samuel Lipsman, Jack Sweetman, Stephen Weiss, et al., *Flags into Battle*, p. 39 and Head, *War Above the Clouds*, p. 65.
72. Morocco, John, *Rain of Fire: Air War, 1969–1973*, p. 144; Marshall L. Michel, *Clashes: Air Combat Over North Vietnam 1965–1972*, p. 244.
73. Michel III, op. cit., p. 284.
74. The first loss of B-52 to a SA-2 is generally attributed to have occurred on 22 November 1972 during Linebacker II though Werell in his book *Archie to SAM* (p. 128) mentions that a B-52 was shot down by a SA-2 on 21–23 April. Most accounts only mention a B-52 being hit by a SA-2 on 19 April 19; the aircraft reportedly managed to return safely. On 9 April 12 B-52D crews took off from U-Tapao and bombed facilities at Vihn. During this mission, an enemy SAM smacked into one of the B-52s, blowing off most of an external wing tank. Even with damage, the crew was able to the fly the wounded bomber south and land at Da Nang air base. See also, Mailes, 'B-52 played major role in Operations Freedom Train and Linebacker I', *Air Forces Global Strike Command Air Forces Startegic – Air*, 4 December 2012.
75. Werell, op. cit., p. 129; Doglione, *Airpower and the 1972 Spring Invasion*, 132; Berger et al., *The USAF in Southeast Asia*, p. 168; Nordeen, op. cit., p. 64.
76. Werrell, op. cit., p.128.
77. Charles T. Fox, *Precision-Guided Munitions: Past, Present, and Future*, Defense Analytical Study, Maxwell AFB, Ala., Air War College, 14 April 1995.
78. Of the total loss of 134, only 104 are attributed as combat losses with 55 of them to AAA. (Ed Rasimus, *Palace Cobra: A Fighter Pilot in the Vietnam Air War*, 2007, pp. 233–48).
79. Werrell, op. cit., p.128.
80. Ibid.
81. Zaloga, op. cit., p. 23.
82. McCarthy, James R.; Allison, George B., *Linebacker II: A View from the Rock*, p. 21.
83. Walter J. Boyne, 'Linebacker II', *Air Force Magazine*, May 1997, Vol. 80, Number 11.
84. The total number of B-52s lost on day three is generally accepted as seven, four in the first wave and three in the third wave although some sources,

including Werrell (*Archie to SAM*, p. 133), give total losses as six on day three.

85. Werrell mentions 'eleven B-52s lost in first three days' but in the breakdown gives the loss as three on day one and six on day three. The Soviet report on Linebacker II claims 17 aircarft downed in the first three days (Drenkowski, Dana & Grau, Lester W., 'Patterns and Predictability: The Soviet Evaluation of Operation Linebacker II', *The Journal of Slavic Military Studies*, Issue No. 20:4, 2007, pp. 559–607). The figure of eleven may be including the severely damaged aircraft on Day One and Two. The figures are otherwise taken from Norman Polmar, ed., *Strategic Air Command – People, Aircraft, and Missiles*, p. 126 and Granville, John M, *Summary of USAF Aircraft Losses in SE Asia*, Report 7409, HQ Tactical Air Command, Langley Air Force Base, Virginia, 1974, p. 18.
86. Werrell, op. cit., p. 134.
87. Williams, Gary H., *Operation Linebacker II: An Analysis in Operational Design*, Naval War College, Newport, June 1997, p. 11; Werrell, 'Linebacker II: The Decisive Use of Air Power?' *Air University Review*, January-March 1987, p. 53.
88. Werrell, *Archie to SAM*, p. 133; Eschmann, '*The Role of Tactical Support: Linebacker II*,' pp. 60, 63, and Clodfelter, '*By Other Means*,' p. 121.
89. Drenkowski, Dana & Grau, Lester W., op. cit., pp. 559–607.
90. The percentage of B-52s getting chaff protection increased from 15 per cent to 85 per cent. In all, US airmen dropped 125 tons of chaff during Linebacker II. (Werrell, op. cit., p. 133).
91. Drenkowski, Dana & Grau, Lester W., op. cit., pp. 559–607.
92. Ibid.
93. The exact details of the total losses remain unknown. This figure is as given by Werrell in *Archie to SAM* (pp. 133–57). Eschmann in *The Role of Tactical Air Support*, (pp. 103–4), lists 30 aircraft destroyed, including three lost in accidents while Futrell in *Aces and Aerial Victories*, at p. 17, states that 27 US Air Force aircraft were lost. The North Vietnamese claimed 81 US aircraft, including 34 B-52s. See also Gareth Porter, *A Peace Denied – The United States, Vietnam, and the Paris Agreements*, pp. 161–2; and Richard Holloran, 'Bombing Halt Brings Relief to B-52 Crews in Guam,' *New York Times*, 2 January 1973.
94. The US Air Force told US Congress that only 13 B-52s were lost. However, what was not disclosed was that nine B-52s that returned to U-Tapao airfield were too badly damaged to fly again and were written off. The exact number of B-52s that managed to barely return to Guam and never flew again, remains unknown. The overall B-52 loss is probably between 22 and 27. Fifteen additional official aviation losses were two F-111s and two F-4 Phantoms of the USAF, two A-7s, two A-6s, one F-4 and one RA-5 of US Navy.

95. Same figures for the total number of sorties launched by NVNAF are given by both the US and North Vietnamese sources although the kills claimed by VNNAF are denied by the U.S., especially the two B-52s claimed by the North Vietnamese. NVNAF on its part claims 9% of the total of all US aircraft destroyed. (Roger Boniface, *MIGs Over North Vietnam: The Vietnam People's Air Force in Combat,* 1965–75p. 214; István Toperczer, *MiG-21 Units of the Vietnam War,* pp.84–6 and István Toperczer, *MiG-17 AND MiG-19 Units of the Vietnam War,* pp. 88–90).
96. Futrell,, *Aces and Aerial Victories: US Air Force in Southeast Asia 1965–1973,* Historical Research Centre, Air University, Washington DC, pp. 122–140; Brad Elward and Peter Davies, *U.S. Navy F-4 Phantom II MiG Killers 1965–70,* and Correll, John T. 'The Vietnam War Almanac', *Air Force Magazine,* September 2004.
97. In May 1965 North Vietnamese Air Force received 8 Il-28s from the Soviet Union. They consisted of 4 bombers, 3 reconnaissance/photographing aircraft and 1 training aircraft. All were assigned to the T-16 squadron of the 929th Independent Air Battalion. See also, Hallion, *Rolling Thunder 1965–68: Johnson's air war over Vietnam,* p. 31 and Staaveren, *Gradual Failure: The Air War over North Vietnam 1965–1966,* p. 143.
98. Shulimson, Dr Jack and Johnson, Maj. Charles M., *U.S. Marines In Vietnam: The Landing And The Buildup, 1965,* pp. 12–14, 39–41, 331.
99. Ibid.
100. Rebecca Grant, 'The Crucible of Vietnam', *Air Force Magazine,* No. 2, February, 2013, pp. 74–8.

Chapter 3: India Pakistan War 1965

1. Mandeep Singh *Baptism Under Fire: AAA in India Pakistan War 1965,* pp. 1–2.
2. Chakravorty B.C., *History of The Indo-Pak War 1965,* History Division, Ministry of Defence, Government of India, New Delhi 1992, p. 26. See also Bajwa Farooq, *From Kutch to Tashknet* p. 76.
3. 'Operation Desert Hawk' http://urbanpk.com/pakdef/pakmilitary/airforce/war/deserthawk.html
4. Bowman, *Cold War Jet Combat: Air to Air Jet Operation 1950–1972,* p. 78.
5. Jagan Mohan PVS and Chopra, Samir, *The India- Pakistan Air War of 1965,* pp. 68–9 and Pradhan RD, *1965 War, The Inside Story: Defence Minister Y.B. Chavan's Diary Of India-Pakistan War,* p.
6. 'Pakistan Army Air Defence in Operations', *Pakistan Army* http://defence.pk/threads/pakistan-army-information.21550/page-23#ixzz3AqaAKj9A. See also, 'History of Army Air Defence' https://www.pakistanarmy.gov.pk/AWPReview/TextContent.aspx?pId=22&rnd=451. Retrieved 27 September, 2011.

7. Bharat Kumar, *The Duels of the Himalayan Eagle – The First Indo-Pak Air War*, p. 42.
8. Jagan and Chopra, op. cit., pp 79–81.
9. Chakarvarty, op. cit., p. 248, Jagan and Chopra, op. cit., pp. 79–81 and Nordeen, *Air Warfare in Missile Age*, p. 138.
10. 'Pak Sabre Jets Destroyed', *The Hindu*, 4 September 1965. Accessed online at https://www.thehindu.com/archives/from-the-archives-dated-september-4-1965/article7612338.ece
11. 'A War Hero Remembers', *The Hindu*, Chennai, 3 September 2015 http://www.thehindu.com/todays-paper/tp-national/tp-andhrapradesh/a-war-hero-remembers/article7610482.ece
11. India was on the defensive in the Akhnoor sector and to relieve the pressure, decided to launch an offensive to make Pakistan 'recoil'. The offensive was to be in Lahore sector, its largest and most important city.
12. Chakravorty, op. cit., p. 146.
13. Chakarvarty, op. cit., p. 249.
14. The warning of the incoming air raid was given to Pathankot and Adampur. While a CAP was launched from Adampur, Pathankot did not take any action. (Jagan and Chopra, op. cit., pp. 103–5 and Chakarvorty, op. cit., p. 251).
15. Ibid.
16. Nordeen op. cit., p. 141 and Chakarvorty, op. cit., p. 251.
17. Bajwa, op. cit., p. 278.
18. 'September 7', *PAF Falcons*, https://www.paffalcons.com/1965war/september7.php
19. 'Squadron Leader Ayamada Bopayya Devayya honoured 23 years after his death',*India Today*, New Delhi, https://www.indiatoday.in/magazine/defence/story/19880415-squadron-leader-ayamada-bopayya-devayya-honoured-23-years-after-his-death-797132-1988-04-15 The loss of a Mystere to Pak AAA is also mentioned by Nordeen in *Air Warfare in Missile Age* at p. 142 and at 'PAF Gallantry Awards' at *Paksitan Air Force* website http://www.pafmuseum.com.pk/heroes/1965-gallantry-awards
20. As with other cases, this loss is shown as due to 'technical failure/accident' and is not attributed to AAA. However, the citation for the gallantry award mentions that his aircraft was hit by AA fire. (Govrnmnet of India *Gazette Notification: 15 Pres. 66 dated 1 January 1966).*
21. Amarinder Singh, TS Gill, *The Monsoon War: Young Officers Reminisce: 1965 India-Pakistan War*, p. 319.
22. Kutub Hai, *The Patton Wreckers*, p. 41.
23. Jagan and Chopra, op. cit., p. 212.
24. Ibid., and Chakarvorty, op. cit., p. 260.
25. 'Air War of 1965 Revisited: Missions against Amritsar Radar: Countering Fishoil' accessed at http://paf-eagles.blogspot.com/2010/09/air-war-of-1965-revisited-missions.html on 22 July 2019.

26. The details can be accessed at http://www.ejection-history.org.uk/ Aircraft_by_ Type/ PAKISTAN/B-57.htm and http://www.defencejournal.com /sept98/ citation_ paf1.htm. Both the pilot and navigator of the ill fated B-57 were awarded Sitara-e Juraat.
27. Abrar Ahmad, *Men of Steel: 6th Armoured Division in the 1965 War*, p. 60.
28. Jagan and Chopra, op. cit., pp. 236–8 and Chakarvorty, op. cit., p. 262. Also Nordeen, op. cit., p. 148.
29. Chakarvorty, op. cit., p. 262 and Jagan and Chopra, op. cit., pp. 241–3. See also '8 pass Charlie' at *https://en.wikipedia.org/wiki/8-Pass_Charlie*.
30. Jagan and Chopra, op. cit., p. 249.
31. This information was given by Major Harnam Grover's son to the author during an interaction with him in 2014.
32. Jagan and Chopra, op. cit., pp. 178–9. See also, GCS Rajawar *The War at Kalaikunda* available at *http://www.bharat-rakshak.com/ IAF/ History/1965War/1071-Rajwar.html*
33. Jagan and Chopra, op. cit., pp. 178–9.
34. Chakarvorty, op. cit., p. 268.

Chapter 4: The Six Day War
1. Werrel, *Archie to SAM: A Short Operational History of Ground Air Defences.*
2. British Military Aviation in 1956 https://www.rafmuseum.org.uk/research/history-of-aviation-timeline/interactive-aviation-timeline/british-military-aviation/1956.aspx
3. Barton Whaley, *Stratagem: Deception and Surprise in War. Vol 1 and 2*, pp. 142–3.
4. Werrel, op. cit., p. 147.
5. Brower, *The Israel Defense Forces, 1948–2017*, Mideast Security and Policy Studies No. 150; https://www.infosperber.ch/data/attachments/TheIsraelDefenceForces1948–2017.pdf
6. Saul Bronfeld *Defense – The Other Face of Marshttps://www.idf.il/media/11774/bronfeld.pdf*
7. Ibid.
8. *Israel Air Force: Air-Defense & Anti-Aircraft Forces* https://www.jewishvirtuallibrary.org/idf-air-defense-and-anti-aircraft-forces
9. The details of IDF's 1967 air defence assets are primarily based on *The June 1967 Six Day War* by Shlomo Aloni (IsraDecal Publications, 2008). There are some accounts by veterans of Egyptian Army which mention that the Soviets did not provide Egypt SAM air defense systems until after the Six-Day War and it was Soviet advisors who were manning these systems during the war. Notable among them is the account by Youssef Aboul-Enein, 'Learning and Rebuilding a Shattered Force: Memoirs of Pre-Yom Kippur War Egyptian Generals, 1967–1972' published in *Strategic Insights: vol. 4, issue 3 (*March 2005) by Naval Postgraduate School, Monterey, California.

10. 'Egyptian general who served in the Six Day War says military was not prepared', *i24 News*, 5 June 2017, accessed at https://www.i24news.tv/en/news/international/middle-east/147068-170605-egyptian-general-who-served-in-the-six-day-war-says-military-was-not-prepared
11. *In Between the Catastrophe, Memoirs of Egyptian Military Commanders from 1967 to 1972.*
12. Ibid.
13. Hammel, Eric, *Six Days in June,* pp. 165–6.
14. Dunstan, Simon, and Peter Dennis, *The Six Day War, 1967: Sinai.*
15. Michael Oren, *The Six Day War, June 1967 and The Making of Modern Middle East*, p. 170.
16. Danny Shalom, *Like a Bolt from the Blue*, pp. 215–20.
17. 'The Visit of the Czechoslovak President's Special Envoy, V. Koucki, to the UAR,' 28 June 1967, History and Public Policy Program Digital Archive, Narodni Archiv [National Czech Archive, Prague], AUV KSC, f. Antonin Novotni (II), Box 93, folder 49. Obtained and translated by Guy Laron. http://digitalarchive.wilsoncenter.org/document/112572 https://digitalarchive.wilsoncenter.org/document/112572.pdf?v=d737ddd0b10081f66b22ec19334b9853
18. Elie Podeh, 'The Lie That Won't Die: Collusion, 1967', *Middle East Quarterly*, Winter, 2004 and Amin Hewedi, *50 Years of Storms*, pp. 408–22.
19. Learning and Rebuilding a Shattered Force – Memoirs of Pre-Yom Kippur War Egyptian Generals, 1967–1972.
20. Ibid.
21. Ibid.
22. Oren, Michael B, op. cit., p. 213.
23. Owen Michael B. op cit, p. 259.
24. Ibid.
25. Two days later he was urgently dispatched to Iraq along with several Jordanian pilots to defend the Iraqi air bases against the Israeli Air Force. He was one of the pilots who intercepted the IAF raid on H-3 air base. Flying an Iraqi Hunter, he shot down two of the Israeli attacking planes. Ali Younes, 'Pakistani Pilots in Arab Israel War,' *Opinion*, Aug 10, 2012 accessed at http://pakfauj.tripod.com/article-paf-arab-israel.html on 22 July, 2019.
26. Michael B. Oren, op. cit., p. 213.
27. While the unclassified sources do not specifically mention a break-down of the type of aircraft shot down by Israeli air defences, an Israeli HAWK shot down an IAF A-4 on 5 June. The damaged fighter bomber apparently penetrated a restricted area around the Israeli nuclear facility Dimona and was shot down when it failed to respond. Luttwak and Horowitz, *The Israeli Army,* pp. 229–30; Nadav Safran, *From War to War – The Arab-Israeli Confrontation, 1948–1967,* pp. 324–5; Rubenstein and Goldman, *Shield*

of David, p. 100; Jackson, *The Israeli Air Force Story,* p. 218; Wetmore, 'Israeli Air Punch Major Factor in War,' *Aviation Week,* 3 July 1967, p. 22; and O'Ballance, *The Third Arab-Israeli War,* pp. 67, 75, 82.
28. There were some 'coincidences' that day which helped Israel. In northern Jordan, Egyptian radar operators on duty picked up the radar signature of a large Israeli air force flying low over the Mediterranean and sent a flash message to their headquarters in Cairo. However, the encryption codes for their unit had been changed the previous day, but nobody had updated the codebooks in the decoding room of the command post. The duty officer tried to decipher the message using the previous day's code and failed. To add to his problems, when Marshall Amer and his staff flew to the Sinai for a meeting with high-level Iraqis the next day, the Egyptian soldiers manning the anti-air defense systems effectively shut down their systems for fear of shooting down their commander. 'Miracles in the Six-Day War: Eyewitness Accounts', *Israel National News,* 14 May 2007, accessed at http://www.israelnationalnews.com/News/News.aspx/122435#.V1TrovkrLDd and 'Miracles of the Six-Day War', *Koinonia House eNews,* 6 June 2016 accessed at https://www.khouse.org/enews_article/2016/2513/print/
29. 'Six Day War', *Israel Air Force* website accessed at http://www.iaf.org.il/2557-30101-en/IAF.aspx
30. The EAF carried out the following number of close support missions over five days. These do not include the air defence missions flown over Egyptian air bases. A very small number but to claim that they did not operate at all may also be incorrect.
    June 5 – 22
    June 6 – 49
    June 7 – 20
    June 8 – 22
    June 9 – 02
31. Jackson, op. cit., pp. 153, 248; James Hansen, 'The Development of Soviet Tactical Air Defense', *International Defense Review,* May 1981, p. 532; and 'Off the Record', *Journal of Defense and Diplomacy,* January 1988, p. 63.

Chapter 5: The War of Attrition
1. Nordeen, *Air Warfare in the Missile Age,* pp. 206–7.
2. O'Ballance, *Electronic War in the Middle East,* p. 26 and A. Dor, *The Mirage IIIC Shahak*- IAF Aircraft Series No 3, p. 14.
3. Nasser later added a fourth 'No' to these: '*No compromise on the legitimate rights of the Palestinian people*'.
4. '*Egypt Will Fight, Nasser Shouts*', *Pittsburgh Post-Gazette, November 24, 1967, p. 2.*

5. Field Marshal Mohammed Aly Fahmy 'Fourth power – the history of the Egyptian Air Defense Forces.' *Al-Ahram*, 20 February 2016 accessed at https://web.archive.org/web/20160220180644/http://www.ahram.org.eg/Archive/2005/10/5/INVE2.HTM And 'War of Attrition' *Encyclopedia Britanica* online accessed at https://www.britannica.com/event/War-of-Attrition-1969-1970
6. Nasser wanted to have a Soviet Anti-Aircraft Forces General as the Chief of Egyptian Air Defence Command but the Russians refused the suggestion. (Herzog, *The Arab Israel Wars, War and Peace in the Middle East*, p. 199).
7. Edgar O'Ballance, *Electronic Warfare*, p. 71 and Fredrick Cox, *'The Russian Presence in Egypt'*, *Naval War College Review* Volume 2, 1970, pp. 45–52.
8. John Bentley, 'Inside Israel Air Force', *Flight International*, 19 March 1970, pp 2, 'The Enemy We Face", *Flight International*, 23 April 1970, p. 669.
9. Chaim Herzog, op. cit, pp. 199–200.
10. *Aloni, Shlomo, Israeli Mirage and Nesher Aces, pp. 46–53.*
11. While Herzog claims the MiG-21 was shot down on May 24, some other accounts mention the date to be 21 March. 'HAWK Missile System', *Israeli Weapons*, accessed at https://web.archive.org/web/20051125121834/http://www.israeli-weapons.com/weapons/missile_systems/surface_missiles/hawk/Hawk.htm This was not the first time HAWK had successfully shot down an aircraft. In an unusual incident an Israeli MIM-23A shot down a damaged Israeli Dassault MD.450 Ouragan that was in danger of crashing into the Negev Nuclear Research Center near Dimona, making it the first combat firing of the HAWK and the first combat kill attributed to the HAWK system. The HAWK batteries shot down between 8 and 12 aircraft during the war of attrition though *Jane's* reports 12 kills (One Il-28, 4 Su-7, 4 MiG-17 and 3 MiG-21).
12. Nordeen, *Air Warfare in the Missile Age*, p. 215 quoting the *zsx* 3 July 1969.
13. Herzog, op. cit., pp. 210–11, Katz, *Israeli Elite Units since 1948*, pp. 31–2, Shalom, Danny (2007). *Phantoms over Cairo – Israeli Air Force in the War of Attrition (1967–1970)*, p. 333 and *Norton, Bill, Air War on the Edge – A History of the Israel Air Force and its Aircraft since 1947*, p. 250.
14. Nordeen; Nicolle, David, *Phoenix Over The Nile – A History of Egyptian Air Power 1922–1994* p. 239 and Shalom, op. cit., pp. 328–9.
15. Nordeen, op. cit., p. 215.
16. Shalom, op. cit., pp. 343–51. The Israeli claims are as mentioned by Nordeen in *Air Warfare in the Missile Age* at p. 215.
17. Shalom, op. cit., pp. 351–2 and Aloni, Shlomo, *Israeli Mirage and Nesher Aces*, pp. 46–53.
18. Aloni, *Israeli Mirage and Nesher Aces*, op. cit., pp. 46–53.
19. The use of Israeli Air Force as 'flying artillery' had been forced upon it even though the IAF was not keen on the same but the success it wanted

to keep away. Reluctant it may have been, subsequent operations were to draw in the IAF more into the conflict. And have an adverse impact on development of artillery in Israel Defence Forces (*Nordeen, Lon; Nicolle, David, Phoenix Over The Nile – A History of Egyptian Air Power 1922–1994. p. 239*).
20. Nordeen, op. cit., p. 211 and 'Commanding the Skies', *Time*, August 22, 1969.
21. O'Ballance, *Electronic Warfare in Middle East*, p. 85.
22. The F-4E was shot down by Jordanian AA guns (Yisgal Nokdemon, 'Two Decades of Phantom', *Israeli Air Force Magazine,* June 1999).
23. 'War of Attrition', *Israel Air Force* official website, http://www.iaf.org.il/2557-30098-en/IAF.aspx
24. McCarthy, Don, *The Sword of David: The Israeli Air Force at War*, pp. 13–16.
25. The aim was to cause so much damage that the mounting public pressure would force Nasser to seek a ceasefire. (Norton, Bill, *Air War on the Edge – A History of the Israel Air Force and its Aircraft since 1947*, p. 30).
26. O'Ballance, op. cit., p. 87.
27. Carter Malkasian, *A History of Modern Wars of Attrition*, Praeger, 2002, pp. 207–8 and 'War of Attrition', *Isarel Air Force* website accessed at http://www.iaf.org.il/2557-30098-en/IAF.aspx
28. 'War of Attrition', *Isarel Air Force* website accessed at http://www.iaf.org.il/2557-30098-en/IAF.aspx and Tom Cooper, 'Operation Kavkaz', *Aeroplane Magazine* January 2016 accessed at www.aeroplanemonthly.com
29. Andrey Pochtarev, 'How to cut the Wings of Phantom', *Red Star*, 1 April 2000, accessed at http://pvo.guns.ru/news/n000114.htm and '18th Special Air Defence Missile Division', https://ru.wikipedia.org/wiki/18-я_особая_зенитно-ракетная_дивизия
30. Isabella Ginor, Gideon Remez, *The Soviet-Israeli War, 1967–1973: The USSR's Military Intervention in the Middle Eas*t, p. 133.
31. 'Operation Kavkaz', *Council of Egypt War Veterans*, accessed at http://www.hubara-rus.ru/kavkaz/ and Adamsky, Dima (2006). Operation Kavkaz – Soviet Intervention and Israeli Intelligence Failure in the War of Attrition (in Hebrew). ISBN 978-965-05-1363-4
32. ibid.
33. On 26 March two Phantoms flew directly over a SA-3 missile site while on 14 April the Shilkas defending the missile unit failed to open fire as the F-4Es *buzzed* them. In another incident, the twin barrelled ZU-23-2B managed to engage the IAF aircraft only to have the guns jammed after firing just 20 rounds('18th Red Banner Special Purpose Air Defence Division', *Council of Egypt War Veterans* accessed at http://www.hubara-rus.ru/gruppirovka-voisk/18zrd/).
34. Nordeen, op. cit., p. 121, Sheldon Kirshner, 'War of Attrition: 50 years On', *The Times of Israel* (Blogs), 2 March, 2019, accessed at https://

blogs.timesofisrael.com/the-war-of-attrition-50-years-on/ and Operation Kavkaz' accessed at http://www.hubara-rus.ru/kavkaz/
35. Bill Norton, *Air War on the Edge: A History of the Israeli Air Force and Its Aircraft Since 1947*, pp. 231–13 and 'Operation Kavkaz' accessed at http://www.hubara-rus.ru/kavkaz/
36. Cooper, 'Operation Kavkaz', *Aeroplane Monthly*, January 2016.
37. Schiff, Ze'ev, 'The Isareli Air Force', *Air Force Magazine*, 1976, p. 36.
38. Kolcum, Edward H., 'Soviets' Shifting Middle East Balance', *Aviation Week and Space Technology*, 11 May 1970, p. 21.
39. US Defence Intelligence Agency, *Free World Intelligence Brief*, 'United Arab Republic (Egypt)' AP 240-3-1-69, 1 February, 1969.

Chapter 6: The Bangladesh War 1971
1. Chakravorty, *History of The Indo-Pak War 1965*, pp. 249–52.
2. Prasad, *India Pakistan War of 1971: A History*; Cooper, with Syed Shaiz Ali. 'India-Pakistan War, 1971; Western Front, part I', *Air Combat Information Group*. Retrieved 4 July 2008 and '1971: Pakistan intensifies air raids on India', *BBC News*, 3 December 1971. Retrieved 20 October 2009. The *Newsweek* in its report on 20 December 1971 mentioned that IAF was alert and that the first strike by PAf was a failure: 'Trying to catch the Indian Air Force napping, Yahya Khan, launched a Pakistani version of Israel's 1967 air blitz in hopes that one rapid attack would cripple India's far superior air power. But India was alert, Pakistani pilots were inept, and Yahya's strategy of scattering his thin air force over a dozen air fields was a bust!'
3. Tufail, *In the Ring and On Its Feet*, pp. 67–9.
4. Ibid., pp. 90–3; and Tufail, 'Air Defence in the Southern Sector', *Aeronaut*, 29 December 2010, http://kaiser-aeronaut.blogspot.com/2010/12/air-defence-in-southern-sector-1971-war.html
5. Gole, Air Marshal CV, 'Reflections On An Air War – The Air Operations of December 1971', *Vayu*, Vol Vi/91, New Delhi, pp. 15–17.
6. Prasad, op. cit., pp. 205–8 and pp. 354–5 and Tufail, op. cit., pp. 43–5.
7. 'History of Pakistan Army Air Defence', *Pakistan Army Air Defence* accessed at Paksitan Army website at https://www.pakistanarmy.gov.pk/AWPReview/TextContentdc89.html?pId=22&rnd=451
8. Ibid.
9. Jagan Mohan and Samir Chopra, *Eagles over Bangladesh, The Indian Air Force in the 1971 Liberation War*, pp. 59–63.
10. Prasad, op. cit., pp. 209–10.
11. Jagan and Chopra, op. cit., pp. 59–63.
12. Ibid., pp 59–60, Air Mshl Inam-ul-Haq Khan, 'Saga of PAF in East Pakistan', *Defence Journal*, May 2009 with Kaiser Tufail, 'The Last Stand', *Aeronaut*, 2012, http://kaiser-aeronaut.blogspot.com/2012/10/the-last-stand-air-war-1971.html

13. Prasad, op. cit., p. 352; Jagan and Chopra, op. cit., pp. 83–91 and Jagan Pillai, 'Boyra Encounter, 22 November, 1971', *Bharat Rakshak*, accessed at http://www.bharat-rakshak.com/IAF/history/1971war/1269-boyra-battle.html. The Boyra incident is also mentioned in 'The War of December 1971' at *Indian Air Force* website accessed at http://indianairforce.nic.in/content/1971-ops
14. Tufail, The Last Stand, *Aeronaut*, 2012 http://kaiser-aeronaut.blogspot.com/2012/10/the-last-stand-air-war-1971.html and Jagan & Chopra, op. cit., pp 90–91. The presence of AAA is also mentioned in a book by Khalil Ahmed '*Legend of Tail Choppers- 50 Years of Excellence 1948–1998,*' PAF Book Club, 2007.
15. Jagan and Chopra, op. cit., p. 109.
16. Tufail, op. cit., pp. 141–2.
17. Prasad, op. cit., pp 356–7, Nordeen *Air Warfare in the Missile Age*, pp. 163–4, and Jagan and Chopra, op. cit., pp 150–1.
18. Jagan and Chopra, op. cit., pp 150–1.
19. Ibid.
20. Ibid., p. 140.
21. Ibid., pp. 160–1, Prasad, op. cit., p. 357.
22. Prasad, op. cit., p. 356 and Jagan and Chopra, op. cit., p. 179.
23. Jagan and Chopra, op. cit., pp. 190–2.
24. Ibid.
25. Prasad, op. cit., p. 358.
26. Jagan and Chopra, op. cit., p. 199.
27. Ibid., p. 209–10.
28. Ibid., p. 235.
29. Ibid., p. 285.
30. Prasad, op. cit., pp. 367–8.
31. Tufail, op. cit., pp. 67–9.
32. Prasad, op. cit., pp. 205–6, Nordeen, op. cit., pp. 162–316.
33. Prasad, op. cit., p. 206; Tufail, op. cit., pp. 60 and 78–9.
34. Ibid.
35. Tufail, op. cit., pp. 51–4 and Prasad, pp. 213–14.
36. Ibid.
37. Prasad, op. cit., pp. 213–14.
38. Ibid.
39. Tufail, op. cit., pp. 51–4.
40. 'Citation of Flight Lieutenant Israr Ahmad, PAF' at Pakistan Air Force website accessed at http://pakdef.org/1971-war-heros/
41. Prasad, op. cit., p. 214.
42. The Official history mentions a raid on Sargodha by Canberras (Prasad, op. cit., p. 214) during which only one aircraft is acknowledged to have been lost to ground fire. The version as given at https://web.archive.

org/web/20131215001937/http://www.bharat-rakshak.com/LAND-FORCES/Army/History/1971War/PDF/1971Chapter10.pdf does not mention any raid on Sargodha and instead mentions that the Canberras raided Malir and Masrur. Raid over Sargodha is however mentioned by Kaiser Tufail in his blog http://kaiser-aeronaut.blogspot.com/2011/02/air-defence-in-northern-sector-1971-war.html

43. Prasad, op. cit., pp. 214–15.
44. Tufail, Air Defence in Northern Sector, *Aeronaut*, 2011, http://kaiser-aeronaut.blogspot.com/2011/02/air-defence-in-northern-sector-1971-war.html
45. Prasad, op. cit., p. 214.
46. 'Gallantry Awards', *Ministry of Defence, Government of India*, website accessed at http://gallantryawards.gov.in/awardees-0
47. Tufail, op. cit., pp. 73–4.
48. 'Gallantry Awards', M *Ministry of Defence, Government of India*, website accessed at http://gallantryawards.gov.in/awardees-0
49. 'History of India Pakistan War 1971', *Bharat rakshak*, accessed at https://web.archive.org/web/20131215001937/http://www.bharat-rakshak.com/LAND-FORCES/Army/History/1971War/PDF/1971Chapter10.pdf
50. Tufail, op. cit., pp 106–7.
51. Prasad, op. cit., p. 216 and 'The Battle for Airfields', *Pakistan Defence*, accessed at at http://pakdef.org/the-battle-of-airfields/
52. Kaiser Tufail, op. cit., 86–7.
53. Prasad, op. cit., pp. 222–4.
54. Tufail, op. cit., p 101 and Prasad, op. cit., pp. 222–4.
55. The Land Battles http://pakdef.org/the-land-battles/
56. Prasad pp. 224–6.
57. Ibid.
58. PC Lal in his book 'My Years with IAF' mentions the firing of SA-2 and claims that one PAF aircraft was hit. The citation of Squadron Leader Abdul Basit, available at http://pakdef.org/ 1971-war-heros/ mentions the incident.
59. 'The Land Battles', *Pakistan Defence*, accessed at http://pakdef.org/the-land-battles/
60. Tufail, op. cit., pp. 86–7.
61. Ibid., pp. 103–8, 'PAF War Heroes', *Pakistan Defence* accessed at http://pakdef.org/ 1971-war-heros/
62. Tufail, op. cit., p. 108.
63. Ibid., pp. 86–7.
64. Squadron History of 'No.1 Squadron', *Bharat Rakshak*, accessed at http://www.bharat-rakshak.com/IAF/History/1971War/1. Also, Chaitralay Deshmukh, 'Wife of missing Air Force officer believes he's still alive in Pak jail', *DNA*, 5 May 2013, accessed at http://www.dnaindia.com/pune/report-wife-of-missing-air-force-officer-believes-he-s-still-alive-in-pak-jail-1830812
65. Tufail, op. cit., pp. 103–10.

Index

.050 calibre M55 Quad, xi, 1
1er Bataillon Étranger de Parachutistes (BEP), 29
12.7mm DShK M1938 AAMG, xviii
14.5mm Quad AA Guns, xviii, 128, 133
18th Special Air Defence Missile Division, 115
2e Régiment Étranger d'Infanterie (REI), 29
20th Parallel, 36–7, 56
20mm quad AA guns, 71, 77, 90, 129, 152
35mm AA Gun, 32
37mm M-1939 anti-aircraft guns, 9
37mm Vigilante Gatling gun system, xvii
38th Parallel, xix, 1–2, 6
40mm L/60 AA Guns, x, 71–2, 79, 85, 127–9, 132
40mm L/70 AA Gun, 71, 127–8, 132, 137
40mm M41-mounted Duster, xvii, 65, 71
57mm AA Gun, xviii, 17, 33, 36, 39, 44, 89, 102, 178
75mm Skysweeper, xvii
76mm AA gun, 5
8 Pass Charlie, 82
85mm AA gun, 9, 13, 34, 36, 39, 44, 99, 102, 110, 152–3, 157, 178
88mm Flak AA Guns, xii, xiv, xviii, 31, 153

A-4 Skyhawks, 52, 107, 110–11, 113, 116, 119

Adampur, 75, 82–3, 125, 141, 202
Abdel-Razek, Hussein, 92
Aboul-Aez, Madkoor, 92
Accidents, 116, 200
 Losses to, 25, 85–6, 103, 182–3
AGM-45 Shrike, 45, 51
AGM-62 Walleye, 52, 157
Air to air combat, 57, 75, 77, 99–102
 Losses to, 86, 103, 160, 163, 182
Akhnoor, 68, 72–4, 202
All-Gun Belt, xiii
Allied Air Force, x, 10
Alpha strikes, 46
ALQ-51 deception jammer, 50–51
Ambala, 83, 128, 137
Amman, 100
Amritsar, 125, 136–7, 141–2, 144–5, 147, 149, 159
 Signal Unit, 124, 140
Anti-Aircraft (AA), xiv, xvii, xix, 6, 8
Antonov An-12, 79, 105
Ap Bac, 30, 32
Arab Air Forces, 88, 90, 92, 101–103, 158

B-29 Superfortress, 3, 8, 11–12, 15–16, 21–3, 25
 RB-29, 16, 20
B-47 Stratojet, xv
B-29, 3, 8, 11–12, 15, 21–2, 25
 RB-29, 15–16
B-52, 44, 48, 56, 58–64, 158, 165, 167–73, 177, 179
B-57, 74–7, 79, 82–6, 126, 137–43, 146–7, 159, 183
 RB-57, xvii, 75–6, 81, 83, 143, 164

Badin, 69, 73, 125, 147, 159
Bac Can, 46
Bar Lev line, 108
Bangladesh, xxi, 124, 131, 136
Battalion 681, 28
Battle of Britain, xiii, xviii, 159
Battle of Stalingrad, xiv
Beijing, 33, 164
Boeing KC-97G, 122
Bofors 40mm L/60 AA gun, x, 71–82, 85, 127, 129
British Anti-Aircraft Artillery, xiii, xviii
Boyra, 124, 129
Boxer, Operation, 110–11

Cairo, 94, 98–100, 114, 116–17
Calcutta, 72, 84
Central Intelligence Agency (CIA), 30–1, 179, 195, 197
CH-21 Shawnee helicopter, 30
Chaff, 58, 60, 62, 96, 154, 170–3
Chain Home, xviii
Chawinda, 82
Chengiz Khan, Operation, 124, 136
Chhamb, 72–3
Chittagong, 84
Chosin Reservoir, 17
Combat Air Patrol (CAP), 40, 69, 78, 96, 130
Counter air operations, 76, 78, 130, 134–5, 139–40, 142, 144, 148–9, 159, 162–3
Communist Party Volunteer (CPV) anti-aircraft artillery units, 11, 15, 17

Dacca, 84, 125, 128, 130–1, 133
Dassault MD.454 Mystère IV, 108, 182
Dassault Mirage III, 94, 106, 111, 122–3, 126, 139–41
Dassault Super Mystère, 70, 77–80, 82, 85, 94, 100, 104, 108, 111, 126, 144–5, 182, 202

Dassault Ouragon, 94, 111, 126
Dayan, Moshe, 114
de Havilland Vampire, 68, 84–5, 89, 126, 182
de Havilland Venom FB4s, 89
Delhi, 71–2, 79, 83, 128
Demilitarized Zone, 3, 35, 58
Democratic Republic of Vietnam, 36
'Dentist' Tactical Air Defence Centre, 19
Desert Hawk, Operation, 68
Detachment X, 1–2
Dien Bien Phu, 27–9
Dimona nuclear reactor, 21, 90, 92, 96, 204, 206
Division Air Defence (DIVAD), xvii
Dumbo radar, 14
Durandal bombs, 95

E-1 Tracer airborne-early-warning (AEW) aircraft, 35
EA-1 Skyraider, 35
EA-3 Skywarrior, 35
Eastertide Offensive, 56
EB-66B Destroyer, 41, 60
EF-10 Skyknight, 35, 44, 179
Egypt,
    Egyptian Air Force, 89, 92–6, 99–101, 103, 105, 107, 111
    Egyptian AAA, 103
    Egyptian Army, 92–3, 102, 114, 122, 203
        Air Defence, 21, 88, 96–7, 107, 110–16, 118, 120, 123
            Air Defence Command (ADC), 115–16, 118, 120, 123, 206
Ehsanul Karim, 69
Electronic Counter-Measures (ECM), 21, 23, 58, 61, 112, 116, 121, 156–7
Electronic Intelligence (ELINT), 20, 22, 76, 81, 110, 116, 168

Index

Electronic Warfare (EW), xviii, 20, 23, 41, 61, 96–7, 115, 121, 156, 181
Electronic Warfare Officers (EWOs), 61
EW Suites, 157
English Electric Canberra, 82, 84–5, 89, 126, 129, 135, 137, 139–43, 147, 164
Enzian, xvi, 152

F-104 Starfighter, 44, 69, 77–8, 80, 86, 124, 136–7, 140–1, 146, 179, 183
F-105D Thunderchief, 41, 43–5, 50, 60, 65, 161, 175, 179
F-4 Phantom, xxi, 34, 40–2, 44, 48, 56, 58–9, 63, 65, 107, 112–15, 119–22, 157, 161, 170, 175, 179, 200, 207
F-6 (Shenyang J-6), 126, 144, 148, 183
F-80 Shooting Star, 1, 7–8, 25
RF-80, 16
F-86 Sabre, xix, 3–4, 16, 69–70, 73–7, 79, 82–6, 124, 126–7, 129–30, 133–5, 139, 141, 144–7, 183
Fairchild C-123 Provider, 30
Flakartillerie, xiii
Flak rockets, xvi, 10
Flak suppression, 8, 12, 153, 155, 157
Flak trap, 7
Flaming Dart, Operation, 47
Foehn, xvi
Folland Gnat, 73, 85, 124, 126–9, 133–6, 147, 182
FPS-20 radar, 125, 142–3, 147
France, 88–9, 107
Army, xii, 27
First Vietnam War, 27–9
Fratricide, 159
India Pakistan Wars, 79, 81, 132, 149
Korea, 14, 24

Six Day War, 103
War of Attrition, 117
Freya early-warning radars, xviii, 20, 154
Ferozepur, 74–5, 79
Fouga Magister, 96

Giap, General Võ Nguyên, 27, 57, 59
Gibraltar, Operation, 70
Gloster E.28/39 Whittle, ix
Gloster Meteor, ix, 3, 89
Golda Meir, 110
Grand Slam, Operation, 68, 70
Ground control interception (GCI), 14, 20–2, 72, 154, 193
Guangxi, 33–4
Gulf of Tonkin, 29, 32–3, 164, 175, 195
Gurdaspur, 82

H-3 air base, 100, 204
Haifa, 99
Haiphong, 38–9, 48, 52–4, 56–7, 59, 62, 66–7, 169
Hanoi, 27, 31–4, 38–40, 43, 46–8, 52–7, 59–60, 62, 67, 166–7, 169–70, 172, 176, 198
Hanoi Habit, 33
HAWK (Homing All the Way Killer) missile system, 21, 65, 91–2, 107–108, 111, 114, 117, 123, 204, 206
Hawker Hunter, xv, 77, 79, 84–5, 99, 126, 130–1, 133–5, 139, 142–7, 182, 204
Hawker Sea Hawks, 85, 89
Hecklers, 19
Helle Nachtjagd (Illuminated night-fighting), 21, 154
Helmond, x–xi
Ho Chi Minh Trail, 34, 39
Hunter Batteries, xv
Hunter-Killer Teams, 62

Ichogil Canal, 74
Identification Friend or Foe (IFF), 18, 20
  Mark X IFF program, 20
Ilysuhin Il-28, 64–5, 90, 94–5, 100, 107, 117, 201, 206
Inchon, 2, 19
Indian Army, 74, 80, 82–3, 86, 124, 135, 138, 140, 142, 163
  I Corps, 74
  IV Corps, 133
  XI Corps, 74, 143–4
  Air Defence/AD Regiments, 71, 73, 75, 128, 134
Indian Air Force, xxi, 69, 75, 78, 82–4, 124–6, 128–39, 142–3, 145, 147, 149–51, 208
  Air Defence Direction Centre (ADDC), 72, 128
  411 Signal Unit, 72
  55 Signal Unit, 72
  Base Air Defence, 126
  FAB-500 M-62 bombs, 132
  Losses, xxi, 70, 75, 82, 85–6, 131, 142
  No. 1 Air Defence Direction Centre (ADDC), 72
  No. 2 Air Defence Area Headquarters, 72
  No. 3 Air Defence Direction Centre (ADDC), 128
  No. 3 Squadron, IAF, 78
  No. 14 Squadron, IAF, 127, 133–4
  No. 16 Squadron, IAF, *The Rattlers*, 129
  No. 22 Squadron IAF, 124
Indian Anti-Aircraft Artillery, 71, 73, 75, 128, 134
  22 (Independent) Air Defence Brigade, 71
  26 Air Defence Regiment, 137
  27 Air Defence Regiment, 137
  33 (Independent) Air Defence Brigade, 71
  48 AD Regiment, 129

Indian Navy, 146
Indochina, 27, 29
Interdiction, 6–8, 11–12, 15–16, 25–6, 38, 79, 138, 143–4, 148, 154–5, 160
Iron Hand, Operation, 45–7, 66
Israeli Air Force (IAF), 88–92, 94–5, 97, 99–103, 110–12, 122–3, 158–9, 162, 204–206
Israeli Defence Forces, 89, 91, 108, 110
Italo-Turkish War, xi

Jammu, 68, 71, 79, 140, 147
Jamnagar, 75–7, 79, 126, 141–2

Kadesh, Operation, 88
Kalaikunda, 72, 84
Karachi, 125, 127, 145–6
Kashmir, 68, 70–1, 124–5
Kasur 74, 79, 82
Kavkaz, Operation, 115, 117
Kim Il-sung, 2, 7
Kimpo, 5, 7, 11, 18–19
Korea, xiv, xviii
  North Korea, xiv, xv, xix, 1–2, 4, 8, 12, 15–16, 18, 25–6, 152, 160
    Air Defences, xix, 5–6, 9–10, 13–15, 20–2, 25, 153–4
    Air Force, 1–3, 5, 10, 12, 17, 19
    Army, 1, 5–6
    Hunter Group, 7–8
  South Korea, 1–4, 18, 24
    Army, 1, 5, 24
Kurmitola, 129–32, 135

Lahore, 74, 79, 82, 145
Laos, 27, 35, 48, 60, 160
Lavochkin La-9, 3
Lichtenstein, xviii
Linebacker, Operation, xx–xxi, 56–64, 66, 180–1
  Linebacker II, 158, 161, 165, 169, 172, 177, 199–200

Longewala, 143–4
Luftwaffe, x, xii–xiii, xviii, 21, 159

Mao Zedong, 14–15, 33, 191
Messerschmitt ME.262, xi–x
MiG-15, 3, 7, 11–12, 15, 17, 36, 55
MiG-17, 48, 63, 66, 94, 99–100, 105, 107, 111–12, 206
MiG-19, 63, 66, 90, 100, 107, 139, 145, 148, 183
MiG-21, 36, 55, 63, 66, 85, 90, 95, 98, 100, 105–107, 109, 111–12, 115–16, 118, 121–2, 126, 130, 132, 135, 139, 145, 147, 163, 182, 206
MiG Alley, 16
Mafraq, 100
Mauripur, 69, 75
Mobile Observation Units (MOU), 72–3, 128
Moked, Operation, 94–5
Mukti Bahini, 124, 136
Murid, 139, 143–5
Musketeer, Operation, 89
McNaughton, John T., 40

Nam Dinh, 47
Nasser, 93, 106–107, 109, 115, 122, 205, 206
Nike Ajax, xvi, 152, 164
Nixon, Richard, 55–6
North Korea,
    Air Defences, xix, 9–10, 14–15, 20–2, 153–4
    Air Force, 1–2, 5, 10, 17, 19
        Air Divisions, 12
    Army, 1, 5–6, 14
North Vietnam,
    Air Defence, 31, 33, 37–8, 53, 57–8, 60–1, 64
        236th Missile Regiment, 47
        361st Air Defence Division, 52
        365th Air Defence Division, 52
        367th Air Defence Division, 52
    Air Force (NVNAF), 31, 52, 57, 63, 201

Anti-Aircraft Artillery, 27–33, 36, 38–40, 44–5, 47, 178
SAM, 40–58, 60–4, 66–7, 157–8
People's Volunteer Army, 14, 17
    People's Volunteer Air Force, 65

Opel RAK.1 aircraft, ix
Operation NGUYEN HUE, 56

P-30 (M) radar, 72, 125, 136
P-80 Shooting Star, 3
Pakistan Air Force (PAF), 73, 75, 77–80, 82–3, 86, 100, 124–7, 131, 135–9, 141, 143–9, 162, 183
    No. 14 Squadron, PAF, 127
    No. 17 Squadron, PAF, 69
    No. 19 Squadron PAF, 86
    No. 24 Squadron, PAF, 76
    Air War Plan No 6, 74,
    Control & Reporting System, 72–3, 125, 128
    Fratricide, 81
    Losses, 86, 183
    PAF Regiment, 71, 77
    Sector Operations Centre, 125
Pakistan Army,
    I Corps, 74
    Anti-Aircraft Artillery, 70–2, 77–8, 80–1, 87, 126–7, 129–31, 133, 135, 139, 141, 145–6, 148
    6 LAA Regiment, 129, 135
    19 LAA Regiment (SP), 72
    29 LAA Regiment, 68
    Anti-aircraft *Mujahid* companies, 127
Pathankot, 75–6, 79, 136, 140–4, 146, 202
Paul Doumer bridge, 52, 56
Peshawar, 75–6, 78
People's Liberation Army, 6–7, 33
    67th Anti-Aircraft Artillery Division, 34
People's Republic of China, xix, xx, 3, 6–8, 10–12, 18, 26, 31–3, 38, 54–5, 63, 84, 126, 164

Anti-Aircraft Artillery, 11, 14
People's Liberation Army Air Force (PLAAF), 3
Perumal C, Havildar, 73
PGM, see *Precision Guided Munition*
Phillaura, 81–2
Pierce arrow, Operation, 33
Polikarpov PO-2, 18–19
Porbandar, 75
Port Said, 109–10
Precision Guided Munition (PGM), xxi, 52, 156
Project Nike, xvi
Project Shoehorn, 50
Protivovozdushnaya Oborona Strany, PVO Strany,
see *Soviet Air Defence Forces*
Puazo fire-direction equipment, xv
Pusan Peninsula, 1–2, 18–19
Pyongyang, 4, 8, 20–1, 155

Qadri al-Hamid, 105
QRC-160 jamming pod, 50
QRC-335 jamming pod, 66

Radar Warning Receiver (RWR), 67
Rahwali, 81
Ramat David, 100
Rampurhat, 72
Rann of Kutch, 68–9
Rashid, Operation, 99
RB-66C Destroyer, 48–9, 179
RB-57D Canberra, xvii, 164
RF-51, 8
Republic F-84F Thunderstreaks 89
Republic of Korea, 1–3, 24
Rheintochter, xvi
Rolling Thunder, Operation, 35–8, 46–9, 51, 53–5, 66, 180
Rooster 53, Operation, 113
Route Packages, 38, 53
Royal Air Force, x, xi, xiii, xviii, 89
  Royal Air Force Regiment, x

S-25 Berkut surface-to-air missile, xvi, 164
SA-2 Dvina missile system, xvii, xx–xxi, 36, 40–6, 48–53, 55–6, 58, 60, 62, 66–7, 72, 79, 83, 92, 95–6, 99, 104, 106–107, 109–10, 114–16, 118–23, 146, 156–8, 154, 164–5, 168–9, 178–9, 181
SA-2F, 66
SA-3, 115–23, 178, 207
SA-7, 56, 58, 116, 119–20, 165, 169, 171, 178–9
Saigon, 35, 64
Sakesar, 73, 125, 142–3, 147
SAM,
  Effectiveness, 66, 164–8
  SAM box, 118, 120–2
  Use in Indian-Pakistan Wars, 79, 83–4, 146–7
  'SAM break' manoeuvre, 49
  SAM-suppression, 60
Sargodha, 69, 75–8, 86, 139–42
Saifzul Alam, 100
SCR-584 Gun Laying Radar, xiii, 154
Searchlight, Operation, 124
Searchlights, xi, xv, xviii, 11, 14, 21–22, 65, 154
SEAD (Suppression of Enemy Air Defence), 8, 12, 64, 120, 153, 155, 157, 159
Shcherbakov, Lieutenant Vadim Petrovich, 42
Schmetterling, xvi
Shock, Operation, 108
Short Range Navigation (SHORAN), 11, 21, 154
Signals Intelligence (SIGINT), 33, 35, 116
Sinai Peninsula, 88–9, 93–4, 96–8, 100–102, 105, 108–10, 112, 114, 120
Strangle, Operation, 16, 155
South Vietnam Air Force, 37, 47

Soviet Union, xiv–xvii, xix–xx, 2, 5–8, 12–13, 18, 33, 36, 40, 42, 63–4, 90–2, 105, 115, 122–3, 153–4, 158, 164–5, 192, 201
  Soviet Air Force, 3, 12, 17, 195
    5th Guards Independent Air Division, 12
    Air Divisions, 12
  Soviet Anti-Aircraft Artillery, 13
  Soviet Air Defence Forces, xiv, 33, 115, 122–3, 165
    64th PVO (Air Defence Forces) Corps, 13
    10th Searchlight Regiment, 13
    AAA Divisions, 13
Srinagar, 78, 140–1, 144, 146–7, 149
Su-7 Fitter, 100, 107, 111–12, 118, 120, 126, 130, 132, 146, 150, 182
Suez Canal, 88–90, 93–4, 98, 106, 108, 110–17, 120, 122
Super Fledermaus radar-fire-control system, 91
Suppression of Enemy Air Defence, see *SEAD*
Surface to Air Missile, see *SAM*
Suwon, 1, 5

Tail Choppers, 84
Taifun, xvi
Tata Pothu Raju, Haviladar, 73
Tet Offensive, 55
Tezgaon, 84, 127–32, 134–5
Thai Nguyen, 39, 46
Than Hoa, 52, 56
Token radar, 14, 21, 154, 193
Trenchard, xii
Truck Hunters, 8
Tu-4 Bull, xv
Tu-16, 90, 94–5, 100, 107, 116
Tu-95, xv

United Nations, xix, 1, 26, 106
  Losses in Korea, 26
  United Nations Security Council, 2

United States Air Force xx, 1, 3, 5–6, 11–12, 14–15, 18, 22–3, 38–40, 45–8, 55–7, 60–3, 65, 153–6, 158, 161, 165, 168
  3rd Bombardment Group, 6
  49th Fighter Bomber Wing, 8
  Far Eastern Air Force, 10–11, 14–15, 23
  Fifth Air Force, 11, 17, 19
  Losses, xx, 65–6, 153, 168, 180–1
  Strategic Air Command, 415, 40, 60–1, 154
United States Army, xi, xiv, 2, 5, 15–16, 65, 152
  216th Anti-Aircraft Artillery Group, 16
  22nd Anti-Aircraft Artillery Group, 16
  441 Anti-Aircraft Battalion, xi
  507 Anti-Aircraft Artillery (Automatic Weapon) Battalion, 1, 5
  605 Tactical Control Squadron, 18
  90mm Gun Batteries, 19
  Air Defence Artillery (ADA), 18–19, 64–5
  Eighth US Army in Korea (EUSAK), 2
United States Marine Corps, 25, 55, 64
United States Navy, 25, 33, 35, 38, 40, 44–5, 49–50, 52, 154, 175
  Losses in Vietnam, 49, 56–7, 200
  USS *Constellation*, 33
  USS *Independence*, 46–7
  USS *Liberty*, 97
  USS *Maddox*, 33
  USS *Ticonderoga*, 33

Viet Cong, 29–32, 39–40, 42, 54, 156
Viet Minh, 27–9, 194
  Viet Minh Self Defence Forces, 27
Vietnam People's Air Force (VPAF), 32, 36, 48, 65

Vinh, 39, 56, 58
Volkel, xi
Voyska Protivovozdushnoy Oborony,
 Voyska PVO,
 see *Soviet Air Defence Force*

Wasserfall, xvi
Weizman, Ezer, 91

Wild Weasel, 47, 58, 60, 178
Würzburg, xviii

Xom Bang, 35

Yakovlev Yak-9, 1, 3, 5